CLIENT TESTIMONIALS

'You bring exceptional insight, experience and challenge to a coaching relationship. You guided us to appreciate and then to release the power of individuals' and teams' potential in a unique and engaging way. Our relationship has had a positive and direct impact on performance.'

Andy Cosslett, CEO, InterContinental Hotels plc

'You have been particularly enlightening in the way you link business challenges to personal goals and aspirations. Quite simply you brought a clarity of purpose and confidence thereby increasing my ability to achieve my goals in a stimulating and enjoyable manner.'

Ian Ellis, CEO, Land Securities Trillium

'We have had a successful partnership centred around team intervention and coaching for more than ten years. You have had a significant impact whether working with our Executive Committee Business Unit teams, One-to-One Executive Coaching or through the introduction of your SuperCoaching methodology across our global business.'

Bob Stack, Group HR Director, Cadbury Schweppes

'You helped communicate the critical importance of work–life balance in a creative and inspirational way and I would recommend your approach to anyone.'

Pierre Danon, CEO, BT Retail

'You have been key to enabling us to establish a coaching approach aimed at helping people in the organisation reach their full potential.'

Dr Phil Lewis, Director of Production,
Rolls Royce Defence Aerospace

'You provided our team with common direction and purpose. You demonstrated great flexibility and understanding in adapting to our front-of-mind issues and helping us to understand these better.'

Alistair Gilmour, European Marketing Manager,
Shell International

SuperCoaching

THE MISSING INGREDIENT
FOR HIGH PERFORMANCE

GRAHAM ALEXANDER
AND
BEN RENSHAW

RANDOM HOUSE

BUSINESS BOOKS

Published by Business Books in 2005

3 5 7 9 10 8 6 4 2

First published by Random House Business Books in 2005

Random House Business Books
The Random House Group Limited
20 Vauxhall Bridge Road, London SW1V 2SA

Random House Australia (Pty) Limited
20 Alfred Street, Milsons Point, Sydney
New South Wales 2061, Australia

Random House New Zealand Limited
18 Poland Road, Glenfield
Auckland 10, New Zealand

Random House (Pty) Limited
Endulini, 5a Jubilee Road, Parktown 2193, South Africa

The Random House Group Limited Reg. No. 954009

www.randomhouse.co.uk

A CIP catalogue record for this book is available from the British Library

Papers used by Random House are natural, recyclable products made from
wood grown in sustainable forests. The manufacturing processes conform to
the environmental regulations of the country of origin

ISBN 1 8441 3701 5

Typeset by SX Composing DTP, Rayleigh, Essex
Printed and bound in Great Britain by
Bookmarque Ltd, Croydon, Surrey

CONTENTS

ACKNOWLEDGEMENTS

Graham: One of the main ingredients lacking in the business world is giving recognition. When it is authentic it has a powerful impact. So here is my heartfelt thanks to those who have contributed to this book. Firstly, to Ben Renshaw. You have been the perfect writing partner, friend and colleague, and I hold you in the highest regard. I thank you sincerely and warmly for everything you have done. You introduced me to Random House, structured our writing, added to and polished my material and pulled the book into shape. Not surprisingly, you are also a great coach and presenter. To my wife, Anita. You have stood by me through our endless twists and turns in life and have always been supportive and believed in me – profound thanks. Thank you to the other main joys in my life – my three children; who make everything worthwhile. Thank you Reina for supporting me as a PA in the early stages of writing this book. Thank you Elan for your research and typing skills. Thank you Lara for constantly being excited at the prospect of this book, and for repeatedly saying how 'cool' it will be to see it on the bookshelves.

Thank you Deborah Tom for introducing me to Dr Robert Holden, PhD, and for your contribution to the book. Thank you Robert for suggesting that I should collaborate with Ben to write SuperCoaching. It turned out to be an inspired idea. Thank you Clare Smith, our editor. Your initial faith that we could produce this book made it possible and you have been a delightful and easy partner throughout. Thank you Kate Tham, my PA. You ensure that our office and my hectic schedule run smoothly and that we have happy clients.

Thank you Timothy Gallwey. Your seminal book, *The Inner Game of Tennis*, influenced me and countless others. Thank you to the great coaches and colleagues past and present I have known: Jinny Ditzler, Philip Goldman, Mike Manwaring, Charles Sherno, Nic Shugar, Anne Wright *et al*. Thank you Susan-Lucia Annunzio and Sasha Song at the Center for High Performance in Chicago. You have been so supportive and are an inspiration to work with. Thank you to all my multiple clients for helping me to explore the art and magic of coaching (and pay me to do it!). You have provided me with an extraordinarily fulfilling career. Thank you John and Diana Whitmore. You introduced me to the then weird and wonderful worlds of eastern philosophy and western psychology. Thank you Tony and Val Morgan. You introduced me to the great, the good and the alternative.

Finally thank you Mother and Father. My mother always struggles to understand what I do, but seeing that I have an office and a letterhead feels it must be okay! My father, sadly no longer with us, in his own quiet way, was always fascinated by what I was up to.

Ben: Coaching provides the opportunity to get into important conversations that we're normally too busy to have. Acknowledgements allow me to thank important people that I'm normally too busy to thank! Thank you Graham Alexander for your vision and commitment. You have created an extraordinary coaching philosophy and approach that inspires and helps countless people. You are a true example of your work. Thank you Dr Robert Holden, PhD, for your inspiration and friendship. Your initial introduction and suggestion to co-author this book made it possible. Thank you to my wife, Veronica, for encouraging and believing in me – it makes the difference. Thank you to my daughter, India. Your cuddles and playfulness were a great antidote to writing! Thank you to my mother, Virginia Renshaw, for your dedication and support. The many hours that you spent editing the text and helping me think were invaluable. I truly appreciate it. Thank you to my father, Peter Renshaw, for introducing to me to so many of these ideas before I could fully appreciate them.

Thank you to the world-class coaches who have supported me along the way: Avril Carson, Beechy Colclough, Philip Goldman, Mike Manwaring, Paul Donovan Rossa, Charles Sherno, Nic Shugar, Deborah Tom, Nick Williams and Anne Wright. Thank you to my corporate and private clients for having faith in me. Thank you to Kate Tham for managing Graham so well and delivering excellent graphics, and thank you to our editor, Clare Smith, for your expert guidance and advice.

INTRODUCTION

Graham: How did someone who was acutely shy, failed his 'A' levels, served petrol and drove mini-cabs turn out to develop the world's best-known business and life coaching model? How did this person end up working with many of the largest organisations and most successful people of our time? Sometimes I still have to pinch myself to remind me that it's true.

It was in the late 1960s when I started to take an interest in the field of psychology, then emerging from the west coast of America, and the religions and philosophies of the East. They became a passion, as I attempted to answer the perennial big questions: What is the meaning of life? Does God exist? Who, and what, am I? I read widely, participated in workshops, became familiar with Gestalt therapy, psychosynthesis and encounter groups, and explored the teachings of gurus and philosophers throughout the ages. I spent hours struggling to focus as I meditated or untangled myself from a yoga position.

Parallel to this journey, I was experiencing success in my first real job with IBM. After my first year, and at a relatively young age, I became a manager and was fascinated by the challenge of bringing the best out in my people, which at the time was not a fashionable issue. Thus these twin tracks combined a life interest with a way of making a living.

After five years at IBM, I took a two-year sabbatical and worked with a charitable organisation, the Trident Trust. The Trident Trust provided disadvantaged young people, nearing the end of their schooling, with opportunities outside the classroom, including work experience, community service and an adventure experience, similar to that run by the Outward Bound scheme, which was intended to broaden their horizons and prepare them for life after school. The combination of my self-exploration through humanistic psychology and Eastern routes, my discoveries as a leader and manager, and my learning from working with youngsters, showed me that within all of us lies not only a great potential but also the capacity to interfere with it.

Having worked with the Trident Trust for two years,

rather than going back to IBM, I decided to continue exploring a wide variety of approaches to human performance and learning. What did great sports coaches do? Did business training add value, and, if so, how? What were the characteristics of world leaders old and new? During this time, I set up a charitable trust with a friend and, after taking several deep breaths, jumped off the diving board and started to run self-awareness programmes. These were opportunities for the general public to attend a weekend workshop in a beautiful country house (borrowed rather than owned!) to explore their lives. We had overworked businessmen, single mums trying to make ends meet and students struggling with their parents and education. The stuff of life. Thus, with no formal training, I embarked on my vocation – working with people in intimate settings on important issues that are relevant in their work and lives.

Much to my surprise, these workshops proved to be an enormous success. It appeared that I had a talent for helping others. I discovered that by creating a safe and non-judgmental environment, and by making small and often subtle interventions, such as asking a question or giving some feedback, I could make a big difference. I learnt that by keeping quiet when people were emotional, listening and being there for them, and simply caring, had profound effects. People then began to approach me and asked if I worked on a one-to-one basis. My answer was, 'I do now!' Thus I began to work with people in confidential relationships to see how I could help with their dilemmas or challenges. I was doing what is now known as life coaching.

At around the same time, I read a book that was to have a huge influence on my coaching career – *The Inner Game of Tennis*. When I first read Timothy Gallwey's seminal book it was like a homecoming. There in front of me was a text that reflected my own discoveries in terms of what appeared to help people raise their awareness, define goals, remove interference and release potential. Coaching became the driving force in my life. Witnessing remarkable results in the sporting world achieved through Inner Game coaching, and experiencing rapid breakthroughs through my own 'life coaching' organisation called, 'Results Unlimited', I began to wonder if the business world was missing a trick. Therefore, in the early 80s, on a quest to introduce coaching into the world of work, I became one of the pioneers of what is now omnipresent in business.

In 1986, I decided to get serious and set up The Alexander Corporation, which became the market leader in business coaching in Europe. The Alexander Corporation offered a broad range of services, including one-to-one and team coaching, building managers' and executives' coaching capability, and supporting organisations in developing coaching cultures. We focused at the top end of large businesses and linked our work to their strategic agenda and measurable performance outcomes.

Then, in 1999, with the consensus of my fellow share-holders, we sold the company to an American consultancy. Since then, I have built a close-knit team of highly capable associates and have continued my exploration and delivery of coaching in its many forms.

Ben: My first memory of high performance was punching the air for joy as Alan 'Sniffer' Clarke scored with a powerful header in the 1972 FA Cup Final when Leeds United beat Arsenal. My family was living in Leeds at the time, as my father was working at the university. Unfortunately, the passion for Leeds United stuck and I have now had to acclimatise myself to constant under-performance and poor management since those heady days of the 70s. However, my interest in high performance grew as we moved down South to Surrey, with my parents taking over the running of The Yehudi Menuhin School of Music.

We were already playing family quartets, as my sister and I had started on the violin aged six and five respectively. It was certainly not our parents' intention to send us to the school, but within a year we'd made friends with other pupils and decided to audition. We went through the standard process and got in. Looking back, I am extremely grateful that I did attend such a unique learning environment. I recognise that being exposed to some of the greatest musicians of our time has been a great influence on me. However, there were other consequences of being in a 'hot house' environment that I didn't appreciate. The covert competition, constant comparison and high expectations left their mark, so when I faced the reality of the music profession I began to have other thoughts about the direction of my career.

I didn't possess the overwhelming drive and passion to become a top soloist, but, equally, I was not able to conform enough to become an orchestral player. By the age of 18, I felt that I had achieved a great deal in music and wanted to seek other pastures. My soul searching took me into the field of psychology and I realised that my real interest lay in people and, in particular, solving problems. I landed up in America, studying an eclectic approach to personal development, and didn't look back. I returned to London and set up a private practice as a 'problem solver', to the extent that if anybody told me that they were happy and successful I would reassure them that they were in denial and that it would soon pass! Fortunately, in 1995, I met Dr Robert Holden, PhD. Here was another young male, quite a rare phenomenon in our field, who was doing pioneering work in the field of positive psychology. We compared stories and realised that we shared a similar outlook. Rather than making the elimination of problems our ultimate goal in working with people, we recognised that by exploring desired outcomes, such as success, happiness and high performance, we achieved better results.

In 1996, the BBC used Robert as their psychologist for

a QED documentary entitled, *How to be Happy*, which took three subjects through an eight-week personal happiness programme. Thankfully it worked and soon after we launched The Happiness Project, which specialises in applying positive psychology and wellbeing to achieve high performance in work and life. We then developed Success Intelligence as our corporate arm and have worked with numerous blue chip companies including Accenture, BAE Systems, The Body Shop, Boots Plc, BT, Football Association, Jaguar, Kingfisher, LandRover, Rolls-Royce, Shell International, Telewest and Unilever, helping them to develop success-focused cultures.

In 2001, I had the opportunity to partner Graham on an extensive coaching project. Working with him and benefiting from his vast knowledge and experience has added another dimension to my work. It has also confirmed that seeing the potential in others and believing in their inherent ability provides the optimum conditions for achieving high performance.

For the purposes of clarity, we have written *SuperCoaching* in a logical sequence. However, in reality, coaching is not a linear process. Its different aspects emerge in fluid and unpredictable ways, which would be confusing, if not impossible, to describe. So whether you dip in and out, or read it cover to cover, our goal is that whether you are a leader, a manager or a coach, you receive new insight, heightened awareness and the tool kit to inspire you to adopt coaching as a leadership style, become a world-class coach and thereby sustain high performance.

SuperCoaching draws upon the latest research from Susan Lucia Annunzio and her team at the Hudson Highland Center for High Performance, in conjunction with Richard Day Research, of Evanston, Illinois, who examined knowledge workers from around the world to determine the factors that accelerate or inhibit high performance in work groups. The study is distinguished by its scope and breadth compared to other studies, and the rigour with which it was conducted. The Center and Richard Day Research developed a research design to systematically reach the greatest number of knowledge workers ever contacted for one study.

Whilst most of the book is written with a joint voice, whenever we have wished to include personal coaching stories we have used the first person. Please note that whenever someone is referred to within the text as 'he' this is merely a useful shortcut and a potential 'she' is naturally implied. All names have been changed to retain confidentiality. With regard to the exercises at the end of each chapter, we have purposefully positioned them to speak to you directly. An effective coach would not ask his coachees to do an exercise that he has not done himself and derived benefit from. If you do gain value from them we encourage you to use and apply them in your coaching work.

Chapter 1 explains what coaching is and discusses the

variety of topics where it can be applied. Chapter 2 looks at the phenomenon of coaching and why it is so relevant in these unpredictable times. Chapter 3 explains our style of coaching and what makes it so unique. Chapter 4 shows how coaching is a relationship model and presents the building blocks required for creating relationships conducive for coaching. Chapter 5 describes the essence of coaching and illustrates the characteristics necessary to become a world-class coach. Chapter 6 gives the essential skills for coaching. The reason they come at this stage in the book is because unless a relationship lends itself to coaching, and a coach embodies certain qualities, then all the skills in the world will not produce effective coaching results. Chapter 7 shares the story of the creation of the GROW model, the world's most popular business coaching model, and how to use it. Chapter 8 offers a series of advanced tools to add to your coaching practice. Chapter 9 covers how to ensure best practice and monitor the effectiveness of coaching, and, finally, Chapter 10 discusses how to derive the most benefit from having a broad coaching vision.

SuperCoaching brings together over 30 years of coaching expertise in helping to draw out the potential in others and achieve high performance. We hope that your performance will benefit as a result of reading it and that *SuperCoaching* will inspire you to embrace coaching as a leader and manager, and also, most importantly, in your life.

CHAPTER 1

Super Success – What is Coaching?

SuperCoaching is an enabling process to maximise performance, development and fulfilment.

Graham: Early on in my coaching career, I landed one of the world's leading management consultancies as a client. They asked me to present at their next annual worldwide partners' conference, a daunting task in front of such an analytical and demanding audience.

I carefully prepared my slides, in the full knowledge that they would never be as good as theirs. I also intended to give a coaching demonstration, to bring the process alive, if anyone was willing to volunteer as a coachee. It wasn't long into my presentation that one of the partners raised his hand. Hoping and expecting that he would build on something I had said, he instead exclaimed, 'This is all nonsense!' I took a deep breath and asked him to say more. 'We hire the brightest and the best. They are highly motivated and capable people. We throw them in at the deep end and they either sink or they swim. I never had any of this coaching. I learnt how to swim. This touchy-feely stuff is all nonsense. All we need to do is tell our employees what to do, let them get on with it and either they succeed or fail.'

Trying not to sound defensive, I asked the partner, whose name was Peter, if he was interested in sport. He replied in the affirmative. Thankfully, we shared some common ground. I asked him whom he most admired, and he responded, Nick Faldo. At the time, Faldo was one of the world's leading golfers. I continued, 'Do you believe that Faldo has a coach?'

'Yes.'

'What is the purpose of that coach?'

'To help him iron out any difficulties and take his game to the next level.'

'That is what I am talking about. Coaching in business is not just for those under-performing. It is also for the high flyers to help them go beyond where they are currently performing and to assist their learning, growth and development. It is not a soft activity. It is directly linked to explicit business needs and challenges people to think differently.'

The analogy had caught his attention, but I also knew that just talking about coaching was unlikely to be as effective as experiencing it. I decided to take a risk and asked him if he would be willing to be coached there and then. There was an air of anticipation. I felt I'd taken my life into my hands. How was he going to respond? To give Peter credit, he agreed and sat down in front of his peers. I said the only way it would work would be for him to put on the table a real issue that he was wrestling with. We contracted the partners to confidentiality and proceeded to spend the next 20 minutes working through his issue in front of a captivated audience.

At the end of the session, I asked Peter for his observations. He said that he would never have believed that somebody who didn't know him or his situation could have provided so much value with a major issue that he had been struggling with for several weeks. More importantly, he said that he now had a completely different view of what coaching was. Peter had previously seen it as a remedial activity to correct under-performance. He described what happened as a radical paradigm shift whereby he now recognised that coaching was predominantly a non-directive method of working with people to enable them to tap into their own capability and, in the process, to find ways to perform more effectively, to resolve issues and to learn and grow. He put it better than me!

Over the years, there have been a variety of coaching definitions used, including:

Unlocking a person's potential to maximise their own performance.
Whitmore (1996)

The art of facilitating the performance, learning and development of another.
Downey (1999)

Meant to be a practical, goal-focused form of personal, one-on-one learning for busy executives and may be used to improve performance or executive behaviour, enhance a career or prevent derailment, and work through organisational issues or change initiatives. Essentially coaches provide executives with feedback they would normally never get about personal, performance, career and organisational issues.
Hall *et al.* (1999)

A collaborative, solution-focused, results-orientated and systematic process in which the coach facilitates the enhancement of work performance, life experience, self-directed learning and personal growth of the coachee.
Grant (2000)

A coach is a collaborative partner who works with the learner to help them achieve goals, solve problems, learn and develop.
Caplan (2003)

Primarily a short-term intervention aimed at performance improvement or developing a particular competence.
Clutterbuck (2003)

> The overall purpose of coach-mentoring is to provide help and support for people in an increasingly competitive pressurised world in order to help them:
>
> • develop their skills
>
> • improve their performance
>
> • maximise their potential
>
> • and to become the person they want to be
>
> CIPD coaching courses definition (2004)
>
> Source: Chartered Institute of Personnel and Development (2004)

Our definition is:

Coaching is an enabling process to increase performance, development and fulfilment. SuperCoaching differs from coaching in that it maximises performance, development and fulfilment through achieving measurable results in alignment with explicit business needs. A Super Coach differs from a coach in having the experience and capability to ensure value in every coaching interaction and in enabling people to go beyond what they thought was possible. This chapter discusses the core elements of SuperCoaching in order to build understanding for leaders, managers and coaches.

'You're being promoted from Ordinary Guy to
Ordinary Guy Who's Been Here Awhile.'

VALUING PEOPLE

Valuing people is essential for achieving high performance
within an organisation.

Graham: When I take up a new assignment I always like
to read the company literature, annual reports, recent
press coverage, internal strategy and culture statements
in order to place coaching within the context of the
business. To this end, prior to starting coaching the CEO
of the Europe, Middle East and African division of a
global manufacturing and services business, I agreed that
I would speak to the global CEO and COO, who were
based in the US.

Kate, my PA, attempted to get half-hour phone calls
booked where I could quiz the executives on the busi-

ness, their aspirations and strategy for the future, and for their perceptions of my coachee. Kate came back, rather crestfallen, to tell me that she had failed to book these meetings. She explained that the two respective PAs had both said that there was no time in the foreseeable future. We assumed that this was a 'brush off', and that the executives did not realise the potential value of the conversations. I thus sent an email to each of them underlining the benefits to be gained from speaking.

We got no response, so Kate followed up. Apparently the emails had been received. It went quiet again. Given that the coaching was about to start, I decided to call the PAs myself, in an attempt to get some time in their diaries. This tactic worked up to a point. I got two 20-minute slots in six weeks' time. I went back to my coachee, explained the situation, and asked him whether I was being 'fobbed off' or whether this was standard practice. He said that he was not surprised and that even he could never get the amount of time he needed with the leaders in the organisation.

Six weeks went by and then, on the day in question, both PAs telephoned to say that the conversations could not take place and would replacement slots in four weeks' time suffice? I responded by saying that this was too far off and would seriously erode the value of the coaching assignment. Could any other solution be found? After some pondering, one of the PAs suggested that I send over the questions that I had been planning to ask so that she could ride out to the airport with the executives and get their input. Thus, more than 12 weeks after my initial request, I got a diluted version of what I was seeking.

Here was a culture where the relentless task focus and permanent busyness of the top executives meant that key relationships were undermined, people felt devalued and the quality of conversation was limited, which ultimately led to a detrimental impact on performance.

This story is symptomatic of the world in which we live. In *Success Intelligence*, Dr Robert Holden, PhD, describes this condition as 'The Manic Society', which confuses hurry ('speed of life') with success ('quality of life'). He writes, 'The paradox of The Manic Society is that no matter how fast we go, and how many shortcuts we take, there never seems enough time. The faster we speed up, the faster time speeds up also. More haste, less time – so our perception tells us.' People will not feel valued if no time is invested in them.

In *Re-imagine!*, Tom Peters expresses the current state of affairs in his uniquely provocative style, 'The phrase has rolled off many a corporate lip: "People are our most important asset." The problem: It's mostly been . . . BULLSHIT. Subject of lip service, to be sure, and believed at some level, to be sure; but not . . . the Essence of What Enterprise Does. Not . . . the Essence of . . . HOW LEADERSHIP SPENDS ITS TIME. I don't mean to say that most enterprises ignore the "people thing".

Of course they don't. But there is a special meaning to the word "first", as in "putting people first". It means that "getting the people thing right" is alpha and omega . . . and every letter, Greek, or non-Greek, in between.'

For the first time, there is quantifiable proof of a direct correlation between how you treat people and financial results. Upon recently completing the largest and most in-depth global study ever conducted of the factors that accelerate or stifle high performance, The Hudson Highland Center for High Performance showed that to sustain profitable growth, you need to create an environment where people feel valued. As Susan Lucia Annunzio, the chairman and CEO of the Center, writes in *Contagious Success*, 'One of the most striking findings in our research is that hard work and high expectations do not differentiate high-performing workgroups. They are necessary, but not sufficient, for high performance. What made the high-performing workgroups stand out was that they linked respect for people with those factors. If the members don't feel valued for their contributions, all the hard work and high expectations in the world will not be enough for the group to be high performing . . . The best way to value people is to show respect by treating smart people as if they are smart people. You don't tell them how to do their job; you trust them to do it well.'

Coaching provides a tangible way of valuing people and putting them first. A coach trusts that people have their own solutions and that they have inherent talent. He will help them realise that they matter by applying the essential coaching skills of listening, asking insightful questions, giving feedback and making suggestions. People feel valued if leaders and managers make the necessary investment of time and attention required for coaching conversations to take place.

A UNIQUE RELATIONSHIP

'I absolutely believe that people, unless coached, never reach their maximum capabilities.'

Bob Nardelli, CEO, Home Depot

Ben: Gerry was a hardened manager. He'd been around the block several times and had over 25 years experience of managing people. There was nothing that he hadn't encountered or dealt with. I wondered how I could help. I asked Gerry why he wanted coaching. He proceeded to explain that it was lonely at the top. He believed that people saw him as having all the answers and only sought him out when they had a problem. He felt that he had to live up to this image, which only compounded the situation. He wanted to reinvent his relationships so that they could be two-way traffic and needed a situation in which he could practise. Coaching gave Gerry the opportunity to experience a relationship in which he could express himself freely, explore ideas and make important decisions to change his current reality. He was able to take this blueprint and implement it with his direct reports, peers and customers, which added a new dimension to these relationships.

In a society where many relationships are fragmented, due to dog-eat-dog environments, fast-tracked leaders and managers, virtual teams and severe politicking, the coaching relationship has a unique place. Based on trust and respect, support and challenge, openness and honesty, the coachee is able to be himself. There is no hidden agenda. The coach has no other motive than to be helpful. This creates a 'safe space' for authenticity, exploration and discovery. It allows the coachee to bring anything to the table without fear of exposure or judgement.

It is extremely rare to have this type of relationship with anyone – even our nearest and dearest. Most people have an opinion that they are more than willing to share; they give their views rather than helping to clarify ours. In a coaching relationship, the overriding intention is to help. Not in a soft, woolly way, but to concretely enable an individual to heighten awareness, gain new insight and generate motivation to act.

Coaching provides the context in which the human touch can be brought back into relationships. Even when a business is going through difficult times, it is the quality of the relationships and the ability of people to connect with each other that makes the difference. Creating an environment in which people open up and engage with each other is at the heart of coaching.

AN IMPORTANT CONVERSATION

> The key to elicit the brilliance of human beings is through conversation.

We were recently working in a leading strategic management consultancy. The managing partner had just received feedback in a staff survey that showed his leadership style was perceived as weak. He found this difficult to understand and was distressed, given how much effort he had put into ensuring the economic strength of the business in difficult market conditions. We suggested that he needed to discover the underlying need that wasn't being met through his actions. We therefore conducted a number of interviews throughout the company and uncovered what appeared on the face of it to be an easy thing to fix. Consultants felt that he didn't really care about them as human beings and treated them as units of production. One of the main things that they were looking for was for him to acknowledge them in the corridors, in the lifts and, from time to time, to strike up a conversation.

We fed this data back and asked the managing partner

what he planned to do as a consequence. Strangely, he was reluctant to start talking to people on a daily basis, and initially put it down to his heavy workload. We challenged him to see if this was the only reason. Finally, after a certain amount of probing, he admitted that there was another obstacle. He agreed that it was a worthwhile use of his time to chat to the consultants about business and their lives, but he had gone for so long without doing it that he didn't know who people were. His reluctance was not due to his workload, but, rather to the embarrassment he felt starting conversations when he was unsure to whom he was speaking. An initial step round this was to introduce security nametags, so that people were easily recognisable. By helping the managing partner break the ice in chatting to colleagues, it led to them feeling like human beings rather than cogs in a machine.

It is ironic that most business success is dependent on conversation. Yet we live in an age where it is sparse. The pace of modern life means that we barely have time to connect. Everybody is rushing, rushing, rushing. When we do pause to converse, the potency of the interaction is often weak. Our power of listening is shallow. We listen to argue, we listen to agree, we listen to interrupt, or we listen for an in-breath so that we can jump in with our point of view. What we often fail to do is to create the space for meaningful conversations to take place.

Coaching is a uniquely focused conversation, which enables the coachee to gain new understanding and solutions. The quality of the conversation is determined by the coach's positive intention. Because he intends value to be added, the coachee will experience a qualitatively different conversation to those that he is used to having in his everyday life.

ENABLING PEOPLE

The age of command and control is largely over.

There was a time, namely the Industrial and post-Industrial Age, when business could be viewed as a machine. Thus, we could disaggregate it into its component parts and, if we were sufficiently demanding, output would be guaranteed, profits made and success achieved. Businesses also tended to operate on a psychological model that said that people left to their own devices would lose motivation and become slack.

This old working model no longer applies. The JFDI (just f***ing do it) school of management is over. Businesses are no longer seen as machines, but as living systems, which exist within a dynamic, unfolding and unpredictable world. There is now ample proof that individuals are, by nature, self-motivated, assuming that a certain set of conditions are in place in their organisations.

The enormous challenge that faces leaders and managers today is how to enable people to operate at their best in a speeded-up, constantly changing and uncertain environment, particularly where, as is often the case, a manager has less knowledge, experience and understanding of the job than an employee. This situation is exacerbated by a radical shift in expectations, where the accent on personal freedom and choice means that people resist either overtly or covertly the imposition of control over them. Any readers that have or have had teenage children will bear testimony to this fact!

Coaching is an enabling process. It fits perfectly into the world in which we now live because it is diametrically opposed to a command-and-control approach. A coach assumes that people have inherent capabilities, can learn quickly and, when correctly focused and inspired, will give of their best, even, in many cases, out-perform what they and their manager thought was possible. An effective coach enables his coachee to discover his own way of moving forward.

LIBERATING TALENT

In 1997, a groundbreaking McKinsey study exposed the 'war for talent' as a strategic business challenge and a critical driver of corporate performance. Then, when the dot-com bubble burst and the economy cooled, many assumed the war for talent was over. It's not. We live in an age where, in certain sectors of industry, employees call the shots – they hire their employer. The race to be employer of choice has never been hotter and an organisation that invests in developing its talent is employing a key factor for success. If it doesn't, the best and brightest will go elsewhere.

The conversation about talent must no longer be confined to the world of arts and sport. As much as discussing the immense talent of Maria Sharapova, Roger Federer, Wayne Rooney and Nicole Kidman, we need to talk about nurturing and developing the talent in our organisations. Ed Michales, a McKinsey director, said in an interview with *Fast Company* magazine, 'For many companies, people are the prime source of competitive advantage. Talented people, in the right kind of culture, have better ideas, execute those ideas better – and even develop other people better.' As Larry Bossidy, the CEO of AlliedSignal, put it, 'At the end of the day, we bet on people, not strategies.'

Looking after talent becomes even more important in a climate of constant change and uncertainty. Stable employment is gone. We're on our own. Morgan McCall noted in *High Flyers: Developing the Next Generation of Leaders*, 'Personal change is an emotional undertaking. Uncertainty, fear, loss, damage to self-esteem, intimidation and humiliation are significant and potentially debilitating emotions . . . As with any weighty challenge, knowing that people care about you and will offer support, can help someone hold on, try again, get back up and otherwise persevere.' Coaching bridges the gap. It provides the necessary focused attention, support and challenge to ensure that we continue to move forward in a positive direction.

If we take the opposite route, operating in a macho, bullying and manipulative environment, where no coaching takes place, it will have a damaging effect on our performance and health. According to Cary Cooper, Professor of organisational psychology and health at Lancaster University Management School, the most recent large-scale study of workplace experiences in the UK found that as many as one in four people were bullied at work within the last five years. He says, 'People who are bullied may experience increased anxiety, depression, a loss of self-confidence and self-esteem, an impulse to blame themselves and a sense of powerlessness.' Where there is limited development of talent, companies will incur a high price in absenteeism, recruitment and training. Coaching is a small investment to make to retain and develop our best people.

REALISING POTENTIAL

Is it possible for someone who has never played tennis to have a 50-ball rally from the baseline within 30 minutes of picking up a racket? Timothy Gallwey posed this question to some of the UK's leading tennis coaches in the early days of an Inner Game tennis demonstration. The overwhelming response was one of disbelief. Tim then went on to explain that by holding on to a limiting point of view, coaches might never find out the potential of their coachees because they were unlikely to create the appropriate conditions in which a new pupil could realise it. To prove his point, he proceeded to coach somebody who had never played tennis before and created such a level of relaxation and focused attention that, after 20 minutes, the coachee was able to sustain a 50-ball rally. Although the demonstration failed to reach the level of an Andy Roddick rally, Tim Gallwey nevertheless achieved a goal that the tennis coaches believed to be impossible.

We have tremendous potential. Yet we also have the ability to interfere with it. Limiting beliefs is one form of interference. Other internal factors include a negative inner dialogue, confusion, a feeling of being overwhelmed, fear and an inability to focus. External distractions can include our boss, an excessive workload, a lack of communication and unclear expectations.

A useful equation when thinking about fulfilling potential is:

Performance equals Potential minus Interference
$$(P = Po - I)$$

Our performance is our inherent potential minus inter-ference. In other words, reverting back to the tennis court, if we have the potential to hit a great backhand, then a lack of confidence or inability to focus will interfere with our potential and mean that our perfor-mance is diminished.

Watching Goran Ivanisevic become one of Wimbledon's most improbable champions, beating Pat Rafter in five riveting sets after barely getting into the tournament, was a stunning example of what's possible if we overcome interference. Two points away from defeat, he fought back to lead 8–7 in the fifth set. He fell behind 15–30 in the last game, then fired a 116-mph ace on his second serve to tie it. He wiped his face, then asked for the same ball for his next serve. His 27th ace, and a 40–30 lead, followed seconds later. One more point and the championship would be his. Again, he wiped his face as he fought to hold back his tears. Then he double-faulted. He got the advantage again, but, once more, he double-faulted. Rafter hit a ball wide and Goran had his third match point, only to lose it again. Ivanisevic got to his fourth match point and reached back for one last big serve. Rafter hit it into the net and Ivanisevic was off, running through the cheering crowd to embrace his father.

Coaching helps to eliminate or bypass any interference

so that performance becomes closer to the inherent potential of an individual. Through the process of shining the light of awareness on the possible obstacles involved, the coachee is able to devise new, winning formulae to achieve higher performance.

ACHIEVING HIGH PERFORMANCE

Graham: I had been coaching the partner of a management consultancy firm. Although Peter was only in his 30s, he had achieved a great deal and was destined for further success. It therefore came as no surprise when he was headhunted to become the UK MD for a global transport company. We explored the pros and cons of making this move and he decided to take up the offer. He also expressed a desire to continue our coaching relationship for the first 12 months of his new job and wanted my opinion as to what would work best. I suggested that the most critical time was his first hundred days in the new role, and that his future success was heavily dependent on his initial leadership impact and early accomplishments.

Before commencing his new role, we agreed that the purpose of his SuperCoaching programme was to ensure and accelerate his success. Peter defined his intended results and success measures as:

- The achievement of identified key milestones in his first hundred days.

- To develop an effective leadership style and process for delivery.

- To ensure a work–life balance.

We agreed that the targets for his first hundred days would include:

- Structure defined and decisions made on senior individuals.

- Identification and achievement of quick wins in order to establish credibility and an output focus.

- Articulated vision and culture for the organisation

- Buy-in and commitment to the vision and culture from the board, executive team and employees.

- Clearly defined 12-month goals, strategies and plans agreed with the board, executive team and direct reports.

- Cascaded communication process in place.

- Individual 12-month objectives and development needs agreed with direct reports.

- Effective working relationships with executive team, direct reports and broader network with agreed communication processes in place.

- Delivery of agreed quarterly targets and outputs.

- Optimal time usage and life balance.

With the agenda set, I asked him if he had any particular questions about how to play his leadership role and any observations he had on potential pitfalls. Peter's questions were:

- What was the best use of his time?

- What was the best way to evaluate the people in the business, particularly his senior colleagues?

- How to move away from the existing command-and-control culture?

His main observation was that it was vital to provide a clear direction and to communicate it effectively. He saw that it was important to get out and about amongst his staff in order to understand the business and for them to get to know him. I suggested that a step often missed by people in new roles was to have open and in-depth discussions with senior colleagues about how to work best together and to forge some agreements. I also pointed out that another potential pitfall would be to dive in and rescue operations which he had done in his previous role.

Thus, from the outset, Peter had clarity about what might constitute success in his first hundred days, some key measurable milestones, early thoughts about his leadership style and how to work best with others.

Having accomplished this preparatory work, Peter hit the ground running. He was perceived as a highly capable leader and a breath of fresh air. Consequently, he achieved an outstanding start, which exceeded both his and the company's expectations.

There is a strong argument that coaching should be positioned at the top of an organisation for the people already achieving high performance. Our experience in running programmes such as The First Hundred Days is that it ensures that executives receive the necessary support and reflection time to optimise their performance. It also provides a context for addressing the three key elements of achieving high performance, as shown in Diagram 1:

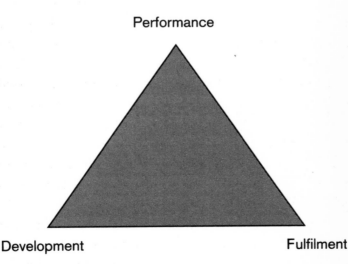

Diagram 1: High Performance

The route to sustaining high performance is ensuring that all three facets of the triangle are receiving attention. Coaching helps in this regard by heightening awareness in those areas which may not receive sufficient attention, especially development and fulfilment. The recent report, *Who Learns at Work?*, published by the Chartered Institute of Personnel and Development, showed that learning at work is now increasingly important. Research has also frequently demonstrated that people are more motivated and learn best when they see that it is relevant to their job. Coaching, with its focus on work issues and improving job performance, fits in well with this.

With regard to the significance of fulfilment The Institute of Work Psychology at Sheffield University produced some remarkable research in 1998 which looked at whether the satisfaction of the workforce as a whole related to an organisation's productivity and profitability. Their findings showed a surprisingly clear link, which shed new light on the imperatives and priorities of management. It highlighted the fact that the job satisfaction of the workforce was a very good predictor of subsequent productivity, and a reasonably good predictor of profitability. More satisfied workers are more likely to control the behaviour and influence the efforts of less satisfied workers by encouraging them to aim for higher productivity. It suggested that companies need to focus much more on the attitudes of the workforce in order to perform well. Coaching covers this ground by ensuring that people derive fulfilment from what they do.

RAISING AWARENESS

Graham: I once coached the CEO of an Irish manufacturing company which had fallen on hard times. Gary had spent most of his first nine months in charge developing a strategy and working with senior colleagues to improve execution in both the sales force and the factories. The business was improving and, as a result, Gary recognised the need to get around, spread the word and build confidence for the future.

We decided to break his job down into its component parts and look at how much time over the next six months Gary should spend out and about with colleagues. He set a target of 40 per cent, which amounted to two days a week. I asked him to estimate how much time he had already spent going around the business in his first nine months. He estimated about 20 per cent. I wanted to check the reality of this figure to help Gary see whether his perception was accurate and to recognise how big a step he was suggesting. My concern was that if it was too big a change from his past schedule it might be difficult to implement.

Gary asked his PA to track back through his diary and tell him how much time he had spent out of his office. She came back with a figure of 8 per cent, which surprised him so much so that he double-checked it to ensure that it was right. Sure enough, it was correct and consequently he realised that shifting from less than half a day a week to two days was too big a jump. He ran the risk of missing his target, which he realised was unrealistic in the first place. Eventually, Gary decided to set up an incremental increase over a six-month period so that he could successfully reach his goal.

The power and effectiveness of coaching comes from helping a coachee raise his awareness of his goals, current reality, possible options and action steps. In many cases the mere act of becoming more aware of what is being discussed can lead to change. By helping a coachee pause the busyness of his life and shine the light of awareness on his situation, a coach can help him to see things more clearly, resolve outstanding issues and take conscious steps forward, secure in the knowledge that he has thoroughly explored his situation.

GAINING INSIGHT

**'You were a gingerbread man in a past life.
That's why your boss is always biting your head off.'**

Ben: I hit a turning point in my life about four years ago. My wife, Veronica, said very firmly that she wanted a child. We had been married for about four years and, although children had been discussed, we were enjoying our careers and lifestyle. As a result, I'd put the idea in the background. My initial response was, 'No way. I'm already too busy. How can I put a child on top of my schedule? What about the responsibility and financial pressure?' This made little impression on Veronica and she once again stated her desire to have children, with or without me! It was time for some soul searching. I put it top of the agenda with my coach and committed to looking at it.

It was a powerful process exploring what having children meant to me; my hopes and fears and my resistance. My coach continued to probe until I realised that one of my blocks was connected to a family joke that my father had never wanted children and had always put his career first. There are some definite similarities between my father and myself, so I committed to talking it through with him to get his input. We went out for dinner and I asked him about the impression I had that he hadn't wanted children because his career was so much more important. His response surprised me. He said that he had taken it for granted that he'd have children, therefore it was never an issue. Although he was wrapped up with his work at the time, he admitted that having children was the best thing in his life.

Gaining this insight had a major impact on my decision-making. I felt a weight lift, as if I'd been given a green light. Suffice to say, four years later, having my daughter, India, in my life is my greatest joy.

One of the great values of coaching is to enable reality to be faced clearly in order to create the possibility for new insights to emerge. The capacity of people to solve their own problems and move forward never ceases to amaze us. Coaching provides the opportunity for a coachee to gain new insights into his strengths and weaknesses, what's working and what isn't, and what he does and doesn't want. An insight is when we see something in a new way or uncover something we were previously unaware of. It is a way of seeing the world anew and can result in giving new options, providing relief, or even making life-changing decisions. Gaining fresh insight is like clearing away a fog. As we dig down to a deeper level of awareness within ourselves, realisations that may have been sitting there for a long time can become uncovered.

CREATING COMMITMENT

Graham: Many years ago, I worked with a coach on going beyond what I thought was possible for myself in order to achieve some of my dreams. One of my desires was to give my family a lifestyle free from financial worry. My coach got me to connect emotionally with how I felt about my current reality of being unable to provide for my family in the way I wanted. A rage generated within me about my unwillingness to carry on with my life as it was. A passionate commitment was stirred to do things differently. That year my income rose considerably and I have never looked back in relation to giving my family what they want. At the time I set those goals, it seemed ridiculously over optimistic. However, I came to learn that, through effective coaching, the power of commitment can be tapped into, which then unleashes the inherent ability of the coachee.

As the German poet Goethe said: 'Until one is committed, there is hesitancy, the chance to draw back, always ineffectiveness. Concerning all acts of initiative (and creation) there is one elementary truth, the ignorance of which kills countless ideas and splendid plans: that the moment one definitely commits oneself, then providence moves too. All sorts of things occur to help one that would never have otherwise occurred. A whole stream of events issues from the decision, raising in one's favour all manner of unforeseen incidents and meetings and material assistance, which no man could have dreamed would come his way. Whatever you can do, or dream you can, begin it now. Boldness has genius, power and magic in it.'

Coaching creates commitment by impacting the will of an individual. As the coachee explores his reality, he is faced with a test of his commitment about different aspects of his life. By staying open and honest, he is able to identify any blocks that may have prevented him from taking previous action, such as cynicism, anxiety or a lack of confidence. By resolving these issues, a new level of commitment is generated, enabling him to take steps about which he had been vacillating. He is able to move from a position of 'could do' to 'will do', from 'problem' to 'project' and from 'powerless' to 'powerful'.

ESTABLISHING MEANING

Ben: Charles worked as a manager within an engineering department. He put in long hours and delivered the required output, but was deeply frustrated. He described his situation as comparable to being on a conveyor belt. He felt trapped by his responsibilities of managing his team, hitting his objectives and providing for a family. He was jaded and exhausted.

Our coaching sessions provided temporary relief from the relentless pressure and enabled him to address the critical issue of meaning in his life. Charles admitted that he felt confused about what really mattered to him and had let himself be dictated to by the influences around him. Through asking important questions about what he wanted, who he was, his identity, core values and the purpose of his life, he was able to reconnect with a sense of meaning.

It transpired that his core value was love, which he had never been able to reconcile with business. Through a process of unpicking what love meant to him, Charles was able to see how he could begin to translate it into his life. He started to invest more time and energy in his family. He began to take a genuine interest in the development of his people. He committed to doing a daily check-in to see how he was going to apply love specifically each day. Ultimately, he changed companies, which enabled him to become more overt about what really mattered. He started to challenge his new manager, peers and team to broaden their focus from simply making money to making people development a key business objective.

Probably the most significant crisis in society and the work environment today is a crisis in meaning. In 2004 *Time* magazine reported that approximately 75–90 per cent of all visits to primary care doctors are for stress-related problems, with job stress being far and away the leading source. The Health and Safety Executive stated that work-related stress costs society about £3.7 billion every year at 1995–96 prices. Research from the National Institute of Mental Health in America reports that 'Everyone will, at some time in their life, be affected by depression – their own or someone else's.'

So many of the planks on which previously life was built have fallen away or become unbalanced. Our modern society suffers from what physicist David Bohm called 'the virus of fragmentation'. The break-up of the traditional family unit, and the resultant broken bonds between children, adults and the elderly, are well documented and familiar to us all. Societal values are often driven by individual preferences and choices, which result in greed and selfishness. The future seems ever more uncertain and fearful. Either religions have lost their currency, or people have become more fanatical and unbalanced in their behaviour. Employment for life is a thing of the past, and people view their careers as a series of staging posts, of their own choosing if they're lucky or, if they're unlucky, visited on them in the latest round of downsizing.

A fundamental human need, as part of a balanced and fulfilled life, is to have a clear sense of meaning. Unfortunately, many businesses seem to lose a sense of purpose, and thus meaning for their staff, in attempting to increase shareholder value. Creating a value-led organisation is not at the top of their agenda. Coaching helps companies and individuals reconnect with what is most important for them by clarifying their vision, mission and values. A coach can then ensure that this becomes the inspiration to drive both their work and life forward.

CREATING RESULTS AND WELL-BEING

Many people share with us their experience of being out of control, constantly rushing to catch up with themselves and getting lost in a set of future goals. The attempt to juggle the different parts of their life in a frantic quest for some tranquillity and equilibrium leaves them exhausted. Stress levels are high, tempers are short, there is no white space in the calendar and time appears to be running out. Clients report how they struggle to get to the finishing line late on a Friday evening. They then experience the wrath of their partner's frustration as they collapse for most of the weekend. When Sunday evening arrives, they desperately try to catch up with what wasn't covered in the previous week, only to start up all over again on Monday morning.

As Madeleine Bunting writes in *Willing Slaves: How the Overwork Culture is Ruling Our Lives*, 'Thinkers predicted that the 21st century would be an Age of Leisure; in the 1970s increasing automation even led policy-makers and politicians to worry about how people would usefully fill their time. For some, this dawning era promised abundant opportunities for human beings to reach their full potential. We would finally be freed from long oppressive hours of toil. Marx's dream of society reaching a point where people could spend the morning thinking and the afternoon fishing would be within reach of us all. It never happened. Quite the contrary: the historic decline in working hours has gone into reverse in the past two decades.'

A 2003 report by the Health and Safety Laboratory revealed that the UK workforce works some of the longest hours in Europe; on average a total of 44.7 hours a week, and that 11 per cent of people in the UK work 49–60 hours per week. In the United States it's even more extreme. A report by the International Labour Organisation stated that employees work nearly 2,000 hours per capita per year. Attempts to overcome this phenomenon have resulted in a surge of interest in achieving a work–life balance. In 2002, a survey carried out by the Department of Trade and Industry's Work–Life Balance Campaign and Management Today revealed that one in five workers want a better work–life balance.

In the midst of this dilemma, coaching provides an opportunity for people to look at the balance between achieving results and well-being. The majority want both; great achievements, and to feel good. Yet this is a difficult balance to navigate. Coaching helps to assess whether the price of our work–life strategy is worth the return. This does not imply that coaching leads to armies of people riding off into the sunset to grow mangel wurzels in the Outer Hebrides. What it does mean is that people can constantly monitor their progress, make adjustments when required and ensure that they are successful and stay sane!

COACHING APPLICATIONS

We will now look at the different applications for coaching and the main topics that it covers.

Coaching has its origins in the fields of sport and the arts. It was a matter of course that great sportsmen and women, musicians, artists and actors had personal coaches to help them achieve peak performance. It is only just over 20 years since coaching has been seen as a useful activity outside these environments. Since then, there has been exponential growth in business, education and life coaching. *Start Ups* magazine revealed that coaching is the number two growth industry, right behind IT jobs, and that it's now the number one home-based profession.

In a business context, coaching can be applied to individuals, teams, and as a style of leadership in developing coaching cultures. It is also possible to apply self-coaching – using coaching principles for strategic and operational thinking, and co-coaching, creating a mutually supportive relationship with a colleague.

As coaching is an enabling process, it is not necessary for the coach to have advanced content knowledge in the field he is coaching. One school of thought suggests that it can be more valuable to coach in an area with no prior content knowledge because it means that the coach is able to remain objective and less inclined to offer a viewpoint. We have worked in many businesses, in many business sectors, in many business divisions, in many countries, with 'grey hairs', in education with young people, with families, relationships and in the sporting world. We would not claim to be experts in all of these areas in a knowledge sense, but our well-developed coaching skills and capability enable us to support others throughout this wide range of situations.

COACHING TOPICS

Coaching, with its universal appeal, can be applied to almost any subject. The following are some of the most common topics that we encounter as coaches:

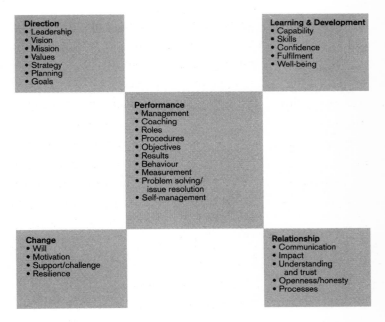

Direction
- Leadership
- Vision
- Mission
- Values
- Strategy
- Planning
- Goals

Learning & Development
- Capability
- Skills
- Confidence
- Fulfilment
- Well-being

Performance
- Management
- Coaching
- Roles
- Procedures
- Objectives
- Results
- Behaviour
- Measurement
- Problem solving/ issue resolution
- Self-management

Change
- Will
- Motivation
- Support/challenge
- Resilience

Relationship
- Communication
- Impact
- Understanding and trust
- Openness/honesty
- Processes

Diagram 2: Coaching Topics

Success Coaching is about helping individuals and organisations become more successful, more effectively. It is probably the most important topic on the list. One reason why people often feel less successful than they are is due to the fact that they have simply failed to define what success means. It is essential for an organisation, team and individual to establish clear criteria for success. Without it we come off track and fail to recognise when we've achieved it.

Vision, Mission and Values Probably the two most important questions in life are, 'Who am I?' and 'What do I want?' It is all too easy to have a picture of our 'ideal' life imposed on us, to adopt a pseudo-purpose and pay lip service to values in which we don't believe. Consequently, we suffer from burn-out because we play a role in our work and life, rather than following our own personal vision. Often the starting point in coaching is to help the coachee clarify who he thinks he is and create a clear vision of what he wants; in other words what he would see, hear and feel in his desired future state. He is then able to plan a more defined route and to live a more authentic life. It's often a wake-up call for a coachee to realise that he doesn't need to suspend his vision, but that by following it he performs at a higher level.

Performance and Personal Effectiveness Coaching is all about helping people produce fulfilling results in their personal and professional lives. In organisations performance issues include:

- Heightening self-awareness and self-management.

- Developing astute relationship management.

- Building strengths and mitigating weaknesses.

- Accelerating results and clarifying decisions.

- Improving execution of the task.

- Being receptive to learning and development in general.

- Focusing on new skills and capabilities.

- Increasing enjoyment and satisfaction.

Coaching has measurable goals and each session ought to achieve tangible outcomes in the area of performance and personal effectiveness.

Leadership Who gives a leader feedback? How does a leader know how he is perceived? How does a leader identify his strengths and weaknesses? Given the confidential nature of coaching, it is sometimes the only way in which a leader will receive direct feedback about his performance. He can gain valuable information on his blind spots by using tools such as 360-degree feedback. Using this insight, a coach can help him adapt his style appropriately to support the success of the business.

Management Managers need to adopt flexible approaches to meet the needs of their people. In a knowledge economy they simply cannot afford just to tell people what to do. Given that in many situations their teams have expertise and experience over and above what they themselves possess, it is essential for managers to reinvent themselves as enablers, rather than controllers. Coaching provides the opportunity for managers to re-evaluate their style and make any necessary changes.

Coaching In *The War For Talent*, the authors Ed Michaels, Helen Handfield-Jones and Beth Axelrod cite the fact that, 'Every manager should be a coach, but most aren't.' One way of developing managers as coaches is for them to receive coaching. It provides a chance for them to explore what coaching is and what it isn't, to receive direct benefits from coaching and to see how they can use it in daily interactions and also in formal interventions, such as annual appraisals and performance management reviews.

Strategy Coaching serves a vital role in pausing action and providing think time. We have almost never worked with a leader or manager who claims that he is spending too much time on strategy and too little on execution; it is almost always the other way around. Coaching enables high-level business thinking and strategising to take place. Time for thinking and planning are crucial to success. Coaching ensures that they happen.

Resilience One of the characteristics of successful businesses, business units, teams and individuals is resilience, which means responding constructively in the face of adversity. It's not that successful businesses have fewer problems, it's the fact that they have developed the ability to 'ride with the punches', to see that most problems are not as life threatening as they appear and that most situations are transitory. Coaching helps to create positive meaning out of the randomly occurring events in life. Positive meaning leads to resilience, which in turn leads to further positive meaning. It is an upward spiral that enables people to overcome obstacles and improve their performance.

Behaviour In recent years, attention has been focused on the development of behaviour, as distinct from skills. It has been recognised that the way an individual behaves in his leadership or management role is a critical determinant of the culture of an organisation and has a very significant influence on the performance and results achieved both by himself and others. Coaching can use leadership or management behavioural frameworks, as well as 360-degree feedback or psychological and personality assessments, to enable an individual to review his behaviour and modify it where necessary.

Skills Coaching lends itself well to the development of skills such as running meetings, leading teams and making presentations. Specific coaching inputs include role-play, video, shadow coaching (observing the coachee in action) and introducing models, frameworks or processes. These interventions provide an opportunity to review current skill levels, to identify options for the future and to commit to action. As we will see later, they can sit at the directive end of the coaching spectrum but are highly effective in the right context.

Relationships and Communication It has been said that business would be simple if it weren't for people! We all have different personalities, working styles, strengths and weaknesses, wants and needs. This often leads to sub-optimal working relationships and ineffective communication. Since business consists of a series of conversations, it is vital to develop effective working relationships and communication processes.

Understanding and Trust Many relationships fail through a lack of understanding. Assumptions are made and mental pictures of colleagues are formed, which then become 'the truth', and needs, frustrations and resentments, because they remain unexpressed, fester. Respect, trust and perceived value can only grow if we build a deeper understanding of our boss, peers and customers. Coaching can help us cut through our assumptions, develop greater empathy and devise strategies to open communication channels.

Problem Solving and Issue Resolution You're probably familiar with the saying that each solution is the next problem. We all confront problems, obstacles and issues on a daily basis. Often we're unable to see our way through this morass. Coaching helps to shine the light of awareness on to situations, starting with a broad sweep and then drilling down until an issue is seen clearly, with the underlying cause correctly identified. Many problems remain unresolved because they look too big. Recognising a first step, a 'bite-sized chunk' turns a problem into a project and helps us to get unstuck.

Planning and Self-management In 2002, Boots conducted the largest ever survey into the state of the nation's well-being. The report identified 15 key factors that made up 76 per cent of our optimum well-being. Number one on the list was to have a sense of control over our destiny. We can handle almost any level of stress if we feel in control and able to choose what we do. Coaching enables us to play to our strengths, particularly in difficult environments, and to learn to manage ourselves in constructive ways. We need to recognise that we can influence our circumstances rather than being controlled by them.

Motivation, Commitment and Will Would you rather have what you want in life, or the reasons why you don't have it? Many of us have dreams, things that we'll do one day, steps that we know we should take and 'mouldy oldies' that sap our energy. Even the most effective people sometimes procrastinate. Coaching is a useful aid to looking clearly at intentions and choosing whether or not to act. It can help a coachee consciously to take a step now, not take a step, or put off taking a step until a later date.

Confidence In our experience, even the most confident coachee is either different behind the mask or has moments of self-doubt. It is part of the human experience. Coaching helps people overcome a lack of confidence by resolving the issues that cause it, such as a low self-image, negative self-belief and unhelpful self-dialogue. It can enable people to take calculated risks and, in the event of failure, it allows reflection and review.

Change and Transformation As Anthony Muh, the Head of Investment for Citigroup in Asia said, 'Uncertainty is the only thing to be sure of.' Coaching helps people respond to change in positive ways, overcoming potential barriers such as scepticism, cynicism, anxiety and fear. It challenges people to make changes at times of need. Although transformation has become a rather hackneyed word in business, it can be triggered into being by coaching through the high level of intention, laser-like awareness and trust in allowing a breakthrough to emerge. This process is often outside the realm of rational thinking and emerges as a consequence of the relationship between coach and coachee.

Happiness More than two thousand five hundred years ago Aristotle posed the question: 'What is the good life?' The pursuit of happiness is enshrined in the Declaration of Independence as a basic right of all Americans. Yet as Oliver James illustrates in *Britain On The Couch*, we are unhappier than we were in the 1950s – despite being richer. Coaching is a useful environment in which to explore the nature of happiness. Sometimes we find it difficult to recognise that we are already happy; we know when we're unhappy, but fail to pay attention to when we are. Verbalising those parts of our work or life that give us satisfaction can increase our overall sense of happiness. Identifying any blocks to happiness and finding ways to overcome them can do the same. We only have one shot at this life, so let's at least feel good!

SUPER SUCCESS SUMMARY

- Coaching is an enabling process to increase performance, development and fulfilment.

- SuperCoaching is the world-class practice of coaching to maximise performance, development and fulfilment in alignment with explicit business needs.

- A Super Coach ensures the achievement of measureable results and enables people to go beyond what they thought was possible.

- At its highest level, coaching is about valuing people.

- Coaching provides the opportunity for the important conversations we're normally too busy to have.

- The most effective way to liberate talent within an organisation is to coach the best and the brightest.

- Performance = Potential − Interference.

- Achieving high performance requires a balanced focus on performance development and fulfilment.

- Coaching shines the light of awareness to create new insights.

- Coaching increases the will and commitment of an individual to act or not to act.

- Coaching can be applied to a multitude of disciplines and a range of topics.

SuperCoaching
Exercise 1: Establishing a Vision for Coaching

A coach believes that people have a vast capability to discover their own solutions. The starting point to becoming an effective coach is to discover your own vision for coaching. This exercise is designed to help you reflect upon your intention and purpose for coaching. As Carl Jung once said, 'Your vision will become clear only when you look into your heart. Who looks outside, dreams; who looks inside, awakens.' Ask yourself, What is my intention for coaching? What are my core beliefs about coaching? Describe your five characteristics of an effective coach. Develop a vision statement expressing your purpose for coaching and desired future state. Use *SuperCoaching* to test and expand your views.

CHAPTER 2

Super Times – Why Coaching Now?

Graham: I had coached an extremely capable business unit director in a major British organisation. Knowing that he had been headhunted for the CEO position of a competitor, I made contact whilst he was on 'garden leave' to see if he would like support in his new role.

Upon meeting, he said that he could envision one-to-one support over his first 12 months on a weekly basis. The purpose of my work would be to serve as a sounding board, to ensure that he focused on the right things, to coach him on how best to lead the organisation, because, in his words, 'I'm going to need a friend. It's going to be a difficult ride.'

When he commenced his new role, it was described in

the business press as possibly the UK's most difficult CEO challenge. It had been an outstanding business, but now had both strategic and operational problems on every front. We worked together to help him decide on the key criteria for deciding who would be on his top team and whether his preferred leadership style was appropriate to manage the urgency and depth of the problems. We created weekly lists to help him achieve his priorities and prevent him from getting dragged down by the countless other areas vying for his attention. What was probably most critical was to ensure that his home life wasn't eroded by his vast workload.

While I'm sure that in former times a confidant or mentor might have been helpful in this situation, the ferocious pace of change, the complexity of the issues on the table, the ruthlessly competitive global market, the consumer and supplier demands, the pressing need for more sophisticated technology and supply chain processes, the high expectations of employees, and the culture that could no longer be dominated by a command-and-control leadership required an entirely new approach. As the CEO of Coca-Cola put it, 'If you think that you can run an organisation in the next ten years as you've run it in the past ten years, you're out of your mind.'

These conditions are common to most organisations today. A friend of ours, the owner of several boutique hotels, upon returning from his summer break, was pulled into crisis meetings with his bank. They were nervous about the unstable market and his burgeoning costs. Steel prices had rocketed at his latest development in Brighton due to the increased demand from China, where building enterprise is soaring. This was on top of a devastated tourist industry following foot and mouth disease and 9/11. It's a crazy situation. Futurists are running scared. In the past, analysts could safely predict a decade ahead; nowadays it's risky to suggest the state of play in six months' time. With the threat of terrorism and hurricanes, the impact of globalisation, corporate mergers and downsizing, leaders and managers are forced to make up the rules as they go along.

In its comprehensive report, *Coaching and buying coaching services*, The Chartered Institute of Personnel and Development highlights the widespread use of coaching in organisations. 'Almost four-fifths of respondents now use coaching in their organisation (79%). Use of coaching as a development tool has seen rapid growth in recent years – in fact 77% of respondents reported that their organisation's use of coaching had increased in the last few years'.

This chapter explores the drivers of the rise in the popularity of coaching, why it is a vital feature of modern business life and is likely to remain so for the foreseeable future.

FEATURES OF MODERN ORGANISATIONS

Success In *Success Intelligence*, Dr Robert Holden paints a picture of the new world of work that involves organisations having to achieve more success, at a faster pace, with fewer resources, more competition, constant uncertainty and in a global marketplace. He then challenges people to think if they want to play this game or not. If they do, he suggests that they will not be able to succeed unless they are prepared to commit themselves whole-heartedly. Coaching provides an opportunity for individuals and organisations to clarify their success criteria within a business context and life in general. This gives companies the best chance that their people will achieve what is expected of them and thus reach the overarching business goals.

Another feature of coaching is that it encourages people to recognise and celebrate their success. When we reached the new millennium, the number of calls we received from IT departments requesting support for their teams was staggering. They had hit a crisis in morale because there had been no big bang, so people questioned whether their previous 18 months of hard labour had been a waste of time. All too often we measure our success against a zero per cent failure rate, which leaves us far from satisfied. In other words, if there are no problems, how do we know if we're successful or not? Clarifying what success looks, feels and sounds like sets us up to win.

Talent As we wrote in Chapter 1, being in the midst of a war for talent involves winning and retaining the best people. Organisations which authentically demonstrate a coaching approach, whose leaders and managers are committed to supporting their people in succeeding and thriving, and are committed to their long-term learning and development, are magnets of employment. In the film *Field of Dreams,* Kevin Kostner captured this idea when he exclaimed, 'Create the conditions and they will come', referring to the idea that if he built an ideal playing field outstanding baseball players would materialise for a game. This idea is backed up by hard data from a study conducted by the Hudson Highland Center for High Performance. As Susan Lucia Annunzio writes in *Contagious Success,* 'If people believe they can make a difference, they will come. If they are given the opportunity to do their jobs well, they will stay, and most importantly, if the right environment is built, they will perform.'

Employees now have a different view of their careers. They will shop around to find an environment where their talent can be realised and where there is a commitment to increasing their abilities. Coaching helps in all aspects of the war for talent. It helps in the attraction of talented people in the first place. It helps them integrate quickly into the business. It brings out their inherent talent. It develops future capability and, crucially, it indicates how highly they're valued and what the organisation will do to retain them.

Coaching also offers an alternative to investing heavily in recruiting new people when an organisation is suffering from skills shortages. Developing the skills of current employees through coaching saves considerable funds. As Davis A. Thomas Fitzhugh, Professor of Business Administration at Harvard Business School, has commented, 'Data shows the quality of the relationship between boss and subordinate is a major predictor of intentions to remain. Coaching – which can help managers talk with subordinates about their developmental needs – absolutely affects the relationship positively.'

Performance As discussed in Chapter 1, there has never been a more critical need for companies to maximise performance. In light of this, the growing body of research about the impact of coaching on organisations illustrates its value. One of the most comprehensive examples, reported in *Business Wire*, January 2001, was compiled by Manchester Consulting Inc. and demonstrates the impact of executive coaching on the organisation's bottom line. It describes a chain of impact originating in coaching: 'Coaching translates into doing, doing translates into impacting the business, this impact can be quantified and maximised' (McGovern *et al*, 2001). The results of the 12-month study showed that there was an average return on investment of more than $100,000 per coachee. Thus, the executive's company obtained 5.45 times its investment in coaching.

Coaching increases personal effectiveness in areas such as time-usage, meetings, corporate presentations, communication, annual appraisals and reviews, as well as across a wide range of leadership and management issues. Following a coaching intervention, it has been demonstrated that coachees spend more time and achieve more in those aspects of their role deemed to be important, rather than in the sea of apparently urgent trivia. It has also been shown that incorporating coaching into the ongoing performance review and management process significantly increases the achievement rate concerning annual goals, objectives and deliverables.

Change John Kotter, Professor of Leadership at the Harvard Business School, captured the proliferation of coaching when he said, 'What's really driving the boom in coaching is this: as we move from 30 miles an hour to 70 to 120 to 180 . . . as we go from driving straight down the road to making right turns and left turns to abandoning cars and getting on motorcycles . . . the whole game changes, and a lot of people are trying to keep up and learning how not to fall off.' As *Wired* magazine reported, 'In a climate where The Fortune 500 list is ever-whirling, today only 13 of the original top 50 from 1955 remain. More revealing than this attrition, however, is the profile of the companies that have replaced yesterday's giants. Where once the list was dominated by businesses that actually made stuff (US Steel, Swift, Gulf Oil), these days the list belongs increasingly to communications, health care, and insurance firms (AT&T, Columbia HCA, Prudential), companies with inventories that can be hard to find.'

In this climate where the pace of change is constantly accelerating, dealing with it is an everyday challenge. The ability of leaders and managers to learn and adapt has become an essential skill. Coaching helps them to build personal characteristics such as resilience, optimism and courage. It supports them in promoting a learning environment, which, as highlighted in the research by The Hudson Highland Center for High Performance, is a major component for high performance. Their study showed that one of the things that distinguish high-performing work groups is that they create a learning environment in which people can seize opportunities, take risks, generate new ideas, make mistakes and learn from them – critical in changing times.

Vision, Mission and Values We live in a multiple-choice economy. McDonald's recently promoted the fact that it had enough meal combinations to select a different meal every day for over 50 years; eBay tantalises us with 25 million products; Sainsbury's has so many varieties of olive oil it's hard to choose. Holidays, cars, clothes, activities and even careers – the list is endless. With the diminishing influence of institutions such as the church, marriage and governments, and organisations no longer representing stability zones, many of the former values that went unquestioned and shaped our destiny no longer have their former power. In this age of personal choice, we demand the freedom to choose how we live. However, we are short on guidance on how to find the purpose, mission and values which would steer our life in the right direction. So it's all too easy to be out of touch with what is most important to us, and our behaviour and actions can lurch about like demented pinballs.

Coaching supports people in clarifying:

- A vision for work and life.

- What is important.

- What their job is really about.

- What they want to be remembered for.

- What is sacrosanct in a changing world.

- What must change.

- What mustn't change.

From our work, it appears perfectly possible to discover a direction within ourselves that feels very real, as if it's our birthright. This does not necessarily need to be a mystical or 'save the world' experience. It can be as prosaic as, 'to perform at my best for the next year', 'to learn and develop', or 'to be in the best possible position for future career advancement'. Once a coachee can clearly articulate his purpose or inner driver, he can then look at the parts of his work and life that are in line with this and those that aren't. In the degree to which he can bring all elements of his life into alignment with his purpose lies his potential for high performance, fulfilment and enjoyment. Constant activity devoid of a personal context in which to place it can result in us running around like headless chickens.

Identity Although Naomi Klein's *No Logo* was a bestseller, the phenomenon of branding is omnipresent. Our children care passionately at an increasingly younger age about whether they are seen in Nike or Adidas. Even the wrinklies can feel it's important to be seen with a Ralph Lauren horse or a Mercedes bonnet badge. But identity goes beyond a product. It tells a story. It's about passion and what we care about. As Tom Peters puts it in *Re-imagine!* 'When one has an "identity" . . . life gets a lot simpler.'

We need to define and represent a personal brand. It's not enough these days to be competent, good or even excellent. We have to be outstanding and unique, so the issue about our personal identity is critical. Coaching helps identify who we are, how we are unique, what impression we want to create and what difference we want to make.

If our external identity is far removed from the real us there is a danger that we'll be acting a part and living a sham. Getting in touch with our authentic self and demonstrating it through our appearance, environment and what we say and do, gives us and those around us a strong sense of identity about who we are in the world. Coaching helps ensure that our personal brand is a clear and strong expression of who we really are. This is equally true for organisations which need to have a strong identity to inspire their employees and provide their customers with a unique experience that fulfils their dreams.

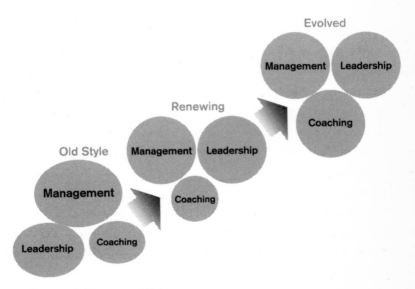

Diagram 3: Management Roles

Leadership The age of 'one-style fits all' is over. Leaders now have to be flexible enough in their approach to adapt to organisational needs, individual preferences and specific situations at a frenzied pace. As Susan Lucia Annunzio writes in *Contagious Success*, 'There is no single personality or style that defines an effective leader. What these leaders (in high performing workgroups) have in common is the ability to create an environment that values people (treating smart people as if they are smart), optimises critical thinking (thinking that is essential to business success), and seizes opportunities (creating learning environments that turn challenges into opportunities). They create environments where people want to go to work every day.'

We still see a large number of organisational practices which are a throwback to a time when businesses were viewed either consciously or unconsciously as machines, and where plans of action could be logically developed to ensure reliable delivery against set targets. In reality, this was probably never quite true, but business undoubtedly used to be more predictable. Examples of redundant processes within organisations might be the strategic planning process, hierarchical organisational structures, the annual appraisal system and almost all command-and-control management. Most leaders do not continue to operate in the old world out of sloth or malice, it is rather that they are not equipped to operate with a new style.

In *Good to Great*, Jim Collins set out to discover how a good company becomes a great company. He identified a hierarchy of executive capabilities a leader must have. At the top was: 'Build enduring greatness through a paradoxical blend of personal humility and professional will.' Coaching provides executives with the opportunity to reflect upon their personal style and make necessary changes. It helps leaders reinvent themselves and their approach to leadership to meet the challenges of this brave new world. It supports their decision-making, as it can be 'lonely at the top', with few people to confide in, develop ideas with and discuss decisions.

Management In what now seems like the dark ages, becoming technically capable and gathering experience in a career discipline sooner or later meant that people would end up as managers. Management was a model based on expertise and tenure. The modern phenomenon is that many managers find themselves in charge of teams who have skills and experiences that they don't have themselves. They operate in under-resourced worlds with constantly changing conditions and where most people have been conditioned to demand a lot of personal choice. It is therefore necessary for a manager to be an enabler not a controller. This does not mean abdication or lip-service empowerment. Instead it means investing significant amounts of time in the same way that sports coaches operate, to ensure that staff fulfil their potential.

Coaching helps management learn new skills and gain

greater understanding to facilitate these important conversations. It helps them identify and implement plans to 'get up to speed', at least partially. More importantly, it enables managers to be clear about how they add value above and beyond technical expertise, so that they have a strong sense of their contribution. This ensures that their credibility and value are maintained.

Behaviour The use of personality profiling models, such as the Myers-Briggs Type Indicator, FIRO-B, OPQ, Emotional Intelligence and Hogan, as well as 360-degree feedback, offer valuable insight into how we function. Most people do not intentionally behave in a way that creates problems for others; it is usually a function of habit, insensitivity, lack of awareness or the result of focusing on the task in front of them rather than on their relationships. Coaching raises awareness about the types of behaviour that limit performance and development. It provides a constructive environment in which to help people face what they are doing and show them how they could behave differently. It is only when people are able to understand the results from profiling instruments that they can begin to self-correct in line with desired outcomes.

Competition Competition is now relentless and global. Businesses spring up overnight and are gone tomorrow. The giants of yesterday have either disappeared in a merger or sunk without trace. New areas of the world, particularly the Far East, are poised to swallow us up. Competition is everywhere and today's new idea is tomorrow's currency. It is almost impossible to differentiate a business via a product or a service offering. The global economy and advent of technology have ensured that one of the few possibilities for organisations to differentiate themselves from the competition is through their ability to maximise the performance and creativity of their workforce. Coaching becomes a strategic factor enabling this to happen.

Less Resource In the past, the resources of an organisation were equal to the task in hand. This is now far from true. Flatter organisational structures, downsizing and virtual teams mean that the workload often exceeds the resource to meet it. Many people are drowning. As the changes multiply, they work harder and harder and put in longer and longer hours in order to cope. Coaching can provide extra precious resource to help them find ways to work more effectively in these people-poor times.

Matrix Organisations Matrix organisations are so antithetical to the traditional way that people have thought about working, and so different to the former organisational chart structures, that employees struggle to understand them, let alone work well within them.

Coaching can equip people to see through the ambiguities and ways that they are supposed to be working and find effective strategies where there is no model from the past and where each situation is unique.

Virtual Teams Working in virtual teams means that there's very little face-to-face contact and most interaction takes place via email, voicemail, telephone or, at best, the occasional video conference. Given that people require a lot of face time for effective teamwork this is quite a challenge. Where does this leave people when almost all of their contact is through technological media? Coaching helps to find effective ways of dealing with this phenomenon, where there are few examples of best practice.

Cost Drive It is generally recognised that you can't shrink to greatness, but it hasn't stopped many people from trying. It is often the easy option and can produce results in the short term. However, it limits future growth and blocks both creativity and innovation. It is essentially a defensive and inward-looking strategy, rather than an optimistic, positive and outward-looking, customer-serving approach. Coaching can help businesses look at the results of potential or actual cost-cutting, eliminate the downside and ensure that if they are going to cost-cut that they also pay attention to the top line.

World Class Is the Old Good It has become axiomatic that a company should aspire to be world class. There is a feeling that unless a business is 'best of breed' then it cannot compete. Clearly not all companies can be world class, but it is an aspiration that many hold. There is a feeling, and much evidence to support it, that if one is not an exemplar of best practice and constantly striving for improvement then one won't last the course. Coaching can help people define what is meant by world class and what is the commercial justification for such a rubric.

Globalisation While international businesses have existed for many years, truly global organisations are a more recent phenomenon. They are not just a function of their size, but of their technological connectivity. Even small businesses, with small numbers of staff, have a global reach. Coaching can help identify where an individual should focus in a far-flung business and can help deal with the diversity of working with people from different ethnic and cultural backgrounds.

Customisation 'Not only do I want what I want, I want it now and I want it the way I want it.' The mantra of the modern customer. The ability of business workers to be hyper-sensitised to and skilled at identifying customer needs, and flexible enough to deliver them, is paramount. Coaching can help businesses see how to be more effective with their customers. It also enables them to identify those employees with mindsets which support customer service and promote them within the organisation.

Knowledge Workers In the heyday of manufacturing, most staff were manual workers. Blue-collar workers ruled. Now it's a different story. Much of modern production is automated, with the result that more and more people are hired for their brains, not their brawn. Several years ago, Peter Drucker coined the phrase 'knowledge worker' to describe the value that these people bring to a business. It's what exists between our ears which contributes to the business, not our dexterity with our hands (beyond the ability to press the right keys on the keyboard). Coaching can help people review their inner world in order to develop the right mental skills to become even more valuable to their organisations.

Mobile Workers We know people who use planes in their working life in the same way that their fathers used buses. People now work from hotel rooms, lobbies, hot desks and home offices; in short, from wherever they happen to be at any given time. Coaching can cover the various aspects of this new way of working. It helps people look at how to use technology to achieve greater agility and flexibility whilst retaining a work–life balance. These are all modern-day dilemmas which require serious consideration.

Technology You may have had the following video clip drop in to your inbox: it's taken by a security camera and pictures a man in an office at the end of his tether picking up his computer and hurling it to the ground. We all know the feeling! We are sometimes uncertain whether our plethora of technological aids has made life more or less effective. A modern-day 'yoga practice' to consider is the effective use of technology. Here lies Nirvana – a still mind! Coaching can help people master technology for huge personal and commercial gain by encouraging them to ask the right questions and get the right support.

Retention The new workforce wants different things. Naturally they want a salary, but in many cases what is even more important is an agreeable working environment, the prospect of being able to learn and develop and a healthy work–life balance. The cost to an organisation of losing an employee, even if they are under-performing, is immense. The cost of recruiting a replacement is high in terms of search fees, the inevitable learning curve, induction and training. By using coaching as a tool, managers and HR can uncover the unique needs and wants of employees which, if accommodated, encourage them to stay

Career Development We have been struck by how few people have had a planned journey through their careers. They have tried to do as well as possible within each of their roles and let the next step emerge. While this may have been a successful strategy in the past, given the volatile climate of constant change it is a questionable attitude to adopt for the future. Although establishing clarity about our motivation and direction does not guarantee an outcome, it can significantly increase the likelihood that we achieve our objectives. Our ability to recognise our future desires and to spot opportunities enables us to plan the direction in which we want to head. Equally, our capacity not to jump at the first approach but to reflect on our needs, beyond those of status or financial gain, will increase the likelihood of a win–win situation for ourselves and the organisation. Coaching challenges people to question whether they should stay in the same organisation or career, or whether they should do something different.

Training The importance of internal and external training and consultancy within organisations has been recognised for many years. There is now a mutual expectation between employers and the workforce that personal and professional development must take place. However, there is also a realisation that what has taken place in the past has not always delivered high value and was insufficiently related to the business agenda. Coaching is, by definition, tailored to the individual and connected to business objectives. It can help people identify development needs, plan development activities and ensure that the training is relevant to their job.

Job Security As we have previously mentioned, one of the predictable planks of certainty in the past was job security. The company provided stable employment and benefits and the employees reciprocated by giving all or a substantial part of their working life to that company. This has almost entirely fallen away. People can find themselves caught up in a downsizing operation that they had not expected. Both blue- and white-collar workers have experienced periods of unemployment, and in some cases this can become a perpetual state. For others, their CVS get constantly longer through numerous job changes. Reports say that most of us face having at least five careers in our working life. One consequence of this volatility in the job market is the enormous proliferation of small businesses and self-employed people, many of whom face daily uncertainty.

Coaching can help in all aspects of this phenomenon. People who fear redundancy can be helped to look at their concerns and options in the event that it happens. Those who have been made redundant can be helped through what is generally a traumatic time and encouraged to move forward. It can supplement out-placement to help people deal with the thoughts, emotions and adjustments that are inevitable if they are subjected to this situation. Coaching can also, in the early days of a new working life, help bring somebody up to speed in the most effective way, whether corporately or setting up on their own.

Time There are many phrases that sum up the experience of time today. 'Cash rich, time poor' or 'The modern currency', 'Time poverty' and 'Hurry sickness' are some of the most common. There is no doubt that time is our most prized possession. How often have we heard in the last week, or said ourselves, that we haven't got enough of it? One of the gifts of coaching is that in a world where there is insufficient time, coaching expands it. It provides the opportunity to stop, reflect, think, gain insight and explore different options free of the tyranny of interruptions, pressing deadlines and spinning plates. Coaching puts time management high up the agenda. As far as we can tell, there have always been, at least in human recorded time, 24 hours, 1440 minutes, 86,400 seconds in each day and this is not about to change, therefore we must prioritise and organise ourselves so that we have enough time for what is important for ourselves, the business and the family.

Graham: When I first worked with George I called him the world's busiest man. As we discussed what should go on his coaching agenda, he kept returning to the enormity of his schedule. Whilst he was making great progress in his business, and had achieved a remarkable amount, his workload felt out of control and was having a detrimental effect on his home life and his health. Something had to change.

George lived by his 'to do' lists. He religiously created them every evening for the next day and every Sunday for the following week. On our second meeting, I asked to see his daily list and he rather proudly passed it to me saying, 'never a dull moment'. Before reading, it I asked him to look in his schedule and tell me how many hours he had booked for meetings. He had eight and a half hours scheduled. I then asked him whether anything might emerge during the day that was unplanned. He anticipated some phone calls, drop-in meetings and possibly one or two additional papers to read. I then went through his list for the day and asked him to estimate how much time each of the items would take to accomplish. When we totalled up all his activity it transpired that George was attempting to accomplish 37 hours of work.

I knew that we had to do something out of the box. My first suggestion was for him to do as little as possible for the space of five working days. He was horrified. I told him that I was not advocating a quiet or irresponsible life, but I wanted him to start being realistic about what he could achieve and, most importantly, to only do those things that would have the biggest impact on his business. Rather than produce his long list, his task was to identify three priorities that were the 'must do's' for the day. With a certain nervousness he agreed and we arranged to review progress five days later.

When we came back together he laughed and said that it had been excruciatingly difficult for the first couple of days, but the discipline of thinking through what was most important was paying off. He reported three types of benefit. Firstly, he gained the satisfaction of accomplishing three vital tasks and consequently moving his business forward in a strategic fashion. Secondly, two members of his staff spontaneously told him that for the first time he looked as if he was on top of the job, which made them feel confident about the business. Thirdly, he had seen more of his five-year-old son in the last five days than he had in the previous three months.

FEATURES OF MODERN LIFE

A Crisis in Meaning Society has changed out of all recognition in recent years and change is, if anything, accelerating. The economy is like a roller coaster, but less predictable. It is at the mercy of whim, rumours and dreams – winning the lottery, the dot-com generation and having security in a pension nest egg.

Our lives are ever more complicated, or at least that's how it feels. We never seem to get to the end of the 'to do' race; never mind ensuring that we realise our hopes and desires. Ironically, it is extremely doubtful whether the bewildering proliferation of technology is simplifying our lives. Certain aspects of technology make things easier. A vacuum cleaner is easier than a dustpan and brush, broadband is faster than snail mail and central heating is more efficient than open fires. But, taken as a whole, where is the increase in leisure that technology promised? Where are the paperless offices? Where is the peace and tranquillity that we believed we would have in the modern world with its miraculous gadgets?

Everything is uncertain in today's society. Will we wipe ourselves out through our bombs, our abuse of the environment, the viruses we unleash, through the use of GM crops, contamination of the food chain, nanotechnology, the breakdown of our complex infrastructure or through something we can't yet see, but which is lurking ready to emerge at any moment? As we were writing these words a TV programme told us that we were likely to run out of electricity in 2010 and that terrorist acts could accelerate this dramatically. Will any of these things come to pass? No one seems to know. The outcome of this condition leads to a perennial state of ever-mounting anxiety, a nagging dread and a reluctance to hear, whilst paradoxically being addicted to the broadcasts that endlessly recite the latest horrors in the world.

While it is delightful to travel by Eurostar and reach Paris from London in considerably less than three hours, has it really made a difference to the quality of our lives?

What do we do with those precious minutes saved? And in spite of the miraculous aeroplanes that can take us wherever we wish to go, the actual experience of flying has deteriorated. Economic measures have led to sardine-can seating, whilst fears of terrorism have led to ever more intrusive security measures and ever longer queues.

Our expectations constantly escalate The salary we aspired to and believed would make a difference to our lives is now not enough, and as soon as we have acquired the latest material addition to our lives we're on to the next. The freedom to choose and purchase material goods is both a blessing and a curse. Most studies in life satisfaction show that graphs are falling in spite of our material well-being and freedom of choice. The slow and steady saving for things in the future is now a thing of the past. We want it and we want it NOW.

Our children have had as much input by the age of ten as our parents had in their entire lives. In the information age input is omnipresent and available. We are never far from advertisements, news bulletins, music and TV channels – stimulus, stimulus, stimulus. Our decisions today include: should I listen to my latest CD, play my latest DVD, watch one of the hundreds of TV choices, watch a tape of a programme from last night, play with my Game Boy or my PlayStation; should I download some songs to my iPod, should I read the latest bestseller or listen to it on CD or download it as an e-book? If these decisions are too much, at least we can keep working!

It is odd living in a world that we barely understand. Almost everything in our homes is beyond our ability to comprehend and certainly to fix. Politicians discuss issues that we barely understand, with implications we cannot comprehend. Something occurs at the other side of the world that affects the stock market, our pension, the price of fuel and food in our local supermarket. What does it really mean to live in a global world? Where is it all going?

Is working for a university degree a good thing or a waste of time? Does an MBA improve our employment chances or shall we be dismissed as being out of touch with the real business world? How do we break into a field where we only ever see adverts for experienced people? And for those of us approaching 60 or 65, will we ever be able to stop work? What are the implications of British call centres being in India and of Britain being both within and outside the European Community? We are told that the world is becoming a safer place than yesterday yet the terror threat seems to be greater. We are told simultaneously that there is more and less crime in our cities. We don't even know what we need to know and whether we need to know it!

Coaching cannot provide definitive answers to any of these dilemmas, but it can provide a context in which to reflect upon and discuss the manic times in which we live. We have found that people experience relief and gain clarity as a consequence of discovering what's important and meaningful for them.

Religion The prevalence and importance of religion clearly varies in different parts of the world. Interestingly, coaching has proliferated both in societies where religion is on the increase and where its hold is less strong than it previously was. Coaching can help us to differentiate between timeless values and unimportant whims, hence giving us a new perspective. It also enables us to bring our focus back to the present, to operate in the here and now and experience a greater sense of peace and security often previously derived from religion.

Marriage In today's Western World, approximately one in every two marriages does not stay the course. More people are choosing to live with partners without the commitment to marriage, and often with the assumption that it's not a relationship for life. Even within marriage and stable partnerships, expectations have changed and in many ways stresses have increased. It is now the norm for both partners to work, either out of financial necessity or career aspiration, with a blurring of the formerly defined male and female roles. In a world without rules coaching can help us see what we want out of our relationships, what we're prepared to give to them and how to take the necessary steps to turn our vision into reality.

Family There is now no typical model for how we should organise our family life. Many of us live apart from our families for part of each week, due to work commitments, financial considerations or a desire to avoid uprooting our children's schooling. Some of us unexpectedly still have our children living with us in their early twenties. Many of us have children from previous relationships. We have housewives and househusbands. We have home working, term-time working, home study and homework. We create caves for ourselves where we can watch TV, use our computer and speak on the phone under the same roof but not in the same space as each other.

We don't often make the time to think sufficiently long and hard about how to set up our family situations and environment. Perhaps there are ways in which our needs can be met. Maybe it is possible to have enough time together as a family, as a couple, with our children, and have our own sacred time alone. Coaching helps us burst through the limitations of our own thinking and consequently helps us to tailor our lives, and the lives of those we love, in a unique and constructive way.

Relationships It's been said that if you can handle sex and money then the rest is a breeze. However, that is not always the case. In our experience, many issues that emerge out of coaching interventions in the workplace are relationship-based. Frequently, we are required to help people focus on the key relationships in their work and life that could be more effective. Coaching encourages people to look into the dynamics of a relationship, at their needs and the experiences of the other person. It also enables people to become more open and honest with each other. Often the fear of broaching a topic is much worse than the subject itself. People frequently report that they are surprised to find that initiating a difficult conversation turned out better than they had expected and that they had made real progress with the other person. Coaching helps to get difficulties on to the table and create new levels of understanding.

Lifestyle We used to be conditioned by our parents, schools, employers, priests and rabbis as to how to live our lives. For most of us this is no longer true – or is vastly reduced. We are now subjected to conditioning from the media, from adverts and from the cult of celebrity. We often live out someone else's version of how we should live (while they make money out of us in the process). Coaching supports people in discovering what they really want. It challenges them to focus on how they would live if they had a free hand to do anything, and what changes they would make. This can be a liberating experience and shows that we can create our lifestyle as we would like it to be.

Health Many of us are experiencing health issues linked to the way we live. Stress is now the number one reason for absenteeism at work, having overtaken back pain. Obesity is rising fast and diseases that not many years ago were virtually unknown are now rampant. For a number of decades life expectancy has risen, yet we are now told that our children may be the first generation to experience a new trend – a fall in life expectancy.

Finding a way to maintain optimum health by building a regime into our lives that ensures our well-being and fitness seems ever more important. However, all of us are aware that just knowing that we need to do something doesn't ensure it gets done. Otherwise we would all be our ideal weight, eating nourishing food, getting the right number of hours sleep, exercising three times a week and feeling calm and relaxed. The support and challenge of an effective coach over health and well-being issues can make the difference between setting good intentions and taking vital action.

Space Without getting too mystical about it, we have always looked upon coaching as a gift. It is a gift for a coach to have open, honest and confidential relationships. It is a gift for coachees to have somebody focused entirely, in a non-judgmental way, on their particular agenda. This enables people to be true to themselves, which is not only refreshing but also means that real issues and truths can be addressed in the absence of any masks or barriers. People can only move forward in a valuable way if they can be themselves and tell the truth.

In many business environments we have to hang our real selves on the peg at the door as we enter. Coaching encourages coachees to be completely themselves, free of any artifice and role-playing.

SUPER TIMES SUMMARY

- Individuals and organisations are being asked to succeed faster than ever before against a backdrop of more competition, fewer resources, more demand and the unpredictable nature of a global market place.

- Coaching helps to ensure that people establish clear and measurable success criteria, maximise available resources and adapt in changing times.

- The days of one-style-fits-all are over. Coaching enables leaders and managers to be flexible, respond to individual needs and engage in important conversations that they would normally be too busy to have.

- Coaching helps to provide an environment in which people can achieve high performance.

- In a world where there is a crisis in meaning, coaching provides an opportunity for people to tap into their own values and define a purpose and mission that is relevant for them.

SuperCoaching
Exercise 2 Success: Creating Success Criteria

We live in turbulent times. The only guarantee is uncertainty. In a climate of unpredictability, it becomes even more important to define your criteria for success — and to acknowledge that they may need to change. As Susan Lucia Annunzio writes in *Contagious Success*, 'We have an important message to send, a message that affects the lives of many around the globe. The message is that companies must respect and value people. This is a must have, not a nice to have.' Think about your criteria for success. What is a must have for you to be successful? How will your coaching contribute to the success of the business and individuals you work with? Describe why coaching is essential now in your work and life? What is your next step to expand your coaching activity?

CHAPTER 3

Super Style – What's the Right Approach?

Graham: I was invited to coach the CEO of the American division of a global transport business. With his approval, I asked the HR department to send me various background documents as preparation for our exploratory meeting, including two personality profiles and three annual appraisal documents. I poured over these in advance of our meeting. They gave a picture of a leader who appeared to know his mind, to be meticulous with detail and to have a directive style of leadership. I wondered how he would respond to a coaching programme with a non-directive approach and to being challenged as and when appropriate.

At our initial meeting, I explained how I worked and

my approach, which proved to be particularly important because he continually used the words 'advisor' and 'expert' when describing his view of a coach. In light of this potential mismatch of style, we agreed to take stock after a couple of sessions and to check the value he was getting and how he was finding my style. Just prior to this review, I received the following email from him: 'Overall, I feel I have gained considerable benefit from our association. As someone who is not always the best at acting upon advice, I think one of your most effective approaches is to lead the discussion towards important aspects or considerations with a series of questions or open comments. Consequently, I have found that I reach my own conclusions, however they are based upon the structure and direction that you have identified and then pursued. Personally, this is much more effective for me than having someone say I ought to do x, y or z.'

It transpired that if I had been highly directive in style he probably wouldn't have responded well to it, but, equally, if I had not explained my non-directive approach it is likely he would have believed that I had nothing to add or was struggling to give input.

Super Style describes the style of non-directive coaching, explains the distinctions between coaching and other types of interpersonal interaction and explores how coaching fits within leadership and management.

**'I haven't read your proposal yet, Bob,
but I already have some great ideas
on how to improve it.'**

DIRECTION VS. NON-DIRECTION

Graham: I was working with a relatively young entrepreneur who, in eight years, had taken a business from nothing to a publicly listed company. His initial vision, tireless energy, big personality and deep understanding of the sector had brought about this success. He had been an inspiring leader, but one who had produced results through having his hand on every lever in the business and involving himself with even the smallest detail. This had worked in terms of growing the business, but had left him with an impoverished senior team that felt dis-empowered.

When I first met him, he was concerned about taking the business forward because he was having qualms about the capability of his key team members. As we talked, he could see that it would become increasingly difficult, indeed impossible, for him to continue to lead with his previous style. I asked him to consider what approach he might need to develop in order to harness the potential of his people. He conceded that he would need to move from a stance of command-and-control to being a more enabling presence.

He was concerned that making this change would leave him emasculated, in other words stripped of his influence and unable to add enough value. He also pointed out that things would probably move slower at first while people found their feet and, initially, in some cases, would not be done as well as if he had done them himself. I had to help him see that the short-term cost to the business was essential to the longer-term gain.

In our coaching sessions we had to contrast his old command-and-control approach against a new enabling style in role-plays around specific issues and conversations that he would have with his people. It was only in this way that he could have a real sense of what this new way would look, hear and feel like. Finally, we constructed a table of various situations and issues, contrasting how his old style would have approached them with how he was going to deal with them in the future. With some trepidation, he started to apply his new enabling approach in situations, which we then reviewed and built upon. After 12 months, I conducted interviews with several of his team members to assess how they had responded. It became apparent that the way the CEO had changed his style over the year had helped them to grow, to the extent where they now felt that there was a strong collective team leading and managing the business and its success no longer depended on one individual.

In hard-driving, task-focused, unforgiving cultures and organisations where managers are largely operational, a classic command-and-control management style tends to predominate. In these environments, managers are led to believe that the most effective way to ensure that the job gets done is to be direct. They tell people what to do, how to do it, and expect everyone to do as they're told. This approach may have worked in more predictable times, but in this changing climate it is a risky strategy.

People become disillusioned, demotivated and de-skilled if they become reliant on their manager telling them what to do. If there is a personality clash there might be a tendency to resist the instructions. If resentment has built up people may feel disposed to undermine the manager. Given that the most important resource in business today is the human brain, directing people along a path without giving full consideration to their individual needs and style is often a recipe for disaster.

At the other end of the spectrum, and particularly prevalent during the empowerment revolution, is a management style of leading from behind. At its most extreme, this style is typically played out with the manager revealing no personal point of view, but serving only as a facilitator for the workforce to define its own targets and working practices. The downside of this approach is that employees can feel let down or unsupported if managers do not offer enough direction, particularly in tough times.

There is a middle way. A style where leaders and managers both direct and facilitate. The key to applying this approach effectively is devising a conscious and well thought-through strategy rather than a default position that leaves people feeling dazed and confused.

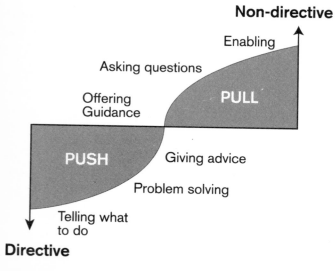

Diagram 4: Coaching Style

By the same token, a coach can adopt a directive or non-directive style, moving up and down the spectrum to greater or lesser effect. The key to success is for the coach to be aware of what he is doing and why. When we initially train managers as coaches we immerse them in a non-directive style. This is because most have been so steeped in telling people what to do that they are no longer conscious of it. They may claim to believe in the theory of drawing out the best from their people, but when the pressure is on they revert to type.

It can be a revealing process as people wean themselves off the default mode of giving instructions. The challenge with adopting a non-directive style is that it can require an investment in time upfront. The purpose, however, is to win it back as people learn and develop at an accelerated rate.

PUSH VS. PULL

In our SuperCoaching training programmes we demonstrate the spectrum of the push/pull axis through a ball catching exercise. We ask for a volunteer who would like to improve his ball catching ability in a 10-minute coaching session. We explain that we will throw some tennis balls, that if he catches them he should throw them back, but if he drops them to leave them. We then proceed to throw several balls, at which point we ask him, on a scale of 1–10 (10 representing outstanding), where he would rate his current expertise and where he would like it to be as a result of the coaching. We throw more balls and then ask him what, if anything, he has noticed. We then encourage him to stay focused on what catches his attention, for example, the direction of the ball, the spin or the pace. At no time do we push him in any particular direction by giving instructions about what he 'should' be doing. Most of the time we witness a measurable performance improvement simply as a result of pulling out of the coachee his own potential.

While both styles have their place, there are great dangers in the push approach. People are already surrounded by family, friends and colleagues; to say nothing of society at large, all of whom are prepared to give unsolicited advice and instructions. One of the key distinctions of coaching conversations, and what gives them power and value, is that a pull approach ensures that what is addressed is highly relevant to the coachee and means that he is authentic in choosing any commitment and action that arises from his coaching. This enabling process taps into people's extraordinary capability, given the chance, to see what's right for them as individuals and to move forward in a way that is appropriate to their own uniqueness. Ownership and buy-in are automatic as they connect with what's most important to enhance their work and lives.

TELL VS. ASK

On one of our development programmes helping managers build their coaching skills we watched the following interaction. The participant in the coach's role, who had a limited understanding of coaching, asked his coachee what he would like to work on. He chose time management. At this point, the coach committed a cardinal error. Assuming that he knew what his coachee meant, he proposed a solution, saying, 'Then you must immediately buy an electric personal organiser. They are terrific, very versatile and much better than the old paper ones.'

Those of us who were observing could see from his body language that this suggestion was not helpful. To give support to the unfortunate coach, we respectfully intervened and asked the coachee what he meant by time management. He replied, 'Well I have just taken on an additional large project, I have lost two of my people and we are right in the middle of the budgeting process for next year. I want to have a look at whether what I'm trying to do at the moment is even possible; if it is, to prioritise and plan and, if it isn't, to go back to my manager and explain my dilemma.'

Hearing that question being asked made the coach realise that not only had he made too quick an assumption, but, more importantly, he had told his coachee what he thought he should do rather than eliciting the real issue from him. If he had pursued his route the session would have been a waste of time and led to frustration.

There still exists a prevailing belief that telling somebody what to do is the fastest way of achieving an outcome. While this may have some truth in it, we've probably all had the experience of telling somebody what to do and finding it does not guarantee the expected result. Consequently, more time is spent having to re-explain and re-work the job than if we had helped to increase their learning and development in the first place. Moreover, when it comes to doing the task again in the future we'll probably again have to tell them what to do rather than have the benefit of any development sticking.

In deciding whether to lead with a 'tell' or 'ask' style it's important to clarify the purpose of an interaction. If a new employee asks, 'Where is the photocopier?' this is not a good time to use non-directive coaching. However, if an employee asks, 'Please help me to prioritise my project', this is an ideal coaching opportunity. The only way we can truly help is by asking open-ended questions to help the employee uncover the real issues and to generate his own solution.

It is important that a leader sets clear expectations with his team about his preferred style. If people are used to being given instructions by management, suddenly having somebody who has a collaborative approach and puts the onus back on to them is very disconcerting. In the worst-case scenario resentment can develop, because people may feel that they're being dumped on by a manager who they perceive isn't up to the job. Giving a clear explanation about our chosen style ensures under-standing and irons out any possible misconceptions.

SPECTRUM OF SUPPORT

There are various other possible interventions on the spectrum between push and pull, including giving advice, making suggestions, giving feedback and asking questions. While the most valuable long-term gain is generally achieved through asking questions, the coachee can also derive benefit from the other inputs. However, they should only be offered if necessary, and if the coachee requests them. The coach needs to be clear that any content he provides is for the purpose of reflection on the part of the coachee, rather than being the definitive or 'right' answer.

We will cover each input in detail in Chapter 6. At this stage, it's important to point out that this is an occasion where the coach's level of self-awareness is vital. For instance, there is a world of difference between giving vague and judgmental feedback and providing descriptive, non-judgmental feedback. The former will wreak havoc while the latter can help to raise awareness. There's also a world of difference between making a genuine suggestion that can be accepted or rejected by a coachee once he has the opportunity to evaluate it, and giving disguised instruction. After 25 years of coaching we still have no desire to play God!

COACHING DISTINCTIONS

It is common to find the term coaching used to describe various 'helping activities' in organisations. One of the difficulties is that terms have been used promiscuously in the past, causing confusion between coaching and other disciplines. The CIPD guide to coaching has identified some generally agreed characteristics of coaching in organisations:

- It consists of one-to-one development discussions.

- It provides people with feedback on both their strengths and weaknesses.

- It is aimed at specific issues/areas.

- It is a relatively short-term activity, except in executive coaching, which tends to have a longer time frame.

- It is essentially a non-directive form of development.

- It focuses on improving performance and developing/enhancing an individual's skills.

- Coaching activities have both organisational and individual goals.

- It assumes that the individual is psychologically healthy and does not require a clinical intervention.

- It works on the premise that clients are self-aware, or can achieve self-awareness.

- It is time-bounded.

- It is a skilled activity.

- Personal issues may be discussed but the emphasis is on performance at work.

We will now make a brief comparison of how the most common terminologies for 'helping activities' are used:

Coaching is:
- Solution and action focused
- Awareness based
- Focused towards task, performance and development
- Non-directive
- Structured
- engaged with a 'boss', peer, colleague or external

Mentoring is:
- Delivered by an experienced and usually senior internal or external manager
- Focused on career development, policy, politics and networking
- Giving advice
- More free-form

Counselling/Therapy is:
- Meaning focused
- Analytically based
- Focused more on feelings
- More free-form

Training is:
- Focused on developing skills and capabilities
- Concerned with imparting concrete knowledge and concrete matters such as products, corporate objectives and processes
- More group orientated

Consulting is:
- Focused on considering problems, arriving at a conclusion and recommending advice
- Specific to the consultants area of expertise

Diagram 5: Coaching Distinctions

COACHING VS. MENTORING

Probably the biggest confusion in terminology lies with the terms mentoring and coaching. Although similar skills are used in both, for example listening, questioning and summarising, there is a clear distinction between them as regards both purpose and provider.

The term 'mentoring' originates in Greek mythology. Odysseus entrusted his house and the education of his son to his friend, Mentor, saying to him, 'tell him all you know'. This is still very much the purpose of mentoring, where an older and more experienced colleague shares his knowledge of an organisation and business with a mentee in order to help him progress in his career development. A mentor tends to be internal to the business and focuses on the long-term development of an individual rather than aiming for a short-term increase in performance.

In a coaching relationship, if a coachee requires some career guidance, it may be appropriate for the coach to either refer him to a mentor within the business or, if he has the relevant experience himself, to step out of his coaching role in order to offer it. The two disciplines are highly complementary, with many people choosing to have a mentor alongside a coach. The 'oracle', or human fortune cookie, is an essential resource in today's business climate. Anyone who has been around long enough to impart some wisdom is a valuable commodity.

COACHING VS. COUNSELLING

One of the major concerns of people in the work environment is that by applying a coaching approach they run the risk of opening a can of worms, since the process will involve delving into a coachee's childhood, family and personal relationships. Once again, although there are some similarities between coaching and counselling, there are very significant differences in the focus and the intention of the interaction.

Coaching is solution-focused and action orientated, whereas counselling is more meaning based. Coaching addresses aspirations, objectives and tasks, while counselling focuses more on feelings. Coaching tends to be structured, while counselling is a more free-form approach. Coaching puts a greater emphasis on gaining clarity about what people want and how to achieve it, whereas counselling aims to help people understand themselves better.

Traditionally, coaches can come from outside an organisation, or within the business in a line relationship, a non-line relationship, or within HR. Counsellors invariably come from outside the organisation. We would not expect managers to act as counsellors, although they may have a very empathetic approach.

COACHING VS. THERAPY

Therapy sets out to enable an individual to cope better in the world. In many cases this will involve modifying behaviours in such a way that he is better able to fit into the normal expectations of business, family or societal life. Therapy is a valuable approach when there are deep and potentially damaging issues within the individual. In those circumstances, organisations should have qualified therapists for referral purposes.

Coaches need to remain alert to the possibility of issues emerging in discussions with a coachee that are outside their capability and that lie outside the boundaries defined for coaching. Coaches should avoid therapeutic issues, as they run a great risk of being out of their depth and potentially causing harm to the coachee and to themselves. Having said that, we have rarely encountered these problems or had to refer coachees elsewhere.

COACHING VS. TRAINING

The purpose of training is predominantly to help people learn and develop skills. The approach tends to be prescriptive, with the trainer delivering the data. It can be extremely useful in building intellectual capability and exposing people to new ideas and approaches for enhancing skills. The downside of some training is that it fails to adapt to the uniqueness of individuals and their business context. It might leave a trainee with valuable theory, but without the ability to use and apply it.

Coaching differs from training in that it approaches learning and development in a highly individual way. In many cases, the coachee is able to learn through his own experience rather than being told the 'right' approach to adopt. Because coaching is unique to each coachee the return on investment should be high, as it specifically targets his development needs. Learning with a coaching approach can take place in a group setting and is usually stylistically different from the 'talk and chalk' training approach. Participants are encouraged to develop their own learning agendas in advance of workshops and, within them, to learn from experience and feedback rather than instruction. It ensures that the implement-ation of any new behaviours and skills are measurable against performance criteria.

Highly effective development combines training and coaching so that people are able to learn intellectually as well as through experience. Once training has taken place, coaching can be the catalyst to help them imple-ment it and gain maximum benefit from it. One of our main contributions to the business world has been to help organisations recognise that they could become more effective at developing their people through coaching rather than just having a rich portfolio of training programmes. While the latter continue to have value they need to be carefully designed and used in order to maximise the return. Companies that invest wisely in their training and coaching programmes reap the benefits.

COACHING VS. CONSULTING

Coaching and consulting can go together, however it's essential to identify which activity is being pursued. We are frequently invited to consult with businesses on their coaching capability and to make recommendations on how to develop a coaching culture. When we agree these contracts, we make it clear that the initial assessment and any subsequent recommendations are made in the consulting role. Then, if we agree a programme to be taken forward, it is done with a coaching approach to ensure that the company does not expect to be told what to do.

One of the reasons why organisations can, initially, be surprised by coaching is that, due to the experience of consultants providing answers and making recommendations, the coach's approach (where their role is to enable the organisation to self-discover and generate its own solutions) is not the norm. This is why finding people who are both effective coaches and consultants is not easy. Coaching and consultancy have different approaches with different intentions and come from different psychological paradigms. However, they can coexist and be a highly potent force when used together.

'My staff just left for a ten-day
stress management retreat.
I'm feeling more relaxed already!'

MANAGER VS. COACH

We believe that a manager wears three primary 'hats' – leader, manager and coach. There is a synergistic relationship between each role, with coaching underpinning and supporting the other two. We're always flabbergasted when asked if coaching should be in a manager's remit. We believe that such uncertainty points to a fundamental lack of understanding of the nature and importance of coaching. It would be comparable to asking if the Arsenal football manager, Arsene Wenger, should be interested and involved in his players' performance and development. Obviously, it is essential for managers to be deeply committed to their staff's performance, learning and development, and the fulfilment of their potential.

A manager needs to lead by defining a clear vision and

direction, then inspiring others to follow it. In essence, a leadership role is about 'creating a game worth playing'; winning hearts and minds so that colleagues become aligned and enthused. Management occurs once the vision and enthusiasm are established. It is the process of assigning resources to deliver the vision and agreeing the strategy, priorities, goals, roles, targets, accountabilities and deliverables. Management also monitors the performance against the goals and objectives. Coaching, however, not only helps staff to achieve those targets, and thus move towards the vision, it also enables them to overcome obstacles, gain insights, build skills and increase performance. In short be the best that they can be.

Thus, from the above, it's clear that coaching should make up the bulk of what a manager does. While the vision, direction and deliverables need constant reinforcement, once established, they do not take up a great deal of time. Once the process is established, a manager is free to adopt the role of coach with his staff. It is important that he is clear with them as to which hat he is wearing and to initially specify when he is having a leadership, management or coaching conversation until people know what to expect. Confusion can arise when an employee is told that he's having a coaching session when in fact it's performance management driven by the manager's agenda. It's equally confusing for an employee, wanting to be given direction, to find his manager asking him what he thinks should be done.

Our intention is to demonstrate that coaching is pivotal in a manager's role. Far from being merely a remedial activity, coaching is an approach that underpins the achievement of objectives by managers and their teams. This is the most effective way for organisations to realise their vision and utilise their most important resource – people.

SUPER STYLE SUMMARY

- Coaching is essentially a non-directive form of development.

- Coaching pulls solutions out of people rather than pushing them towards answers.

- Telling people what to do may achieve short-term results. However, asking their opinion taps into capability and generates long-term development and sustainable performance.

- The primary difference between coaching and other 'helping activities' is that it is more focused towards task, performance and development and has a structured approach.

- Coaching underpins the responsibilities of a manager. It is the glue that binds leadership activities with the achievement of objectives.

SuperCoaching
Exercise 3: Developing a Coaching Style

A person with high emotional intelligence is able to accurately self-assess his strengths and weaknesses and then devise an action plan for self-improvement. Take this opportunity to honestly assess how much you adopt a coaching approach. On a scale of 1–10, (where 10 represents world class), how effective is your coaching? Are you able to be directive and non-directive at the right time? How far are you able to draw solutions out of others? Do you prefer to tell people what to do or to ask their opinion? Now you have increased your awareness about your coaching approach, what specific actions will you take to enhance it?

CHAPTER 4

Super Being – The Essence of Coaching

Ben: I watched the television broadcast of The Labour Party Annual Conference in 2002. A very special moment occurred when the guest speaker entered the room. A hush descended. There was an air of anticipation. The silence was broken by a spontaneous standing ovation and thunderous applause before Nelson Mandela had even addressed the audience. Through the TV screen I could feel his presence. It had a quiet authority. It commanded respect. It exuded calm and a sense of perspective.

We do not need to be world statesmen in order to be Super Coaches. However, who we are as human beings will have a major influence on the effectiveness of our coaching. Language is inadequate to describe the key existential state for a coach, suffice it to say that we need to bring our whole selves to the coaching interaction.

Super Being describes the essence of coaching and positions the coach's quality of being as the foundation from which effective coaching emerges.

SELF-AWARENESS

'The unexamined life is not worth living.'

Socrates

Graham: 'How can you possibly help me?' I was greeted with this opening sentence from an ex-SAS commando who had been physically and mentally scarred in battle and now headed up a division in a major defence contractor. I had been warned in advance that he was a hard-bitten northerner, didn't suffer fools gladly and called a spade a spade. I had also been informed that he had little understanding or interest in coaching, and had only agreed to meet me because he liked to lunch and took a perverse pleasure out of debunking HR initiatives and consultants.

With this encouraging background, I had booked a table at a well-known restaurant. Luckily, he had eaten there before and had been impressed and thus, in spite of being a coach (only marginally above a double-glazing salesman in his eyes), I had scored an initial brownie point. In response to his opening remark I said, 'I don't know if I can help, but I've certainly worked with countless chief executives and they wouldn't have paid the bills unless they had got some value.'

As the lunch progressed, my straightforward approach and willingness to challenge clearly intrigued him. Here was a man who had survived by being tougher than tough. This had carried over into his leadership style and he was unused to having people stand up to him. I could sense a growing respect as we discussed how I might be helpful and he began to reveal a side that I suspected others never saw. Behind the tough exterior lay a surprisingly warm heart. He clearly cared about his people, as indeed he'd had to behind enemy lines, and he recognised that there were things he could learn in order to lead more effectively within the corporate world. It emerged that he had no clear sense of where his career was heading and, being in his early fifties, this uncertainty was troubling him. There was no obvious person with whom he could discuss these issues.

At the end of the meal, not only did he insist on picking up the bill, but said that he would like to proceed with a coaching programme. He recognised that not understanding the detail of his business might not be a disadvantage, and that having a man-to-man, honest discussion about his approach and future could be very helpful. I believe that earlier in my coaching career, when I possessed less self-awareness and confidence, he would have made mincemeat of me. I would have tried to land him as a client rather than focus on his needs and the benefits he might derive from coaching.

We do not subscribe to the view that in order to be an effective coach we must have everything sorted in our own life. However, we think that it's essential for a coach to have a high degree of self-awareness and to continue to deepen it. A coach should know himself sufficiently to understand his inner world, strengths and weaknesses, and have a sense of humour and perspective about himself. This ensures that during a coaching interaction the coach can dedicate his complete attention to his coachee, whilst also having an awareness of himself. This involves being able to observe his thoughts, emotions, body language and reactions so that they are used to support the process, rather than create any interference. A high level of self-awareness also enables the coach to pay attention to his intuition, which can be an accurate monitor of the coaching process and a basis from which he can ask insightful questions, offer feedback and make suggestions.

Unfortunately, many people in organisations are total doers and have not invested in self-reflection. Traditionally the right side of the brain – the part responsible for the more intuitive processes – is not stimulated at business school. Furthermore, people don't learn it on the job. The process of increasing self-awareness usually involves a level of frustration. In our SuperCoaching programmes participants reach a point where they feel so conscious about who they are and what they are doing that it interferes with simply being themselves. This is an inevitable stage in the learning process, as heightened self-awareness initially causes increased self-consciousness and discomfort. Only through hours of practice does self-awareness become an unconscious state creating a powerful arena where coaching can occur.

PRESENCE

In our workshops we sometimes ask participants to think back to the first decisions they make at the beginning of a normal day. A typical list would include:

- What to wear?

- Tea or coffee?

- Hit the snooze button.

- Walk the dog.

- Get the kids off to school.

- Check email.

- Who to call first?

It is a 'to do' list and is characteristic of our action-packed lives from the minute we wake up to the minute we collapse exhausted at the end of a day. It also turns out that most of these decisions are unconscious. We are on autopilot and rarely stop to think about the impact of them.

We then ask our delegates to consider another type of decision. A 'to be' decision. What kind of person do they want to be today? What level of impact do they want to have? What impression do they want to give? How do they want to be remembered? Although 'to do' decisions are important for shaping our lives, 'to be' decisions are essential for determining our presence in the world. Examples include:

- To be inspiring.

- To be empathetic.

- To be generous.

- To be humorous.

- To be reflective.

Recognising that we can influence our own presence means that we can consciously choose the way we impact on others. Super Coaches have an enabling presence that is authentic and helps coachees to be open, honest and trusting. They go beyond any concerns about looking good, getting coaching right or appearing to be an expert. Super Coaches bring all their energy and attention to coaching so that their presence supports and inspires.

EGO-LESS

'To awaken means to realise one's nothingness.'

G.I. Gurdjieff

Perhaps Freud would have argued that there is no such thing as ego-lessness. However, the less a coach pays attention to his own ego, the more he can provide the greatest value to the coachee. We describe the ego as our needs, wants and desires that derive from a place of insecurity, self-doubt and, at its most extreme, from narcissistic wounds – blows to our self-esteem that were usually inflicted in childhood by parents who were either too distant or too indulgent. Typically, people with big egos seek recognition, control and external confirmation to combat their feelings of helplessness and low self-worth.

On a recent three-day programme to develop managers to become better coaches, one participant stuck out like a sore thumb. To virtually every comment we made, he responded in an aggressive manner. Although the points he made were valid, the way in which he made them felt antagonistic and eventually isolated him from his peers. When it came to observing him in action as a coach, he not surprisingly attempted to dominate his sessions, steering his coachee in the direction he thought was appropriate and finding it extremely difficult to allow the coachee space to reflect. Here was an example of a person unable to rise above his own ego through a lack of self-awareness and a chronic need to appear right about his own opinion. It was also impossible to give him any feedback, because he responded to any approach defensively.

Coaching is riddled with paradoxes. A coach needs to be passionate about his coachee gaining maximum value from coaching, but needs to be unattached to particular agendas, processes or outcomes. A coach must have a well-defined methodology and approach and yet be flexible in meeting the needs of his coachee. In other words, a coach is required to surrender and let go on a constant basis so that the coachee owns his own agenda and process. It is only in an ego-less state that a coach can allow a session to unfold in its own unique way, giving rise to increased awareness, insight, understanding and motivation.

BEING NON-JUDGMENTAL

Ben: When I first met Graham I was struck by how easy he was to talk to. Being invited to work alongside him, I wanted to impress, but found that I didn't need to. In fact, I ended up discussing unresolved issues from my own life, which I certainly wouldn't have done if I wanted to look good. I felt free to be myself, unconcerned about his opinion of me. I was not alone in having this experience. Watching Graham in action coaching exec after exec, shows how he brings the same quality of non-judgment to each interaction. It is hardwired into his DNA. Although he has opinions, his level of mindfulness ensures that they don't cause any interference in his coaching relationships.

In the early days of coaching we were intrigued by the challenge of how a coach could create an environment in which a coachee feels trusting and relaxed enough to be open and honest. Why, within 10 minutes of meeting a coach, would somebody reveal aspects of himself, his concerns, hopes and dreams that he may not have previously shared with anyone? Over the years, we have come to recognise that one of the primary factors that enables this to happen is being non-judgmental.

Working in a non-judgmental environment is an unusual experience for many of us, as we tend to operate in worlds dominated by prejudice, personal beliefs and biases. Consequently, we are often on the defensive, feel embattled or strive to impose our own particular point of view. It is refreshing and reassuring to be with a coach who has suspended all judgment. It provides the opportunity for a coachee to behave in accordance with his true self. For some, this is the only occasion in their working life where this could happen. Once somebody feels supported and not judged he can say what he truly means and real issues can be addressed.

This is where it's essential for a coach to have a high level of self-awareness, so he is able to recognise where he is particularly prone to making judgments, what pushes his hot buttons and how to free himself from them. Thinking that a coachee is weak, wrong in his opinion or unskilled will cause serious disruption in the coaching process. A way for a coach to heighten awareness about judgments is to watch out for any thoughts that start with 'should', 'ought', 'must', 'have to', 'right', 'wrong', 'good' or 'bad.' Thinking 'He should confront his manager', 'He's got the wrong team structure', 'He must develop clear direction' will send an energetic signal to a coachee that he's being judged.

This doesn't mean that a coach avoids giving feedback, being discriminating or giving his reactions, but the key is to replace judgmental thoughts with non-judgmental language. Using 'could', 'can', 'maybe', 'perhaps', 'consider', 'possibility', 'option', 'what about' invites a coachee to reflect upon his perception and behaviour in a non-threatening and considered way and ensures that he feels supported and able to say what he thinks.

The job of a coach is to be neutral. He needs to free himself from any prejudices, biases and personal beliefs. In order to be most effective, it is imperative that he becomes a clear mirror and listens through undistorted ears. When his own mind-set intrudes he will listen selectively, become judgmental, manipulate the conversation or attempt to prove to his coachee that he is right. This is dangerous practice. All beliefs are personal and while his particular prejudices and biases can seem to be an ultimate truth, in fact they are only our point of view. Self-awareness helps him suspend these mind-sets during coaching. He needs to observe his own thought processes and head off biases before they hijack him.

BEING ACCEPTING

'Acceptance of what has happened is the first step to overcoming the consequences of any misfortune.'

William James

Related to the notion of non-judgment is the coach's acceptance of anything and everything about his coachee and of what emerges in coaching sessions. It is paramount that the coach accepts it all and then works with what's most useful, without the normal filtering processes that restrict or limit so many conversations and leave them bereft of authenticity, openness and honesty.

As the coach accepts, so does his coachee. He is helped to look objectively at any issues rather than judge them. Many people stay stuck because they can't look at and accept where they are. What we find is that many issues are rooted in some form of self-attack. In other words, people give themselves a hard time, which prevents them from arriving at a solution.

Ben: Lucy was a high-flyer. She was identified as having considerable potential and was being fast tracked through her organisation, due to her insatiable appetite for work and ability to overcome challenges. When we met, I was struck by the way Lucy talked about herself. She managed to put herself down in every other sentence saying, 'I'm not productive enough', 'What's wrong with me, I should be doing better than I am', and when she compared herself to colleagues she always came off worse.

I encouraged Lucy to reflect upon the way she spoke about herself. When I summarised her content, she was amazed at how negative she sounded. I asked her to consider what it would be like if she heard somebody else speaking like that. Lucy realised that she was being highly self-critical and admitted that she had grown up in a family in which she rarely felt accepted. She had a younger sister who got all the positive reinforcement and praise from her parents. Lucy had been told that she needed to set an example. She became a grade A student and was then told not to get bigheaded. Consequently, she appeared to have spent the rest of her life over-compensating for this lack of acceptance and had internalised it. Lucy admitted that, although she had achieved a lot, she derived little satisfaction and that her next step was to learn to accept herself in order to start enjoying her accomplishments.

Accepting a coachee is the ultimate mark of respect a coach can give. For a coachee to know that he can tell his coach anything in the knowledge that he will not think less of him provides the necessary climate of safety for coaching to occur. He is able to look at his reality free of any prejudices or points of view, safe to brainstorm options, including the wacky and unusual, and safe to choose to act or not to act. The relief for a coachee is often palpable in early sessions when he experiences acceptance and the freedom to explore. Unconditional acceptance is a rare and precious thing and is unusual in our judgmental society.

BEING NON-DEFENSIVE

Ben: 'You did not challenge me enough, you can afford to be the bad guy and I felt that initially we spent too long discussing the background of the issue.' Kevin gave me his feedback following an early session in our coaching programme. I could feel myself wanting to defend my position. I wanted to say, 'You told me that you were under considerable pressure, therefore I didn't think it was appropriate to challenge you too hard. I'm happy to be the bad guy, but you didn't give any indication that you wanted to be pushed and I didn't even need to prompt you to talk about the background.' Instead, I listened and asked Kevin what specifically he would need me to do differently in order to feel satisfied. 'What would it look like if I truly challenged you? How would you know that I was being the bad guy? Will you let me know if our discussion appears irrelevant?'

It is vital that coaches are non-defensive in order to create environments in which people can be completely straightforward and have no hidden agendas. If there is something on the mind of the coach or coachee which they think is beginning to get in the way, then they need to voice it without fear. The coach needs to be able to ask the coachee whether he is finding the coaching valuable, whether he is happy with his approach and how could it be more effective. Equally, the coachee needs to feel that he can ask for direct feedback, observations and suggestions from the coach without needing to justify his request.

A coach needs a high degree of internal security in order to be open to receiving honest observations and feedback from his coachees. A Super Coach recognises that he has nothing to prove about himself, nor about his coaching. He knows that there is always room for learning and development but it doesn't mean that he has to be defensive. If a coach feels defensive or vulnerable then he will fail to ask for feedback, or ask in such a way that he will get unclear answers. It is similar for coachees, who need to be prepared to learn, grow and recognise that being non-defensive provides the optimum condition for successful learning and development.

BEING AUTHENTIC

'Live in such a way that you would not be ashamed to sell your parrot to the town gossip.'

Will Rogers

Do you constantly fear that you are about to be unmasked as a fake? That the same employers who gave you your high-flying job are about to wake up to your inadequacies? If the answer is yes, you are suffering from Impostor Syndrome. One manager captured this condition when she described going to Paris on the Eurostar for a business meeting. Helen was wearing her grey trouser suit and starched white Paul Smith shirt, carrying her mobile phone and the latest Sony Vaio laptop. She painted the picture of a professional woman on her way to knock a few heads together and clinch a deal. Inside, though, she was feeling quite different. She was merely acting the part of the businesswoman. In Helen's perception, the other women with their laptops and copies of the *FT* were real. She was an impostor. She kept waiting for the conductor to ask for an ID and then usher her off the train.

The Impostor Syndrome is a surprisingly common complaint and is characterised by the feeling that sooner or later we will be revealed as a fraud. Every achievement is a fluke or a mistake, no accolade deserved. Either we have managed to fool everyone again, or we are simply dealing with an idiot who cannot appreciate just how incompetent we are. Sooner or later, we know that someone will tap us on the shoulder and say: 'Game's up. We all know that you haven't got a clue.' To add to the challenge, every new project, promotion and award only adds to the fear that next time we will be exposed. Paradoxically, the higher we climb up the corporate ladder, the more anxious we become.

The term Impostor Syndrome was coined in 1974 by the American psychologist Pauline Rose Clance, author of *The Impostor Phenomenon*. According to research figures, approximately 70 per cent of the professional population are sufferers to some degree. This means that the majority of us have adapted our behaviour to hide our authentic selves and at times pretend to be something we're not. Given that being authentic is one of the most important prerequisites for effective coaching it poses a real challenge not to play or act at being a coach. If it does happen, the coachee will either sense it immediately, causing him to become hesitant and calculating in his disclosure, or it will create an underlying discomfort due to the insincerity involved.

An important aspect of authenticity is self-awareness. If we know who we are, it is more likely that we will know when we're being true to ourselves. A useful indicator for how authentic we're being is the level of tension we experience in our interactions. If we're feeling relaxed and unconcerned about what others think about us then it's a good indicator that we're being authentic. On the other hand, if we're editing what we say, trying to please and getting caught up in our performance, we're removed from our authentic selves.

A Super Coach is being himself. Like any great performer, he makes coaching look natural and easy. He is able to be confident not arrogant, to combine wisdom with humility and create a natural flow in conversation. The coach may have remarkable skills and capability, but the coachee will feel this as a natural expression of who he is. The failure to be authentic will result in the coachee feeling that he is having coaching done to him through a series of techniques rather than experiencing a natural connection.

BEING FLEXIBLE

We were asked to help turn around a department of an organisation that was consistently under-performing. We undertook a series of interviews with employees to get a view on the business and clarify the issues involved. What emerged was a high degree of consensus about the level of rigidity in the company. People were hemmed in by the working practices, which prevented them from performing tasks outside their function. This led to a silo mentality that erected even bigger walls to be overcome. Although the organisation talked about teamwork, they had a controversial system of individual reward that hijacked employees' attempts at supporting each other beyond what was necessary. It transpired that the department was its own worst enemy through being so inflexible.

Systems, procedures, structures, models, tools and techniques all serve a function. However, we need to be careful how we use them so that they don't detract from the importance of flexibility. The majority of effective coaching sessions travel from A to B without a clear indication of how they were going to get there. Although an underlying structure is required that allows flow to occur, it mustn't imprison the conversation, thus preventing the coaching from creating its own lease of life.

No two sessions are ever the same. No two coachees are ever the same. Every coaching topic, whether it's vision, work–life balance, performance, relationship or motivation is unique. A Super Coach is able to go with the flow and allow outcomes to emerge naturally. Some coachees like a fast pace in their coaching sessions and to move from A to B via logical steps, whilst others prefer a slower pace and are more comfortable proceeding with a mosaic-like conversation. It's important that a coach is able to read a situation carefully and respond to it with a flexible mindset.

BEING INTENTION-LED

Graham: I will always remember the day when my coach helped me to get a clear, strong picture about how much money I wanted to earn in a given year, coupled with an absolute conviction that it would happen. I was unwilling for any other outcome to occur. When I articulated and became passionate about this intention I had no idea of how I was going to get there. (I later found out that the coach didn't either). In the event, I quintupled my income, which was beyond my wildest dreams, and finished the year driving a Ferrari.

Intention inspires action. It is the food of life. It is the creative force that causes extraordinary things to happen. How did we write this book? Through our intention to bring it into fruition. How did you land up reading it? Through your intention to maximise your performance, development and fulfilment.

Patch Adams, MD, is a social revolutionary whose medical career has been devoted to giving away health care – one of the most expensive things in America – for free. For over 30 years he has operated a home-based family medical practice known as the Gesundheit Institute and treated over 20,000 people. His work came to light as a result of a Hollywood movie of his life, in which he was played by Robin Williams. What makes Patch such an inspiring figure is the power of his intention to cut through the barriers of medicine as a business, to address the caring relationship between doctor and patient based on a mutually responsible, loving, creative and even humorous exchange. Several years ago, The Happiness Project, which organises seminars on positive psychology and well-being, had the good fortune to work with him. Meeting Patch in the flesh only reinforces his commitment to his intention. Every conversation he has, every moment he breathes is living testimony to his desire to see a more open and humane world.

What is the right intention of a coach? Does he intend his coachees to gain tremendous value from coaching? Does he intend them to come up with their own solutions and resolve their own issues? Does he intend them to perform beyond what they thought was possible? What is his intention? Firstly, a coach must want to coach. He must be whole-heartedly committed to his coachee gaining value from the interaction. Secondly, he needs to support the coachee in becoming absolutely clear about his intention in a way which engages his head, heart and guts with a passionate certainty that he will achieve it.

BEING AN ENABLER

Ben: I was at a friend's 40th birthday party recently and introduced to the manager of a well-known electrical retailer. Darren had been with the business for 18 weeks and his store had already become the number one outlet in the group, turning over £3 million per month, up from £1.8 million. I was fascinated to learn more. I asked him about his secret for success, he replied, 'Coach your people.' He went on to explain his philosophy that people have answers within them, they need to be encouraged to think for themselves and tap into their own motivation. I thought I was listening to myself! I wanted to know which management school Darren had attended. I was not surprised when he informed me that he had learnt on the job, starting out as an apprentice butcher and staying in food retail for 20 years. Having become slightly stale in the food business, realising that management is about people not the product, Darren decided to change sectors. He applied exactly the same principles in the electrical trade as he had done in food and discovered that seeing himself as an enabler for learning, growth, motivation and action got him similar results.

At the heart of non-directive coaching is a coach perceiving himself as an enabler for change, insight and understanding. At the other end of the spectrum is somebody seeing himself as the answer to others' problems and telling them what to do. How do you see yourself? Do you see yourself as a catalyst for people to discover their own solutions, or as a wise sage who believes he knows what is right for others and is determined to tell them what to do? Knowing where you sit on this spectrum is vital. The coach who is flexible enough to move up and down it can adapt to a wide variety of coachees and coaching needs. The coach who is only in the business of giving advice is unlikely to get it right every time and will fail to help his coachees recognise their own brilliance.

Super Coaches are enablers. It is their job to create environments for learning and insight and to help others generate the will to act. We are not saying that giving advice and making suggestions don't have value. However, the way to make a difference through non-directive coaching is to enable others to tap into their own resources, which creates something useful for them, increases their own ability in the short-term and helps to build their capability for the long-term.

ATTITUDE

'Attitudes are more important than facts.'

Karl A. Menninger

We're sure that you're familiar with Pavlov's experiments with salivating dogs. He rang a bell, produced food and recorded that his dogs produced saliva. He then rang a bell, produced no food and noticed that his dogs still dribbled. Are we the same as Pavlov's dogs? Does life ring a bell and we salivate without making a conscious choice about how we respond to the stimulus? Are we the product of our conditioning, our genes, our environment and our upbringing, with little choice as to how we can respond to life? In other words if our father had a short temper, do we also, is it in our DNA? If, as a child, our teacher told us we were stupid, so that now, each time we make a mistake we 'remember' the emotional pain, is it just tough luck?

Probably the biggest breakthrough in psychology during the last century was moving away from a deterministic view to painting a picture of a cognitive map which suggested that, in between each stimulus and response, is a gap in which we can make new choices. This insight is most poignantly addressed by Victor Frankl, a psychiatrist and a Jew. Imprisoned in the Nazi concentration camps during the Second World War, Frankl was able to retain a level of objectivity, due to his training, that contributed to his survival. He went on to write an extraordinary book, *Man's Search for Meaning*, which describes his horrific experiences in the camps. At one stage, he states how every last human right and dignity can be taken away from mankind, except his ultimate freedom. In Frankls' words: 'The ability to choose our response in any given situation; to choose our own way.'

The effectiveness of a coach is determined to a large extent by the attitude that he brings to it. Since coaching is a function of the 'bubble' in which the coach and coachee exist during a coaching session, his attitude has a crucial influence on this, for better or for worse. Is he absolutely committed to the success of his coachees? Does he believe that they have enormous inherent ability? Does he trust the coaching process and believe that it always adds value?

Super Coaches have an attitude that is optimistic, resilient, humorous and open. They take responsibility for it and ensure that their attitude is in the best possible condition to support their coaching.

BEING CONFIDENT

'As is our confidence, so is our capacity.'

William Hazlitt

Ben: A popular request on our SuperCoaching programmes is for the tutors to demonstrate a coaching session in front of the audience. I shall never forget the first time I got the opportunity to do this. It was comparable to many of those 'first' experiences in life: school, kissing, driving, marriage! I was terrified. I did my best to look cool, sat down and silently asked for help.

I started with a broad question, asking my coachee, 'What's on your mind?' Howard proceeded to present me with a complex business issue that involved looking at the impact of his boss and company structure on his set objectives. I managed to get him to clarify an outcome for our conversation and then asked him to tell me more. I was holding on to the edge of my seat wondering whether I was doomed, when out of nowhere Howard had an 'Ah ha' moment. His demeanour changed as he exclaimed that what he needed to do was quite simple.

Everybody had told him that his problems lay in his relationship with his boss and that he needed to sit down with him and realign his business objectives. This had not resonated with him. He now saw that what he needed to do was address an environmental issue. He used to work in his own office. Following some restructuring, he now operated in an open-plan office in which he couldn't concentrate and get his job done. He thanked me profusely for my help, which caused me some embarrassment – I hadn't done anything. However the beauty of this experience was that it confirmed my faith in the coaching process and strengthened my confidence as a coach.

Unfortunately, there is no magic confidence pill for becoming an effective coach. We know of no quick solution other than getting coaching miles under the belt. Confidence is born out of experience, of learning what works and what doesn't, getting honest feedback from coachees and peers, and collecting evidence of tangible and measurable results.

The confidence level of a coach will be a direct measure of his capacity to coach well. Hence, it's important to be confident in handling a wide range of coaching topics and dealing with whatever arises. Coachees need to feel they are in capable hands, as they entrust their current reality, hopes and dreams to the coach. Any uncertainty or lack of confidence will transmit itself and could erode the coachee's confidence and engagement with coaching.

This does not mean that a coach should fake it. He can demonstrate his confidence by acknowledging when he requires time to think. Saying, 'Let me think about that for a moment', or 'I'm not sure how we should proceed' is a useful way of being upfront. Another option is to check in with the coachee by asking, 'Are we on track?' or 'Is this useful?' A truly confident coach can be honest with his coachee without worrying about not looking good.

We encourage you to take as many opportunities as you can to coach in a variety of situations and with different coachees. Keep notes of what you did, what seemed to be effective, what less so, and of your key discoveries. Find opportunities to do 20- or 30-minute coaching sessions to 'force' you to be both focused and time economic, and to prove to yourself how much can be achieved in a short period. Another useful way to build confidence is to get a colleague to coach you on your coaching skills and to give you feedback, which will enable you to develop faster and more effectively. In the early days of our coaching, we sometimes used to do four or five 2-hour coaching sessions back to back, not a practice to be recommended, but one which afforded a great learning laboratory.

BEING COMFORTABLE WITH THE UNKNOWN

Another aspect of developing confidence is being able to operate effectively in situations of high ambiguity. Initially, all coachees are unknown. Precisely what a coachee means during the early exploration of his coaching needs may not be obvious and might prove to be very different from what finally emerges. The outcomes that he desires may be uncertain or might change during the coaching interactions. While we believe in a basic structure to coaching sessions, they are never identical and can never be predicted. A coach may need to invent a different structure and process 'on the hoof', one that he has never seen, heard or applied in the past.

While the coach wants to get from A to B with his coachee, he may have periods of uncertainty about how he is going to get there, or indeed what should be his next step. For some coaches this is the magic of coaching, to 'trust the force' and to allow it to evolve naturally. For others, it represents stark terror, as they plunge into the unknown. It is comparable to how an acorn grows into an oak tree. It would be hard to explain the exact process of how a tiny seed develops into a towering tree, yet within the DNA of the seed lies the knowledge of its destiny.

BEING COMFORTABLE WITH DISCOMFORT

Discomfort is an important ingredient of coaching. In fact, we believe that it is sometimes the job of a coach to create discomfort. As a coachee faces his reality, confronts his choices and is pinned down to specific actions he may move out of his familiar zone and into uncharted territory. Coaches don't need to be sadists, but they do need to be comfortable with the discomfort of their coachees. A coach needs to ask himself, 'Can I live with discomfort, or do I wriggle?' 'Am I concerned that my coachee's discomfort might cause him to like me less or want to pull out of coaching?' Many coaches and coachees operate within their comfort zone. But real value stems from being stretched through challenging thoughts, attitudes and assumptions or looking into choices which could be changed. Sometimes tough love is the most useful form of support.

BEING SECURE WITH INSECURITY

Beneath the confident-looking exterior of most people lurk insecurities. We do a good job of putting up a sophisticated mask to cover them, however, in a coaching context we cannot derive true benefit from the process unless we're prepared to face them. A coachee may have insecurities in relation to a specific situation, problem, issue or relationship. If so, it's important that a coach allows him to explore his insecurities without projecting his own, so that he can voice them without fear of being judged. There is nothing worse than a coachee discussing a possible job loss, financial disaster or relationship breakdown only for a coach to join him in worrying. Any negative reaction on the part of a coach could close a coachee down and mean that a key area cannot be resolved.

BEING CERTAIN WITH UNCERTAINTY

The most useful coaching agendas and topics have an uncertain outcome. It is unknown how a coachee will react to coaching. Will it enable him to develop some skills, take action, move forward more effectively, or change his life? All that we know is that we do not know. Within this climate of uncertainty, what we can be certain of is that when the coaching process is clearly explained, when an agenda is well formed and where the coachee is passionately committed to change then results are guaranteed. In our experience coaching, if well managed and conducted, always delivers.

SUPER BEING SUMMARY

- The quality of a coach's being determines the quality of coaching.

- The ability to be self-aware through self-reflection is the cornerstone for achieving a high quality of being.

- We are 'human beings' not 'human doings'. To some extent we can choose how we want to be.

- Developing the traits of non-judgment, acceptance, defencelessness, authenticity and flexibility are marks of an effective coach.

- A coach sets an intention to enable his coachee to generate his own solutions.

- A coach develops an infectious attitude of optimism, openness and resilience.

- Being confident as a coach is achieved through doing coaching – there is no substitute.

- An effective coach is comfortable with high levels of ambiguity.

SuperCoaching
Exercise 4: Being a Coach

Who are you being? This is probably one of the most powerful questions you can ever ask yourself and determines the quality of your personal impact. Are you being a support or a hindrance? Are you being non-judgmental or prejudiced? Are you being reflective or thoughtless? The answers you give are direct indicators of the intention that lies behind your behaviour. To increase your awareness about yourself, sit down with someone you trust and get them to ask you the following question for 10 minutes: 'Who are you?' Request that they do not interrupt you and only use that question. After 10 minutes, ask them to proceed with the question: 'Who are you really?' Pay attention to the different levels of your response and notice the impact it has on your self-awareness. What usually occurs is that people start answering at an environmental level, focusing on roles and responsibilities. As they continue, they move on to capabilities and skills, deepen to beliefs and values, and finally tap into innate potential and possibility.

See how this applies to you coaching. Ask yourself, 'Am I playing the role of a coach, or am I being authentic when coaching?' In your next coaching session, commit to being your real self and review afterwards if and when you held back and the impact it had.

CHAPTER 5

Super Relationship – How to Connect?

Graham: A newly appointed CEO of a marketing company asked me to interview his top 40 managers to give him a perspective on their view of the business. I was at pains to point out that I was not going to evaluate them. I wanted to have open discussions and was concerned that if I were perceived to be sitting in judgment it would close them down. In the course of these interviews, I met someone who had been described as the superstar in her field. She was obviously an exceptional talent, with a strong track record, who had entered this large and bureaucratic business to inject flair and creativity.

Clare was extremely guarded in our meeting, saying that she couldn't tolerate 'tree huggers', which reflected her fear about my involvement in the company. It transpired that Clare's cautiousness stemmed from a belief that I would not honour the confidentiality protocols and would report back to the CEO my observations of her. My attempts to clarify that any output from the interviews would be non-attributable were only partially successful. Hence we finished the interview early and I suggested sending her my credentials with some testimonials from other clients referencing my commitment to confidentiality.

A couple of weeks later, I was surprised to discover that Clare had a requested a further meeting. This time she started by apologising for her suspicion, saying how much she had appreciated my understanding and thanking me for sending her the supporting documentation. She proceeded to give an honest account of her view of the business and alluded to the fact that she felt her creative spark was becoming dimmed within the confines of the company culture. It turned out that, although Clare had worked with an executive coach for several years, who had helped her make major career choices and whom she had come to trust and respect, she was receiving no specific support in relation to her current dilemma. Given her initial caution, and the fact that she was already working with a coach, I was hesitant to offer my services. However, I did say that I would welcome the opportunity to understand more about what she brought to the company.

I assumed it would go no further but, again, to my surprise, when I bumped into her in the corridor several days later, she said that she had been thinking about my offer and invited me to spend two days shadowing her as she travelled around visiting other offices, clients and suppliers. I sent her my observations about her contribution and, once again, it went quiet. Eventually, I received a call from Clare, who apologised for not having responded sooner and explaining that she'd been away. She had appreciated the time we'd spent getting to know each other, valued my description of her role and would like to explore the possibility of establishing a coaching relationship. This experience reinforced to me the importance of building a relationship before being able to commit to coaching.

This holds true elsewhere. Since most organisations today prioritise getting the job done over investing in the quality of relationships, performance suffers, morale wanes and motivation declines. We encounter employee after employee who reveals that, because they have a dysfunctional relationship with their line manager or with leaders within the organisation, they are either looking around for a new job or performing below their capability.

We have also found that, in many companies, managers are promoted on their technical capability, not on their relationship skills, hence a large gap can exist between demonstrating effective management practice and what happens in reality. It is often the case that managers are uncomfortable when dealing with people, or are not motivated to manage them well, and so end up avoiding people issues and neglecting their teams.

Having coaching on the agenda provides a powerful reminder to readdress what's important and ensure that relationship is a central ingredient for achieving high performance. Super Relationship explores the component parts that make up successful coaching relationships and provides a blueprint for how to create high quality relationships in general.

TRUST

'The glory of friendship is not the outstretched hand, nor the kindly smile, nor the joy of companionship; it is the spiritual inspiration that comes to one when they discover that someone else believes in them and is willing to trust them.'

Ralph Waldo Emerson

A coaching relationship is sacred. For many people, it is a unique experience to be able to discuss issues without being judged, criticised or having others' opinions thrown at them. The development of trust is the bedrock that allows coachees to reveal information that they may never have told anyone – even their nearest and dearest.

In his best-selling book, *The 7 Habits of Highly Effective People*, Stephen Covey introduces the metaphor of an Emotional Bank Account to describe the amount of trust in a relationship. If we apply this concept to a coaching relationship, and make substantial deposits by demonstrating commitment, integrity, scrupulous confidentiality and openness, then a safety net will exist in the relationship that allows for extraordinary results to occur. If not, there will be hesitancy and reservation, and the coachee will withhold themselves until, eventually, it will be impossible to continue effectively.

Ben: I once coached an HR director who was struggling in her role. Jan had lost motivation and no longer looked forward to going into work. In her mid-30s, she had always been career focused and had achieved beyond her wildest dreams, but she had now reached a crossroads. We started by looking at her career prospects and what options she could consider. As we continued, what transpired was that, above all else, Jan wanted a child. Married for several years, she recognised that she had never allowed herself to acknowledge her deep desire to start a family. She had not even told her husband, who she feared would worry about the financial implications of changing their lifestyle. When I requested feedback at the end of the session, Jan confirmed that it was the trust she had in our relationship, and in the coaching process, that had enabled her to admit to thoughts and feelings she wouldn't have dared to express in the past.

This is not an uncommon story. We're sure that all effective coaches have countless examples where trust has provided the climate for powerful outcomes to occur. Many people come into coaching with low trust thresholds. The amount of politicking, covering backsides, deceit, hidden agendas and blame that takes place in most organisations means that people don't trust each other or, at the very least, are wary of opening up. In addition, the short tenure of leaders and managers makes it difficult to get to know people. The average time in the role of a CEO in America is 18 months. These people are the custodians of vision. They hold the reins to thousands of people's livelihoods, but they're around for such a short period of time that it's hard for employees to believe that they really have their best interests at heart.

A simple yet effective way to start building trust is to invest time in relationships. In our time-poor economy, coaching sends out a powerful message that people are valued and that relationships are important. This alone will begin to restore people's faith that the company is more than just a money-making machine. It will enable better communication, more openness and honesty, more co-operation and collaboration, and, ultimately, higher performance. If trust is broken there is potentially a huge price to pay.

'I've seen the error of my ways and I've decided to start being more respectful to my coworkers. Hey, bozo, I'm talking to you!'

RESPECT

'Probably no greater honour can come to any man than the respect of his colleagues.'

Cary Grant

Companies now have legal responsibilities to provide workplaces free from unfair discrimination, harassment, bullying and victimisation. This also extends to the way employees treat each other when they retire to the pub together after work. It seems remarkable that treating people with respect has had to become a legal issue – however, once we understand the significance of mutual respect then it makes sense.

Respect follows closely behind trust as the glue that binds relationships together. In many ways respect is the practical demonstration of trust. A coaching relationship will be off to a good start if the coachee respects the coach for his skills, experience and track record. By the same token, the coach needs to respect the coachee. Given the nature of what the coachee discloses, it would be possible for the coach to form a negative view of him and believe that he should be able to operate more effectively than he does. Such thinking needs to be *verboten* for a coach. It's always easy to look into other people's lives and think that we know better.

A coach should always remember that most coachees, most of the time, do their best. Sometimes they are outstanding, at other times support is required. This is a natural process and part of being human. We need to respect this and, as a coach, respect those people who trust us enough to spend time with us and, in many cases, part with their own (or at least their budget's) money.

To expand on the principle of respect, the following model illustrates the three positions that can be held within a relationship:

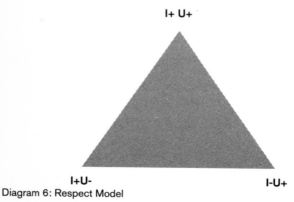

I+ U+

I+U-

I-U+

Diagram 6: Respect Model

The first position, I+ U+, represents 'I respect myself and I respect you'. It is based on mutual respect, where people value relationship as much as task. It is demonstrated through coaching behaviours such as:

- Investing time in conversations.

- Listening and summarising.

- Asking insightful and relevant questions.

- Exhibiting open body language, e.g. eye contact.

- Giving and receiving feedback.

- Being encouraging.

The types of outcomes that are achieved as a result of mutual respect include:

- Job satisfaction.

- Motivation.

- A willingness to go the extra mile.

- The ability to find solutions and resolve issues.

- Flexibility.

- Retention.

- Low absenteeism.

- High morale and performance.

When people operate in an I+ U+ way it is usually due to deep-seated beliefs about the importance of valuing people, involving them in decision-making, working in a collaborative way and believing in their potential. It is the only way to establish an effective coaching relationship.

On the other hand, I+ U- stands for 'I respect myself more than I respect you'. It is symbolised by prioritising task above relationship. This position is common in hierarchical management systems where managers have a tendency to tell people what to do without listening, asking questions or requesting feedback. Although they may subscribe to the idea of I+ U+ in practice, when the pressure is on they revert to a command-and-control style of management. This may lead to a short-term rise in results, but a fallout in the mid to longer term is inevitable, as resentment creeps in, performance decreases and communication breaks down.

I- U+ represents 'I respect myself less than I respect you'. It is usually based on feelings of fear, inferiority and low self-confidence, and manifests itself in behaviours such as saying 'yes' when we mean 'no', constant apologising, being over-polite when asking for help, an inability to delegate and not contributing our opinion. The outcome is that people may be treated like a doormat, feel anxious, depressed and isolated and yield low performance.

Obviously, demonstrating either I+ U- or I- U+ behaviours is the antithesis of effective coaching and will cause a relationship to break down very quickly. We often hear about the challenge to internal coaching of being able to coach upwards within an organisation when people have traditionally adopted more sub-servient positions. This will only be overcome when there is sufficient respect to allow for more openness and honesty to occur.

OPENNESS

We recently worked with a new CEO who took over a failing operation. One of his first requests was for us to interview his top team to get a view on current affairs. It was a fascinating process listening to story after story of frustration, angst and concern about the problems in the business. What transpired was that previously leaders had kept their cards tight to their chest, but, as the business grew, it was no longer possible to operate such a closed regime. People had failed to take responsibility and be accountable for their actions because they had existed in a culture which was steeped in being risk-averse. Capable people would enter the company only to become hijacked by the deeply ingrained habits of passing the buck and not sharing information. The lack of openness was crippling performance and threatening the survival of the organisation.

Thankfully, the new CEO had a very different style.

He led with unusual candour and openness. He spoke from his heart and addressed the issues head on. He held up his hand if he failed to deliver on his promises and explained his reasoning. For instance, one of the requests from the top team was for him to be more visible than previous leaders. Although he pledged his commitment to get around the company, it was virtually impossible given the demands on his time. He acknowledged his inability to do this and sought other mediums of communication. Gradually, his openness set a tone for others to follow, leading to frank discussions and debates that had never taken place in the past.

As we have already shown, the coaching relationship is unusual in its complete transparency. Within a context of trust and respect coachees are able to disclose highly sensitive information. This is not to say that they need to share everything about their lives or that coaches are free to pry into anything and everything. The coachee is always the gatekeeper of the aspects of his work and life he wants to explore. However, it is essential that once a topic has been agreed, both parties are open in their discussions with each other. This is particularly relevant when the point of giving and receiving feedback is reached in the coaching relationship, because any progress can be seriously undermined if either party is not prepared to be completely open.

HONESTY

'No legacy is so rich as honesty.'

William Shakespeare

'Our company lost 900 million dollars last quarter. Your job is to make this look like the best thing that ever happened to us.'

A coaching relationship needs to be straightforward to help people be direct and honest. Otherwise, no value can be gained, because real issues will not be addressed. The way that we help coaches become more comfortable with honesty is to practise in genuine contexts on our SuperCoaching training programmes. They practise coaching sessions using real issues rather than role-playing with an invented topic. This encourages participants to experience the power of being honest with their peers and to take that reference point back into the workplace.

There may be occasions when it feels difficult to be

honest as a coach. Sometimes a coach will be required to challenge the coachee if he 'smells a rat'. The coachee may be playing an old mental record, almost forgetting that it's not true, or be so out of touch with his real situation that he is temporarily blinded. He may talk about his boss as being unapproachable, aloof and disinterested, when in fact he's really talking about his previous boss and running an old script. In this type of situation the coach needs to help him undo his past perceptions and get him to give an honest description of his current reality. A coach can achieve this most effectively by being honest about what he sees, feels and hears, so that the coachee can reflect upon his perspective.

We have always believed that what makes coaching potent is the authenticity demonstrated by coaches. Thankfully, this now fits with one of the latest aspirations in business cultures – to be authentic. We applaud this emergence and encourage the development of this level of honesty within the working world. It is difficult enough to wrestle with the issues and problems in the workplace without having to deal with an overlay of inaccuracy. While, at the outset, there may be a certain level of discomfort for people in being authentic (particularly amongst senior executives who can spend much of their life playing a role and wearing a mask), the feedback we receive is that they find it liberating to let go and be themselves.

SUPPORT

'Our prime purpose in this life is to help others.'

Dalai Lama

One of the traits of an emotionally intelligent person is empathy, i.e. the ability to sense others' feelings and perspectives and to show genuine concern for their well-being. Developing empathy, so that we're able to touch the life of a coachee without stepping over any boundaries, cements the relationship and is a big deposit in the emotional bank account.

It's important to recognise the distinction between empathy and sympathy. Although there may be occasions in coaching when sympathy is appropriate, such as when a coachee has been given bad news about an imminent redundancy, or has suffered a bereavement, empathy is more appropriate in most coaching situations. Although the coach may show sensitivity and be attentive to emotional cues, he is not colluding with the emotional state of the coachee.

Ben: I remember, on one occasion, coaching someone who was facing major challenges. Bill's wife suffered clinical depression and consequently he played an active caring role, ensuring that she received the right support, although he had recently found out that she was having an affair with one of his 'best friends'. Bill was ambitious in his career, but he worked for a manager who gave him little time or attention and overlooked him for promotion. He had let slip many of his friendships, due to the time he had invested in his marriage, and felt alone. It was difficult not to sympathise with Bill in a way that might have resulted in my projecting my own feelings onto him. It was therefore critical that I was able to empathise and support but not divert the attention away from him.

Sometimes, the most effective way to support the coachee is simply to ask him, 'What support would you like?' 'How can I support you?' or 'How would you know that you're really supported in this situation?' Putting the onus on to the coachee encourages him to take responsibility for the type of support he would like, and keeps clear boundaries.

Ultimately, our success is linked to the support that we receive. As Dr Robert Holden writes in *Success Intelligence*, 'The age of the independent person is over.' We cannot succeed on our own. We need to develop our 'A' team, the key supporters who are behind us. Since most people in the workplace find it hard to ask for support, perceiving it as a sign of weakness, encouraging coachees to ask for and receive support is often a big step forward.

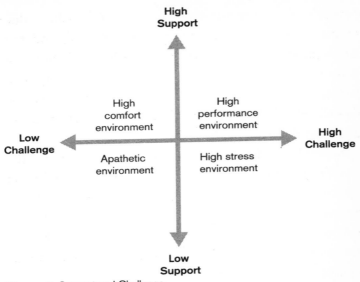

Diagram 7: Support and Challenge

CHALLENGE

'I have little patience with scientists who take a board of wood, look for its thinnest part, and drill a great number of holes where drilling is easy.'

Albert Einstein

Ben: I worked with an HR manager who had to deliver a presenation to senior managers about how to interview employees who have returned to work after a period of sick leave. During the presentation, Kate was hassled, interrupted and talked down. Her lasting perception of the team of managers was that they were 'rottweilers' – threatening, disrespectful and difficult.

She had more presentations scheduled, but was adamant that she was not going to do them. She was furious about how she had been treated and gave the managers a good verbal bashing. Following her outburst, I challenged Kate on her position. What agenda was she running? Had she really stepped into their shoes? Had she considered their reality – understaffed, overworked and then asked to do more paperwork? Could she see that her presentation might imply that they weren't doing a good enough job? Had she built up enough rapport to be perceived as a support rather than an HR policewoman laying down the law?

Through being challenged, Kate began to see the situation through their eyes. She was able to shift her perception of the managers from 'rottweilers' to 'people who needed greater empathy and a listening ear'. This allowed her to return to the team and work with them to find a way forward.

Coaching is sometimes perceived as a 'soft' activity. In organisations it can smack of being 'touchy-feely'. This is far from accurate. While it is a supportive activity, the coach has to be tough and challenging. This is not because he knows what's right for the coachee or because he is attached to his point of view, but because it serves the coachee to be challenged on his perceptions, beliefs, behaviours and actions. It helps him drill down to the truth of the matter and ascertain what he will and won't do.

Many of our senior executive clients specifically ask us to challenge them and tell us how valuable this is when we do. We're often the only people who provide this level of challenge, since other members of the organisation can be wary of treading on toes. The key to being able to challenge our coachees appropriately and with respect lies in the strength of the relationship with them. Given a strong relationship, a coachee will experience challenge as helpful rather than critical. A way of describing the challenging nature of coaching is 'tough love'.

One of the main areas a coach can challenge a coachee is in how he sees things. People often make wild generalisations, use sloppy and imprecise observations, start to believe their own perceptions as if they were the truth, and exhibit other manifestations of faulty thinking and logic. Courteously pointing out to the coachee what he is doing can enable him to see things in a new way and gain fresh insight. It's all too easy to make false assumptions or become imprisoned within fixed mindsets. The job of the coach is to challenge the coachee rather than agree or collude with his thinking.

Effective questions with which to challenge a coachee include:

- What makes you say that?

- Are you sure about that?

- What evidence do you have?

- Is it a fact or a feeling?

- Do other people share your perception?

- What would it look like from another point of view?

- How could you see it differently?

These types of question force a coachee to reflect upon his position. It can also be helpful to make observations such as:

- It seems to me that you are generalising.

- It appears to me that there might be another way to see this.

- I sense that this is your perspective.

As long as a strong relationship has been established, the coachee will find this useful rather than feeling under attack. It's important for the coach to make sure that what he perceives as challenging really is so for the coachee. We have observed situations, whilst training coaches, where the coach poses what he thinks is a challenge only to discover that it is something the coachee has already considered. Clear expectations need to be set with the coachee about the level of challenge during the contracting process (which we cover in detail shortly).

A coach becomes good at challenging others by grabbing opportunities to be challenged himself. When he is being coached he should make sure that he is challenged on his blind spots, such as repeating old stories, indulging his emotions or staying stuck with unhelpful behaviours. It's also a smart move to ask his coachees to challenge him if they perceive anything in his coaching sessions that doesn't work for them. However, a coach has to be prepared to take whatever he gets and not become defensive or try to justify his actions. We heard about one situation where a coach was running a two-day team event and had set an expectation that all opinions were valid and nobody could be wrong. At the end of it, he entered into a conversation with the marketing director in the team and asked for his opinion about the effectiveness of the course. The director gave it, upon which the coach said 'You're wrong'. The director felt that he had completely devalued the whole event by that one statement. The more comfortable coaches are at being challenged, the more effective they become.

CHOOSING A COACH

Having outlined the foundations for establishing an effective coaching relationship, we will now cover the process of choosing a coach and creating a working contract. Since there are more and more coaches available in today's market, it's critical that businesses and potential coachees clarify who is available and choose the coach most appropriate to their needs. It's equally important that a coach works with people with whom he resonates, and where he believes that he can make a measurable difference to the quality and success of the coachees' work and lives.

Chemistry What is chemistry? Is it the experience of compatibility, connectivity, trust, respect and liking that come into play when people meet? While it's difficult to define, we all know it when we experience it. If people are going to spend a significant number of hours with a coach, talking about things that are important to them, and maybe adopting a level of openness and honesty that is unusual, it's essential they feel good with this person. They need to ask themselves if they could open up to him. Would they look forward to spending time with him? What does their intuition tell them? The first test upon choosing a coach is to clarify the potential of the fit, whilst the coach needs to evaluate whether he wants to work with a particular coachee. Does he believe that he can add value? Does the prospect excite and motivate him? If not, he must be prepared to refer the coachee elsewhere, otherwise he could find himself compromised later on.

Experience It's valuable for the coachee to learn about the background and track record of the coach. How long has he been coaching? In what situations? At what level within companies? What evidence does he have of results that his coachees attribute to coaching, and what record of case histories, testimonials and references does he have on file? The coach's ability to flex to the uniqueness of his coachee and the issues being coached, as a result of years of experience and being in a multitude of situations, contributes greatly to his effectiveness as a coach. People need to remember that they are entrusting themselves to the hands of a coach, and need to ensure that those hands have become strong and reliable through many hours of valuable coaching.

Approach The next step is to clarify the coach's approach to coaching. In the early days, it was probably sufficient if someone was skilled at asking questions, listening and making suggestions. Things have changed. It is now critical for these skills to be underpinned by a rigorous, clear and planned methodology and approach. Where does the coach sit on the spectrum of directive and non-directive coaching? Does he believe in tapping into the inherent capability of the coachee rather than telling him what to do? What is the coach's approach to confidentiality? How does he determine what is on and off-limits? How does he formulate an agenda? It's important for a coach to be clear about how he links the agenda to the business imperatives, leadership models, performance appraisals and HR perspective within an organisation. He also needs to have clarity about the documentation of sessions, the frequency of meetings, how the time will be used and if there is any contact between sessions.

Liking We are sometimes asked whether there should be mutual liking between coach and coachee. We believe that it would be inappropriate for them to work together if they couldn't stand each other's company. However, whilst qualities such as trust and respect are essential, a mutual liking isn't necessary unless feelings get in the way of the coaching process. From the coach's standpoint, it is critical that he wants to help an individual and can accept him for who he is. From the standpoint of the coachee, trust and respect override whether he likes the coach. Sometimes the level of challenge required can only be established in a relationship that has an edge and is not overly familiar.

Commitment A basic requirement for successful coaching is for the coachee to want to be coached and to be willing to engage with the coach in an honest, open and straightforward manner. Beyond this, he should be committed wholeheartedly to his own learning, development and performance enhancement. It is not possible to coach someone who does not want to be coached. Coaching must not be an imposed requirement for a coachee. It cannot be demanded by a manager or an HR department. Coaching can only start when there is a commitment on both sides to the coachee deriving value.

Until this commitment is reached, coaching should not be undertaken. Some of us will have validated this view through our own abortive attempts to 'help' our partners, children and others who haven't wanted to be coached.

CREATING A COACHING CONTRACT

Positioning			
Coaching Definition	Success/Leadership/Performance/Talent/Change		Business Control

Agreements			
Confidentiality	Boundaries	Documentation	Timing
Frequency	Expectations	Structure	Environment

Style/process			
Non-directive	Open/Honest	Support/Challenge	GROW model

Agenda formulation			
Self-assessment	360-degree feedback	Stakeholder meeting	Psychological profiling
Appraisals/PDP's	Career data	Leadership competencies/Culture statements	

Success measures

Progress reviews

Diagram 8: Contracting

Positioning The first step in creating a coaching contract is to ensure that there is a common understanding about what coaching entails. Since a variety of interpretations exist, it's important to give coaching a clear definition. It's vital to explain the approach of non-directive coaching; that it's not a soft activity and will require the coachee to arrive at his own solutions through the use of a clear framework. It's also necessary to iron out any potential misunderstandings about the use of coaching, by explaining how it is related to areas such as success, leadership, performance, talent and change within the business context, is not a remedial activity, but is aimed at high-flyers.

Confidentiality Protocols Confidentiality provides the necessary environment of trust, safety and privacy for effective coaching to take place. Havoc can occur if confidentiality protocols are not spelt out at the outset. It's therefore essential to cover items such as:

- How to inform the coachee's boss about progress and give any feedback on the coachee's capability.

- Keeping HR in the loop.

- Note-taking.

- Handling difficult subjects that cause concern, e.g. a coachee's drinking habit, a coachee's boss not giving him the support he needs, a coachee being out of line with the values of his organisation, a coachee secretly planning to leave his company.

- The coach revealing to his colleagues which companies and individuals he is working with.

There are no rules as to how to manage confidentiality. Generally speaking, the agreements that we set up clarify who is privy to what parts of the agenda, and who will be part of the agenda formulating, review process and final success measurement. In some cases, we may agree with the coachee's boss that anything personal emerging out of the sessions stays between coach and coachee, whilst any performance issues relating to the business are shared. We recommend that the coachee should be the gatekeeper of anything that might go beyond the coaching session. It is always a between-four-walls confidential conversation unless he decides otherwise.

Boundaries In addition to confidentiality, it is essential to agree the boundaries of what will and will not be covered. Our standard policy is to encourage the coachee to look into not only those areas that seem to be creating difficulties and leading to sub-optimal performance, but their areas of strength as well. However, what he does and does not talk about is his own choice. Boundary questions can arise at the outset or later on, when issues begin to emerge that the coach feels less qualified to address or feels should be off-limits (such as deeply-rooted emotions, marital or family problems and addictive behaviour). In these situations, it is the responsibility of the coach to ensure that the coachee finds the right person or support structure where they can be addressed. It may be a case of referring the coachee to a counselling service within the company or a recommended provider if one does not exist. If a coach establishes agreements with clarity and certainty at the outset, and sticks scrupulously to them, all should be well. If there are any hazy or omitted agreements, then a coach should not be surprised if, subsequently, there is chaos, bad feeling or fallout.

Documentation The danger in documenting coaching sessions is that it can lead to a break in the flow of conversation and cause a loss of focus on the part of the coachee. However, it is valuable to have a written record of key points, insights and action steps agreed. There are various options to overcome the possible interference of note-taking, such as having a note-taker at the meeting (assuming this doesn't erode the coachee's openness and honesty), taking time out during the session to make notes, jotting down the key points as the session progresses so that they can be expanded afterwards, and letting the coachee make his own notes with prompting from the coach at the end of each session. It's important to agree what is most useful for the coachee and to be flexible enough to deliver what he wants.

Ownership and Personal Responsibility Who is actually responsible for the coaching agenda and the success of the coaching? There are three possible answers to this: the coach, the coachee and both of them. We believe that the answer to this is both coach and coachee. However, in the final analysis, it is the coachees' life at stake. As a coach cannot force him to take action, it is better expressed as 51 per cent coachee and 49 per cent coach. Having said that, coaches must bring their head, heart and guts to the relationship to maximise the effects of coaching.

Since we live in a culture which lends itself to making others accountable for our own lives, whether it is through the government, corporations, unions or management, the value of non-directive coaching is that the coachee owns his agenda, his process and any resulting actions. In other words, effective coaching ensures that people take personal responsibility for looking at their current reality and aspirations, for defining goals, for exploring options and, crucially, for their own performance, learning and development.

The coach needs to take personal responsibility for delivering a service of measurable high value, ensuring an agenda that has both personal and corporate relevance and entering upon a process that is effective and economic in time. It is also up to the coach to ensure that the coachee's action steps are feasible, have been evaluated for implications in advance and that the coachee is committed to them. Ultimately, it is up to both parties to create a huge win from coaching.

Timing It is important to agree how much time is allocated for a session. There will be different time criteria depending on the type of coaching intervention. The following is our recommendation within organisations:

- One-to-one coaching provided by an external coach: 2 hours.

- Co-coaching relationship: 1 hour each way.

- Manager as coach: agree a time at the particular juncture, e.g. 'I have 5 minutes/1 hour for this conversation'.

- Team coaching: agree a time span depending on the situation.

It's useful to clarify the time agreement at the outset of each session. We live in busy times and coach busy people, so it's critical to not make assumptions about the time allocation. The coach should manage the coaching session so as to ensure that the coachee is out of the door at the set time. He will greatly appreciate this because, in many business cultures, this will be the exception, not the rule. It is also a professionally sound practice that demonstrates expertise.

A mark of an inexperienced coach is when his sessions overrun. Excuses are given such as: 'There was so much to cover' or 'I couldn't stop the coachee talking'. This is usually the result of the coach or coachee believing that a lot of background detail is necessary; having a weakly defined goal for the session; or it may be the inability of the coach to cut in and ensure that rigorous focus and momentum are maintained towards reaching a well defined outcome. It is useful to keep a discreet eye on the clock, whilst recognising that there will be occasions when flexibility is required.

Frequency There is no magic answer to the frequency of coaching, although this will be influenced by the urgency of the agenda. Our preference is to coach people at least once a month. Any less and it runs the risk of losing focus and importance in the eyes of the coachee. At the other end of the spectrum we have coached people daily and indeed have 'shadow' coached them (i.e. tracked them through their working days) when the agenda has been particularly vital and urgent. We don't believe in open-ended coaching contracts; at least not initially. We tend to commit to coaching programmes of between 6–12 months duration at the outset. This relationship may then evolve into subsequent programmes with built-in milestones for review. Committing to finite lengths of time avoids dependency, loss of focus and the possibility of it turning into a routine.

Expectations People brought up in a command-and-control style environment may find non-directive coaching an unfamiliar way of working, so it's important for the coach to clarify with the coachee at the outset what to expect in terms of his predominant style of working. By explaining that he will be doing a lot of listening, asking questions, giving feedback and making suggestions, the coach avoids the potential confusion that can occur with the coachee waiting to be told what to do. A further expectation to clarify is the possible outcomes that might occur from coaching. A coachee might have the expectation that his life will be transformed after one session. Without putting limits on the results it's advisable to set realistic and achievable outcomes to manage expectations.

Structure Explaining the structure of coaching sessions provides reassurance to coachees by demonstrating that there are tried and tested rails down which the coaching will be running. These include:

- Checking how much time is available.

- Getting an update from the coachee on any relevant developments in their work and life.

- Reviewing the notes of the last meeting, including action steps.

- Using the GROW mode (see Chapter 7) to frame the session, including agreeing a topic to be covered in the session and a specific outcome.

While this framework isn't intended to restrict the coaching process, it is designed to contribute to a well-managed and productive session that covers a lot of ground with an economy of time. There will be occasions when this goes out of the window, if, for instance, the coachee appears for a session clearly stressed and needing to download, or if he needs to deal with an urgent and unforeseen topic.

Environment The environment in which a session is conducted will play a large part in determining its success. Attempting to work in the office of a coachee can be a nightmare, with the distractions of phones, email and colleagues. Ideally, it's best to find a private location that creates an atmosphere of relaxation and calm and lends itself to generating a high level of focused concentration. We have found ourselves in situations where we've had to improvise, sitting with backs turned away in glass-panelled rooms, creating privacy in hotel lobbies and covering windows with flipchart paper! Most organisations have private meetings rooms, so ensure that the coachee books them in advance.

AGENDA FORMULATION

Graham: 'Roger, I have been coaching you now for six months and I would like us to review your achievements and level of satisfaction with our coaching programme.' In the review, Roger highlighted that his work–life balance had improved, his meetings had become more effective and that he was in a better position to prioritise his workload. He said that he's got more from coaching than he'd expected and that he was very satisfied.

Metaphorically speaking, I gave myself a pat on the back for what seemed to be a job well done. I then asked Roger if I could meet with his manager to ensure that he was happy with our work and, without disclosing confidentialities, to give him an idea of progress made. Roger agreed that it would be helpful.

As I walked into his boss's office, I had to restrain my anticipation of the glowing report that I was about to receive. However, before I could even open the conversation, his boss said that he believed we should have met sooner. He went on to say that he had seen very little change and was concerned about the value of the coaching programme.

In that moment I learnt a big lesson. While an effective coach may deliver what appears to be excellent coaching for a coachee, where the latter is delighted with the outcome, unless it is in line with the organisational agenda for that person there is a risk that the company will be disappointed in their investment. It could even damage the organisation's view of the coachee. Following that incident, I became extremely attentive to ensuring that any coaching agenda met both personal and organisational needs, that clear success measures were defined, and that there were frequent review sessions scheduled to align other stakeholders in the coaching programme and assess any progress made.

We will now look at the various inputs that can feed a coaching agenda. Some of these may depend on the coachee and the culture in which he operates, but a coach should always encourage coachees to have access to as many of the following inputs as possible in order to enrich their coaching agenda:

Self-assessment The first input to consider is a self-assessment. Ideally, this is done in a written format and then brought to the sessions to be discussed verbally. It enables the coachee to look deeply into his work and life with reference to past successes, disappointments, strengths, development needs and aspirations. It must define a view for his coaching agenda, which will be subsequently fleshed out by other inputs. The self-assessment aims to provide value in and of itself by prompting self-reflection and asking important questions.

Stakeholder Meeting The second potential input is a meeting between the stakeholders, usually the boss and/or HR, coach and coachee. Taking this step allows some straight talking to occur between all parties to ensure a common view of the coaching agenda. We would love to receive a five pound note for every time that we have been assured by a boss or HR that an individual has been given clear feedback about where he stands, his strengths and weaknesses and career prospects, only to discover that he has a hazy picture and, in some cases, an erroneous or non-existent one. This is usually due to people giving non-specific feedback with unclear data. A three-way meeting can test understanding and clarify any outstanding issues.

360-Degree Feedback A third possible input is 360-degree feedback. Many organisations already have their own 360-degree feedback processes in place, however these can vary in value depending on how they're perceived, and whether they are an online questionnaire requiring a tick in the box, or a detailed face-to-face interview. If 360-degree data exists within the organisation it should be built into the coaching agenda. Where the feedback is unclear, the coach can encourage the coachee to seek further clarity from his boss, peers, direct reports or HR. If a coachee does not have recent or adequate 360-degree data within the company, the coach can set this up through a paper or email exercise. However, if budgets allow, the most effective feedback process is face-to-face interviews with selected personnel using a series of questions that meet the needs of both the organisation and the individual. To ensure honesty, these feedback processes should be set up as non-attributable, unless it is a very mature and adult culture. The coach wants people to give honest perceptions and not be fearful of the consequences. These perceptions can be synthesised into a report and used as data to influence the coaching agenda. The coach should use the same 360-degree feedback questions with his coachee, so that he can compare and contrast his own perceptions with those of his colleagues.

Personal Development Plans (PDP) and Reports It has become an emerging trend for businesses to encourage their employees to formulate personal development plans and to use personal development reports. These vary enormously in how useful they are, but, on the whole, they tend to form part of an annual review of the individual's performance and how they are perceived within the organisation. If the PDP is completed well, it can serve as an important input into the coaching agenda by ensuring that any coaching fits alongside specified objectives and targets. When a PDP is unclear, it can be a trigger for the coachee to establish greater clarity so that he can benefit from it.

Career Data Many companies have career data on file. They have processes in place and run assessment centres which identify those exhibiting high potential for future progression. However, due to the often-confidential nature of this data, it can make it difficult to use. Thus the best that a coach can sometimes do is to gain an overall steer from a boss or HR about the coachee's future prospects and the areas that he may need to develop to increase his chances of progression.

Psychological and Personality Profiling Many businesses use profiles such as MBTI, Belbin and FIRO-B as part of their recruitment process, and to inform the career development process within the organisation. Our view is that these profiles should not be seen as an ultimate truth, but, rather, as providing a directional steer within a conversation to flush out the characteristics and internal preferences of our coachee. When these profiles are not available, the coach can conduct them himself, if qualified to do so, or suggest where a coachee can get a profile report with the approval of the business.

Leadership Competences and Culture/Value Statements Most organisations have worked hard to define their leadership competences, management expectations and value statements derived from an overall articulation of their vision and culture. If these are authentic they must be reflected in individual coaching agendas, and indeed in any people management process within the organisation in order to have any potency. It's essential for the coach to be familiar with these contextual frameworks. They provide a reference for coachees to check what they need to develop and reinforce to become more aligned with the organisation. When a number of people are coached within a company this information provides the means to ensure that a common framework underpins personal coaching agendas.

Context The coach must understand the business context within which the coaching sits. He needs to discover if the coachee's part of the business is succeeding or failing, how much change the business is going through, how long he has worked for his boss, the current state of play within his team and whether he has a clearly defined leadership expectation and framework. It's important not to embark on 'black box' coaching where the coaching is disconnected from the bigger picture. The danger with working without a clear context is that what may seem to be valuable topics, and, as a result beneficial steps forward, could be inappropriate. The coach does not need to be an expert in the coachee's business, in fact he will never understand a fraction of what the coachee does, but he does need to be 'savvy' to the internal and external context, to ensure that any coaching is both effective and relevant.

Success Measures Once an agenda has been established using some or all of the above set of inputs, the next step is to translate it into clear success measures. Each agenda topic needs to have a defined outcome, articulated in such a way that it is measurable. In some cases this is relatively easy. When a coachee wants help in formulating the correct structure for his part of the organisation, it's clear when he has decided upon it, when he has identified an action plan to achieve it and also when it has been successfully executed. Other topics can be more difficult to measure. Improving communication, developing presence or charisma and exhibiting more passion all have a higher degree of subjectivity and are open to interpretation. Coaches should not embark on working on these types of topics until an agreed way of measuring progress and success has been established. This may involve gaining agreement with relevant third parties to reach a consensus of opinion.

Progress Reviews While every coaching session ought to deliver measurable value, it is necessary to review evidence for progress, set against the original agenda. These reviews can be held at regular intervals and built in to the initial contracting phase in order to manage expectations and deepen accountability. Ideally, any progress review should include the initial people involved in the contracting process. They provide an opportunity to address the coachee's and organisations' overall satisfaction, to identify any benefits that they may have derived that were not on the initial coaching agenda, and to discuss any frustrations or concerns. This helps to clarify what has been achieved with the client and to calibrate the level of value.

SUPER RELATIONSHIP SUMMARY

- Trust, respect, openness, honesty, support and challenge are the building blocks for a successful coaching relationship.

- The process of choosing a coach requires both parties to resonate with each other and feel that measurable success can be achieved as a result of coaching.

- It's critical to draw up a clear contract before commencing a coaching programme.

- The level of detail that goes into establishing a coaching agenda is a rigorous process which distinguishes SuperCoaching from good coaching.

SuperCoaching
Exercise 5: Building Coaching Relationships

You cannot coach someone unless you have a relationship conducive to coaching. Take a moment now and describe the quality of your relationships. Give a percentage to how many are conducive to coaching. What would need to happen for you to create more coaching relationships? Would you need to become more open, honest, supportive and challenging? Seek feedback from your colleagues as to how they perceive their relationship with you, and thus whether coaching is feasible. What is your next step to ensuring that you create more coaching opportunities?

CHAPTER 6

Super Doing – The Skills of Coaching

We recently ran a training programme for a leading recruitment and outplacement company, which wanted to offer their clients a high performance, one-to-one coaching service. During the event, we ran a series of exercises designed to stretch the participants' coaching skills. We made a distinction between asking questions that help a coachee build his understanding, thus raising his awareness of a subject, and the kind of directive questioning that follows a chain of thought held by the coach.

One of the delegates struggled to grasp this distinction. He started off sessions by saying, 'Don't you think we should talk about X?' Followed by, 'I think we can accomplish Y', dressing up his opinion by asking, 'Did you talk to him about Z?' Even after playing him video footage of his coaching sessions, he continued to pollute his questions with opinion. Eventually, somewhat exasperated (thankfully with himself rather than us), he made a telling statement. 'I don't think I've ever asked a genuinely open and non-directive question in my life. I always have an agenda and try to get my coachee to where I think they should be. Although I've had a good deal of success in my outplacement consulting, I can now see the improvement I could make by ensuring that what I think is right for my client actually is. By helping him come up with a solution, through asking open-ended questions, listening and testing understanding, he has the opportunity to evaluate it rather than me trying to convince him.' While the individual in question didn't become an expert coach overnight, this insight set him on the way to honing his skills.

The reason why we didn't begin this book with input on coaching skills is that, however skilled a coach is as a technician, he will not be guaranteed effective results unless he develops the right relationships and the right presence for coaching. Super Doing starts by looking at the optimum mental state necessary for coaching, which includes having an awareness of the type of inner dialogue that takes place during an interaction. It then covers the main skills a coach uses: listening, questions, summarising and feedback.

FOCUSED ATTENTION AND RELAXED CONCENTRATION

Robert Pirsig captures the essence of this essential coaching skill in his classic book, *Zen and the Art of Motorcycle Maintenance*, when he describes the difference between a master craftsman and a novice. He defines a master craftsman as someone who is 'absorbed and attentive to what he's doing even though he doesn't deliberately contrive this. His motions and the machine are in a kind of harmony . . . The material and his thoughts are changing together in a progression of changes until his mind's at rest at the same time the material's right.' This coming together of thoughts and material reflects the state of mind a coach requires. However, this is a challenge, because we live in a world of distraction. Meetings, mobiles, emails and the 'to do' list all vie for our attention, often against a background of emotional anxiety. Thoughts such as, 'What should I be doing now?' or 'I haven't got enough time' continually pop into our minds like emails dropping into our inbox. This can lead to a condition sometimes referred to as 'interrupt driven', where we find it difficult to concentrate for any length of time. It can become an addictive state, where we constantly feel the need for something to distract us. Unless a coach learns how to focus his mind with laser precision it will severely limit the effectiveness of his coaching.

Focused attention and relaxed concentration means being 100 per cent absorbed and engaged in a coaching

conversaion, free from any internal or external interference. In the sporting world, this is referred to as 'being
in the zone' or in a 'peak state'. It is like being in a
timeless bubble where nothing exists other than the
immediate task to hand. A good example of this mental
state in action occurred when David Beckham took a free
kick for England in the last minute of extra time in a
crucial World Cup qualifying match against Greece in
2001. You could see Beckham drawing all his mental
attention inwards as he prepared to shoot. His concentration was completely immersed in the task of kicking
the ball as he unleashed an extraordinary shot to score a
vital goal.

In this state of 100 per cent absorption, coaches lose
all sense of self. With no interference coming from them,
the light of awareness shines freely on the coachee,
helping him to see his reality clearly and allowing
insights to occur, motivation to increase and progress to
be made.

Coaches need to practise skills to aid the development
of this level of absorption. When we give coaching
demonstrations in our SuperCoaching programmes,
delegates often remark that their biggest challenge in
improving their coaching skills is to stay focused and
relaxed, whilst preventing their own agenda from causing
interference. There are several strategies to help deepen a
coach's ability to access this optimal state. He can:

1. Receive coaching either in a co-coaching relationship or with an external coach. Unresolved issues playing on the coach's mind can hijack his coachee's session. If, for example, the coachee is exploring his career ambitions and talking about his frustrations at not moving more quickly up the corporate ladder, and this is a personal issue for the coach, he may identify with it, fail to be completely absorbed in the conversation and end up projecting his own situation on to it.

2. Maintain his own physical health through exercise, nutrition and sleep. It's hard for a coach to be fully present when he is feeling exhausted. Making sure that he is in good shape means that he has more mental energy available for concentrating and paying attention.

3. Prepare for a session adequately by reviewing previous notes. This enables the coach to reconnect with the issues at hand, pick up on any agreed action points and think about a possible agenda for the session.

4. Create an environment conducive to coaching. It's important to remove any external interruptions. The coach can ensure that phones and computers are switched off and that a quiet room is booked. It may be necessary to have sessions in a neutral venue in order to eliminate distractions.

5. Focus on some aspect of the coachee during the session, by making frequent eye contact, looking at his face more broadly, noticing an aspect of his body language, emotion or voice modulation.

It's important that a coach recognises when he has been distracted. This is usually caused by a chain of thought-associations, such as getting caught up in the content of the conversation or wondering what question to ask next. Certainly, in the early stages of learning how to coach, it's common to get distracted by figuring out what question to ask, particularly if the coach is not familiar with the subject matter or feels intimidated by the situation. If this happens, he needs to refocus on his coachee by using the methods described above.

The coach should also notice when his coachee becomes distracted. If this lasts for any length of time, it's helpful to find out what's causing it. By asking 'Where did your attention go?' or 'What distracted you?' the coach is able to help him become aware of his mental state. If it is something relevant to the coaching process then a change of focus may be helpful.

It could be that a coachee recognises that he has become distracted thinking about a team member. The agreed agenda was to discuss his management style, but the issue about the team member is more pressing and needs to be addressed first. Once the new issue is resolved, the coach may then find that there is some link back to the original agenda. If the distraction is an external interference, such as the need to make a phone call or to respond to a pressing demand, this needs to be addressed so that it doesn't intrude. However, if it happens frequently, it is essential to confront it as an issue and agree to avoid distractions.

A further factor in helping raise the level of attention and concentration of the coachee is to ensure that he owns and is committed to the coaching agenda. It's not possible to coach someone on a topic in which he has little interest. If a coachee is not paying sufficient attention, it could be a clear indicator that the agenda doesn't have enough relevance. There is no future in engaging or continuing a coaching conversation when one or other party is distracted mentally, emotionally or physically.

ALLOWING

One of the many paradoxes and subtleties in coaching is that, although he is responsible for managing a session and ensuring value and tangible outcomes, the coach must not impose too much control over his coachee or on the session. We can use a tennis analogy to illustrate the skill necessary to allow a session to unfold. In the game of tennis, there are precisely defined aspects, such as the rules and scoring system, which are not up for debate. There are also recommendations for the best grip, body position, shots to play and strategy to use. However, within these guidelines, each tennis match unfolds in its own way, as players demonstrate their own unique approach.

Coaching is comparable in that there is a recommended methodology, enabling frameworks and particular skills, but an effective coach allows sessions to unfold in their own unique way. This means that a coach must allow coachees to be themselves, to progress in their own time and to let outcomes emerge in their appropriate form. If a coach exerts too much control, he risks alienating his coachee, which can result in him failing to involve himself fully in the process, or feeling manipulated and causing the interaction to be stilted and mechanistic. It is not up to a coach to tell his coachee what he ought to be coached on, to force a pre-determined agenda on the direction of the coaching, or to insist on action steps that he thinks are right.

If a coach can operate in this subtle way and let a natural coaching journey unfold, he will provide some-thing unusual, if not unique, for his coachees: an opportunity to gain their own insights and make their own commitments to moving forward in their work and life. It is always gratifying for both parties when this happens and a coachee reports having gained value from such a coaching interaction. This validates the coachee's inherent ability and demonstrates that considerable wisdom resides within him.

One of the reasons why we do not recommend coaching friends and family is that it is far more difficult to operate in this way with someone to whom we are close. We often have firmly fixed views about who they are, what they need and what actions they should take, so much so that these prevent the process unfolding naturally. A key distinction that distinguishes Super Coaches from those who run their own agenda, lack confidence, or who are caught up with a lust for power, is the ability to transcend their ego to create this optimum state for coaching.

INNER DIALOGUE

Ben: I was giving a coaching demonstration in front of an audience which consisted predominantly of cynical engineers. As I sat down, I became aware of a voice in my head that said, 'Don't mess up. This is your one chance to convince them about the value of coaching. You've now got to be an outstanding example of everything you have been talking about.' The nerves set in. When I asked the volunteer what topic he wanted to explore, he presented a complex issue about his job. My inner voice got louder. 'You've got no chance. You haven't a clue what he's talking about. Quit whilst you're ahead.' Thankfully, another internal voice started, 'You're okay. Trust the process. You know it works. Stay focused on the task in hand. You will know what questions to ask.' As we proceeded, I had a heightened state of awareness of the two voices residing in my head and continued to focus on the second, helpful one.

On another occasion, I was working with a client who brought to the table the issue of achieving work–life balance. His wake-up call happened on his last birthday, when he received a card from his wife asking him who he was married to, his company or her. When we began to explore the subject, two differing points of view emerged. One train of thought went along the following lines: 'I can't work fewer hours. All my colleagues put in 12–14 hour days. We're always there for each other, available to talk in the evenings and help each other out. The only person who doesn't do this is my boss and he's a real bastard. He gets out on the golf course on a Friday afternoon and leaves everyone in the lurch.'

As I asked him to consider alternatives to this reality another train of thought emerged: 'I could explain my dilemma to my colleagues and contract with them to be available two nights a week. I don't have to follow in my boss's footsteps. There is a way of achieving balance and bringing people with you.' He recognised that he had an inner dialogue which consisted of one voice causing disruption and interference and another that led to the natural identification of solutions and a way forward.

Timothy Gallwey, author of the classic book *The Inner Game of Tennis* and one of the pioneers of coaching, introduced the notion of Self 1 and Self 2 to explain this dynamic. He described Self 1 as the voice in the head, the inner voice of thoughts and feelings, and Self 2 as our innate ability. Tim makes a useful differentiation between Self 1 and Self 2's impact on our ability to learn and perform. He shows how if we're not careful, Self 1 becomes a dictator. It judges, instructs, criticises and applauds us and this can distract us from our inherent ability to perform to our optimum capacity.

We have explored this form of inner dialogue extensively and are convinced that the same principle applies whether we're hitting a tennis ball or coaching a life situation, behaviour or skill. Too much mental processing, analysis or problem-solving seems to get in the way. Mental stillness, i.e. Self 2, appears to be the essential coaching state. Any necessary mental processing, analysis or problem-solving takes place at an unconscious level. In the same way that we don't tell ourselves how to walk, we don't tell ourselves how to coach. The coach's ability to still his mind and focus on his coachee is paramount. His capacity to see his thoughts as they emerge, and to let them slide away, is a master skill. The coach doesn't have to be oppressed by the need to solve his coachee's problems and come up with solutions, but he does need to exist in a state of uncertainty, of being rather than doing, and allow solutions to emerge.

Paradoxically, the opposite is true for a coachee. It is useful for the coach to help his coachee to see what is going on with the voice in his head. His inner dialogue either supports his success or hinders it, so it helps him to externalise it, thereby freeing him from interference and enabling him to move forward.

The four inputs of a coach

- Ask questions
- Playback/summarise
- Make suggestions
- Give feedback

It is important to be aware of the purpose of your interventions:

Unacceptable purpose

Fishing for more information for coach's interest

Manipulating the conversation to coach's agenda, ideas or solutions

---

Diagram 9: Coaching Inputs

ASKING QUESTIONS

'The *Star Trek* computer doesn't seem that interesting. They ask it random questions, it thinks for a while. I think we can do better than that.'

Larry Page

Graham: I had been coaching the distributions director of a retail business. To help the person in question raise his awareness about himself and how he was viewed, I requested my trusted collegue, John Burnard, to conduct a life interview and run a series of tests. In advance of the debrief of this psychological and personality profile, I asked John to provide me with the headline messages that had emerged. He told me that in all the years he had surveyed senior executives he had never come across an individual who seemed to be so ill-fitted for his role. This observation had nothing to do with the director's capability, it just appeared that his currrent role didn't play to his strengths and in fact seemed out of line with his underlining drive and aspirations in life.

In light of this, I decided to take the bull by the horns and, rather than work through the report with my coachee as planned, I asked him, 'Why are you doing the job that you're in?' His response took some time and was emotionally charged. He said that it boiled down to the fact that his parents had always had huge aspirations for him, that his siblings had enjoyed great success in the commercial world and that it was never questioned that he would make his way through the corporate world. I then asked, 'Is this the real you?' He replied that he had always felt like a fish out of water as he climbed the corporate ladder and that he had surprised himself by how far he had reached. Unfortunately, it had brought him little satisfaction and he had constantly questioned whether it was what he really wanted to do.

In our subsequent coaching sessions, my coachee looked into what he really wanted to do and what would be a true expression of who he was and what was important to him in life. To cut a long story short, he resigned and opened up a small English language school. Our coaching came to a natural conclusion, but the last time I talked to him he reminded me how those two killer questions had been the catalyst for transforming his life.

The quality of the questions asked in a coaching inter-action will determine the quality of the output. The ability of a coach to ask useful and insightful questions is the key for heightening awareness, unlocking information, exploring realities, opening new doors and establishing actions. It fits with the Socratic method. Socrates's approach was to ask his pupils questions, so as to draw out the knowledge he was convinced they already possessed.

The secret to effective questioning is to know both the right time and the right type of question to ask, so that the coaching process does not turn into an interrogation with the coach firing off one question after another. It's essential that questions are asked with thought given to their purpose, relevance and possible value. There are several types of questions available in the coaching tool kit:

Open	**Closed**
What　How	Did　　Should
	Do　　　Must
	Would　Have
	Will　　Is
	Could
Specific	**Analytical**
When　How many	Why
Where　How much	
Who　　How often	
Which	

Diagram 10: Questions

In the early stages of a coaching interaction, the most helpful questions are open-ended ones that enable coachees to choose topics that they see as relevant and important. 'What?' and 'How?' questions are non-judgmental in their tone and do not imply that the coach is leading the conversation in any particular direction. A coach could begin a coaching session with questions such as:

- What's on your mind?

- What would you like to talk about?

- What would you like to discuss?

- How are things?

These provide a non-threatening climate for the coachee to reflect upon his situation. They help him approach his situation in a broad and general way and keep him exploring ideas until he has identified his most relevant topic or need. If there is a pre-agreed topic of conversation, for example discussing the status of a team, a coach could ask, 'What is the current situation with your team?' or 'How are things with the team?' If, on the other hand, he asks a narrower question, such as 'How are your relationships with your team?', it is clear that, because a direction has been suggested, the range of possible responses is diminished. A closed question in this context would be, 'Are your relationships with your team good?' This limits the coachee's response even further and cuts down the likelihood of generating an answer of any real value.

Once a topic has been agreed, the use of questions helps to define a particular outcome from the coaching session. For instance:

- What do you want to achieve as a result of this session?

- How would you know that this session has been truly valuable?

- What would make a measurable difference for you as a result of this session?

Now that an outcome has been established, the coach can also invite the coachee to describe his situation using a focused request such as:

- Tell me what's going on.

- Tell me about your experience.

- Describe your present situation in more detail.

This helps to heighten awareness and invoke an enriched description of his reality. At this stage in the coaching process questions may help to clarify the history of a situation, draw out any underlying beliefs and assumptions, assess the current emotional state, focus any desires for the future, check what has been tried before and explore possible options for the way forward. It is still most effective to use open questions, and not to drill down too soon, as it keeps the conversation at a higher level. Appropriate questions include include:

- How do you feel about what's happening?

- What and how great is your concern?

- What has happened in the past?

- What do you want to occur in the future?

- What have you done so far?

- What resources do you have? Time, money, people, skill, will, support, etc.?

Through this type of probing the coachee gains further clarity and insight and may have acquired several ideas about how to change his situation. The following open questions can draw out possible options:

- What options do you have available?

- What are all the different ways in which you could approach this situation?

- How could you do things differently?

As a coaching session progresses, the coach shouldn't hold back from asking an off-the-wall or challenging question such as:

- What if there were no limits, what would you do?

- I know that you don't know the answer, but imagine if you did, what would you do?

Once ideas have been discussed, the coach can ask specific and closed questions in order to gauge the coachee's level of motivation to commit to something that he believes is achievable and is determined to act upon:

- Is there anything else that would be helpful to look at?

- Are there any obstacles blocking you from moving forward?

- What are you going to do?

- When are you going to do it?

- Who is involved?

- Where will it take place?

- Will you do it?

The one question with which care should be taken within a coaching context is 'Why?' Moving into analysis too soon may cause a defensive reaction from the coachee, particularly, if he feels judged and criticised. If, for example, a coachee wants to explore his relationship with his boss and the coach asks why, the coachee could land up thinking that he shouldn't look at the relationship and that it's a sign of weakness. Although analysis can facilitate greater understanding it is, ultimately, guesswork and replacing it with questions such as 'What are the reasons?' and 'What do you think happened?' evokes more specific, factual answers.

It can also sometimes be invaluable to ask naïve questions as a non-expert in a particular area. As Socrates said, 'The only true wisdom is in knowing you know nothing', so asking 'What do you mean?' and 'What's involved in this situation?' can help the coachee clarify his perceptions, assist him in re-evaluating them and also perhaps help expand what he thought was possible.

It is essential in the questioning process for the coach to follow the interest and train of thought of the coachee. There is nothing worse for a coachee, when discussing a particular subject, than for the coach to respond with a question which bears no relation to what he has just said. It goes completely against the non-directive approach, which we have discussed earlier, and, because it demonstrates a lack of empathy, will break down trust.

We are often asked for our definitive or magical list of questions. While we have provided some generic questions that are of potentially great value, there is no definitive list. If there were, coaching would become a mechanistic and predictable process. That would be the death of coaching! Great questions emerge out of real attention on the part of the coach and from being at one with the coachee. The most beneficial often occur unconsciously.

LISTENING

'The most basic of all human needs is the need to understand and be understood. The best way to understand people is to listen to them.'

Ralph Nichols

Graham: Many years ago, before becoming a coach, I was very uncomfortable when people expressed emotions, especially anger or sadness. If someone described a difficult situation in his life, I felt pressure about how to respond. I questioned what I could do and feared appearing inept or uncaring. What I discovered, after numerous uncomfortable situations, was that a person just wanted someone to be with who cared, empathised and listened. It was often unnecessary to respond. In fact, sometimes a response, although said with the best of motives, intruded into the person's space and was unhelpful. What transpired was that they needed to feel secure enough to be able to express themselves, which helped to change their state in a positive direction. I thus discovered the power of listening.

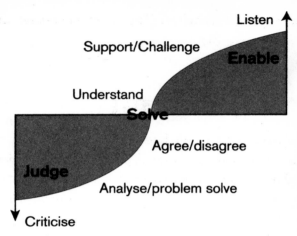

Diagram 11: Listening Spectrum

Most of the time we listen for a reason. We listen to respond, to agree or disagree, to prove a point, to wait to talk, or to complete somebody else's sentence. It's also common to go through life without a consistent experience of being truly listened to – as when the listener has 'become us' and fully 'gets us' at a deep level. The Americanism 'I felt gotten' captures this notion, as does the science fiction book *Dune*, which invented the verb 'to grock', which means to understand somebody at a very fundamental level.

Even the notion of listening to understand throws up the question of who that understanding is for. It is all too easy to think that listening is a device to help the coach understand the situation. However, given that coaching adopts an approach whereby the potential lies within the coachee to problem-solve and find ways to develop skills, is it really necessary for the coach to understand the minutiae of the coachee's situation? Indeed, we have often been in situations where we have not fully understood what the coachee is saying, but have found that this does not diminish our ability to ensure that he gains value from the interaction.

The purpose of listening in a coaching interaction is to aid the coachee's understanding of his situation. It is for the benefit of the coachee rather than the coach. The most powerful way for a coach to think about listening is to listen in order to listen. In other words, the coach has no personal motive beyond exposing his coachee's current reality and enabling him to gain new clarity and insight into his situation.

We all know how to fake listening. Nodding our heads, saying 'yes' . . . 'umm' . . . 'oh really' in between sentences, maintaining eye contact and repeating back to the coachee what he has said, parrot fashion, can make it appear that we're listening. However, listening to listen is a different experience, which combines the coach's intention to be fully present, engaged and focused on the coachee's interest. Although we want to move away from the idea that listening is a technique that can be taught, there are some guidelines that help a coach increase his awareness of his current capability and identify any development needs that he may have. Some of the most important of these are:

- The coach giving his full attention to the coachee by absorbing himself in what is being said.

- Letting the coachee finish his sentences.

- Using silence to allow reflection and think time.

- Paying attention to both verbal and non-verbal communication, including content, tone of voice, pitch and pace, volume and body language, such as eye contact, physical gestures and facial expressions.

- Following the interest of the coachee.

- Noting main ideas. They may be mentioned at the start or end of a dialogue and repeated a number of times.

- Being open and honest. If, for example, the coach has drifted off, having the courage to say, 'Sorry could you repeat yourself, I lost what you said'.

- The coach being aware of his own inner dialogue and letting irrelevant thoughts slide by.

- Asking relevant questions.

- Summarising.

- Offering feedback.

Listening has been described as the greatest gift that we can give to another person. It is a supreme example of true respect, allowing somebody else to be the way they are and to speak their truth.

SUMMARISING

It can be very helpful, from the coachee's standpoint, if, from time to time, the coach summarises and plays back what he believes the coachee has said. This is primarily for the coachee's benefit and enables him to re-hear, reflect upon and thus see more clearly what he has said. It has the added payoff of indicating the extent to which the coach has been attending, and how interested and committed he is to what is being shared.

Summarising is an art which, if used as a mechanical act, driven from a technique base, will be disruptive to the coachee. A complete oneness with the coachee will mean that the coach is nodding, indicating his attentiveness and understanding as the interaction proceeds. What seems to be highly effective, is the coachee realising that he has been 'gotten' as a result of summarising. Alternatively, the coachee, with the benefit of playback, can clarify what he means and restate it, thereby helping to increase understanding.

We do not suggest that a coach should attempt to become a tape recorder, playing back precisely every word that the coachee has uttered. In fact, this would drive him nuts! Effective coaches are able to sum up what has been said in a way that recreates the coachee's statements and captures where they are coming from, without necessarily using the same sentences, and probably being more economic with words and thus time. An expert coach can also encapsulate what wasn't said but was implied, which can give a deeper rendition of the coachee's reality.

It's important, however, that the coach does not put his own spin on things, particularly in the early stages of a coaching conversation. The coach should use the same key words as the coachee, rather than ones that he thinks mean the same thing. We have a videotape of a coaching session in which the coachee used the expression 'time-management' whereas the coach used 'organise your time'. Each time it happened the body language of the coachee indicated that the connection was lost. Upon debriefing, the coachee said that he felt misunderstood and that it was not quite what he meant.

A coach can ensure that his summary captures his coachee's meaning by asking the coachee if it is a fair reflection of what he has said. We find that coachees will spontaneously agree or disagree if the summary hits or misses the mark. The value of summarising is in providing the rare experience for the coachee to hear back what he has said, to clarify his understanding and to expand his point of view.

To summarise summarising:

- It does not need to match what the coachee says word for word.

- The coach puts the main idea(s) into the coachee's or his own words, but includes only the main point(s).

- It presents a broad overview, so is usually shorter than the coachee's original statement.

- It is helpful to use phrases such as 'This is what I think you're saying . . .' 'Let me play back what I think I've heard . . . ' 'Let me check my understanding . . .'

OFFERING FEEDBACK

'I've been making an effort to be less critical.
If you weren't so self-absorbed, you'd see that!'

Feedback in organisations can be highly charged. It often has a history of being delivered as negative criticism and therefore people avoid it like the plague. We could go as far as to say that feedback is usually a one-way exchange of feeling, in circumstances of stress, where failure is the key issue! Unfortunately, this experience robs people of the true purpose of feedback which is the sharing of information about current behaviour that could be changed in order to improve performance or about performance that has been particularly effective. It's important to recognise that feedback is as much about identifying people's strengths and successes as it is about development needs.

Living and working in an environment deprived of feedback is like being in the desert without water. We start to see mirages of our own behaviour, which may be far from the perception of others. A recent survey by the Department of Trade and Industry (Dti), highlighted this condition, which they called the 'Inspiration gap', the difference between how executives rate themselves and how their staff rate them. Most said that they expected workers to show trust and respect both for the people they worked with and for their customers. But, when 700 white-collar staff were questioned, only four in ten thought their MD or CEO had the same characteristics. The same number said they talk more than they listen. Six in ten said they were out of touch, and only one in ten said they inspired them.

In order to achieve high performance, it is essential for people to be hungry for feedback, requesting it from their boss, colleagues, customers and coach. Thankfully, most organisations have 360-degree feedback mechanisms which can add valuable data for individuals to reflect upon their current performance and development needs. Feedback enables us to see ourselves through the eyes of others, it acknowledges and validates us, and serves as an input for learning and change.

In a coaching context, there are several primary sources of feedback. If the coach has a relationship with the coachee outside the coaching interaction, then he can draw upon observations made at other times. For example, a line manager is able to draw upon data in relation to achieving business objectives, behaviour exhibited in meetings and one-to-one interactions. He may also be able to play back a generalised perception of the coachee gained from other colleagues. This needs to be done with caution, framed as 'My understanding of how you are viewed'. It's important that it's not used by a coach to avoid telling the coachee how he views him. Deferring to other peoples' perceptions is weak and does not serve the coaching relationship with the necessary integrity, openness and honesty. The coach can also give feedback within the coaching session itself. The coach may spot many things about the coachee, such as how he presents himself, his body language, energy and interest in particular topics, as well as his physical work environment and his commitment to learning and growth.

We suggest the following four steps to giving effective feedback:

Diagram 12: Feedback Model

1. Set the scene.

- Timing, i.e. make sure that any feedback is given as close as possible to the event.

- Prepare the facts and how to present them, i.e. ensure that any data is accurate, specific and time bound.

- Request permission, e.g. 'I have some observations for you, would you like them?' 'I have some feedback for you, how and when would you like it?'

- Explain the purpose of the conversation, i.e. to provide some specific data which could help the coachee improve his performance or reflect upon what he is already doing well.

- Review the contract of working together, i.e. confidentiality, two-way exchange, open and honest, supportive and challenging.

2. Invite self-assessment.

- Ask open questions to raise awareness, e.g. What is your view? What do you think?

- Listen to understand, i.e. allow silence and reflection.

- Summarise to check understanding.

- Encourage the coachee to take ownership and responsibility for his behaviour and any future actions, e.g. 'My encouragement would be for you to think about the impact of your comments before speaking.'

- Explore understanding of implications of actions, e.g. 'If you do adopt a more open style of leadership what do you think the implications would be for your team?'

3. Give your feedback.

- Offer feedback in a straightforward and direct manner, e.g. 'I notice that in meetings you appear withdrawn and lacking in confidence because you don't contribute your point of view.'

- Focus on behaviour as observed and not personality, e.g. the need to speak more loudly, participate more actively (rather than become more extrovert, which is a personality trait).

- Explain the consequences of behaviour, e.g. by speaking quietly and not presenting your viewpoint, people perceive you as lacking confidence and disinterest. By speaking more loudly and actively participating, people will perceive you as confident and engaged.

- Return to self-assessment to establish shared under-standing, i.e. if necessary, draw upon the coachee's self-assessment to check understanding and close any gaps.

4. Plan action.

- Summarise joint conclusions, e.g. what we recognise is that in group situations such as meetings you tend to speak quietly, avoid eye contact and fail to give your opinion.

- Draw out proposed solutions and offer suggestions on how to improve performance, e.g. attend a presentation skills course to practise voice work to increase volume, expand variation in pitch and pace, increase comfort and confidence in front of groups and maintain eye contact.

- Plan actions, e.g. book the presentation course within one week, request feedback from colleagues after next meeting.

- Offer support and book a review session.

- End positively, e.g. focus on the achievement of receiving feedback and being prepared to act upon it.

It's important to recognise that feedback is merely an input into coaching; it is not coaching. In organisations, we sometimes encounter managers who say, 'I gave him feedback and he hasn't changed; see, he is uncoachable.' We repeat; giving feedback is not coaching. Feedback becomes valuable when coaching is applied to ensure understanding, to apply the 'so what?' test, to capture the learning, to look at the practicality of changing, the motivation to change and to help in the creation of committed action steps.

As well as becoming skilled at giving feedback, it's essential that we learn to receive feedback effectively. The attitude of the receiver is critical in determining the quality and success of the feedback process. A hostile, defensive attitude will deter others from giving feedback. Consequently, and somewhat ironically, those most in need of feedback in organisations are least likely to get it.

In the excellent interview with Manfred F.R. Kets de Vries, the director of Insead's Global Leadership Center, entitled 'Putting Leaders on the Couch', from the January 2004 issue of *Harvard Business Review*, he recalls an incident when he attended a meeting of 30 senior executives gathered for a presentation about the future of their organisation. The CEO was a wealthy man who used to brag that he would need ten lifetimes to spend all his money. He arrived 20 minutes late for the meeting, and came in talking on a mobile phone. Nobody acted annoyed. Eventually, the presentation started, and the CEO's phone rang. He picked it up and talked for 15 minutes while everybody sat there, waiting. Suddenly he got up and said he had to go. This was the most important meeting of the year, and he just walked out. No one objected. Everyone told him what he wanted to hear. It was as if he were in a hall of mirrors.

In order to adopt an attitude conducive to receiving

feedback we suggest considering the following four questions:

1. Do I understand the feedback?

   • Other people see only your behaviour and actions and make judgements on the basis of what they observe. You may have honourable intentions, but other people may have perceived your behaviour differently. That is their reality.

2. Is it valid?

   • You have the right to reject feedback. However, it is valid from at least one person's perspective, so it's helpful for you to ask for feedback from others to check if they have the same perception.

3. Is it important?

   • Even if the feedback is valid, you may decide that it is not important enough to act upon.

4. Do I want to change?

   • The final choice about what to do with the feedback lies in your hands. Even if it is valid and important, you may decide not to change. However, you should consider the consequences of changing or not changing.

Being prepared and willing to receive feedback from the coachee is another dimension of coaching. This can take place during the coaching interaction by checking if the conversation is helpful, if the approach is working and if the coachee is getting what he wants. It can also form part of periodic reviews of the coaching relationship and agenda, with the coach asking such questions as, 'Are you getting the value you want?' 'What do you like about my approach' and 'What could I do differently?' A confident coach will ask these questions and a good coaching relationship will ensure that they are answered honestly.

MAKING SUGGESTIONS

The final input that a coach can offer is making suggestions. This area is fraught with danger as they are often anything but suggestions. The coach may present his opinion as a suggestion, when in fact it is his own personal belief about what he thinks the coachee should do. Suggestions are often disguised in the form of questions, such as:

- Have you thought about doing . . . ?

- What about . . . ?

- Have you considered . . . ?

At worst, the coach may move into proving, convincing or demanding that his coachee take his suggestion on board.

Making unsolicited suggestions is anathema to a coaching approach based on helping the coachee self-discover, build capability and move into a position of ownership and commitment. The suggestions may not be welcome. Coachees may want to figure out solutions for themselves, need deep thought and reflection, and could even be on the verge of clarity and insight. Making a suggestion can intrude into this and spoil their train of thought.

If the relationship between coach and coachee is strong enough, then a coachee will voice this. But the coach must be sufficiently humble and attentive to the coachee's needs to check whether a suggestion would be welcomed before making it. Gaining permission ensures that the suggestion has the best chance of being useful rather than being poked into the coaching conversation because the coach has a 'good idea' that he can't resist 'laying on' the coachee. For instance, the coach could say:

- I have a suggestion, would you like to hear it?

- I have something on my mind that could be valuable, do you want me to share it?

Even where the coachee welcomes suggestions, or indeed asks for them, we recommend that these are left until late in the coaching session, so that the coachee has been given every chance to generate his own ideas.

Making suggestions differs from giving advice, offering guidance or sharing personal experience. It may be appropriate if permission is sought to give them, however we do not endorse it as common practice in non-directive coaching. If advice is requested, it can be useful to agree to give it following the session so that it doesn't cloud the coaching taking place. In regard to sharing personal experience, the coach has to be extremely mindful of his agenda. If he discloses information purely for the purpose of helping the coachee reflect upon his own situation or to create greater empathy in the relationship then it may add value. However, if his motive is to get something off his own chest this is unacceptable and the coach should deal with it by seeking his own support.

A suggestion is no more than what it says it is; a suggestion. It is not the answer, the right way or an absolute. If it applies in his world it provides another option for the coachee to consider and reflect upon. It can either be accepted, and subsequently acted on, or rejected as inappropriate or unworkable. It's vital for coaches to be unattached to any suggestions they offer. The mark of an effective coach is to make very few suggestions, because such a rigorous job has been done in helping the coachee arrive at his own decisions.

SUPER DOING SUMMARY

- The optimum mental state for coaching is achieved through developing focused attention and relaxed concentration.

- Allowing sessions to unfold by transcending the ego and the need to control the direction and outcome are the hallmarks of an effective coach.

- A coach needs to become aware of his inner dialogue. He can do this by paying attention to Self 1 (his inner thoughts and feelings) and Self 2 (his innate natural ability). The goal is to let Self 2 lead his coaching.

- The coach's ability to ask valuable questions determines the level of insight his coachees gain.

- The highest level of listening is to listen for the purpose of listening.

- Summarising is for the benefit of the coachee to re-hear, reflect upon and thus see more clearly what he has said.

- Where requested, providing feedback for the purpose of improving performance or highlighting where performance has been particularly effective supports coaching.

- When appropriate, suggestions can be made for the coaches to reflect upon, however they may or may not be taken on board.

SuperCoaching
Exercise 6: Developing Skills

Begin to assess your level of absorption in coaching conversations. On a scale of 1–10 (where 10 stands for 100 per cent), how focused are you? How much attention do you pay to the quality of the questions you ask? How often do you listen to listen? Describe the impact of your summaries. How effective are you in the area of feedback? What is your intention behind making suggestions? What are the next three steps you will take to develop your coaching skills?

CHAPTER 7

Super Model – The GROW Model

Graham: 'George, we have 30 minutes for this coaching session. What would you like to talk about?'

'Well. I'm 37 years old and I would like to decide on a career plan until I reach 60.'

'So what would you like to cover in the second half of our 30 minutes?' I said jokingly.

I was confronted with this challenge on a coaching programme for managers, which included giving them 30-minute individual coaching sessions on a topic of their choice.

'George, I sense that this is not a realistic outcome for our 30 minutes, would you agree?' He did, but, as I was passionate to see him getting some real benefit, I went on to ask, 'What goal would you like to achieve in this session?'

George responded, 'If I could decide how and when I'm going to generate this plan it would be a step forward.'

We duly approached the session from this standpoint. George achieved what he wanted and then he owned up to the fact that he had been testing me. He said that he had deliberately put an impossible goal on the table to see how I would tackle it. He had done the same thing in an earlier practice session with a fellow manager who had been coaching him and could see now that because they hadn't pinned down a clear goal, the session had been unsatisfactory and had left him no further forward than when he started.

It may sound odd, but, in the early days of coaching, although my coachees gave me positive feedback, I wasn't clear why. I wondered if it was due to my being non-judgmental, my ability to focus on the coachee, who basked in the attention, the questions I asked, the way I listened, or just who I was. What was it? I also questioned if there was an implicit structure in my interactions, or whether I just made it up as I went along. My understanding was further complicated by the different benefits reported by my coachees.

When I started training coaches, including HR practitioners and middle-level managers, I was forced to clarify my methodology. But it wasn't until I landed one of the world's largest strategic consultancies as a client that it really became necessary for me to understand what I was doing. These consultants, in particular, needed frameworks, left-brain methodology and clear understanding before they were able to embark on a development programme which was predominantly experiential.

I commenced a process that involved video and audio taping of countless coaching sessions to analyse what was going on. I had NLP (Neuro Linguistic Programming) practitioners watch me in action and provide feedback on what they observed. We mused endlessly about what coaching was, what we did and what happened. Gradually, we saw that there was an inherent structure to what I was doing. There was a beginning, middle and end. It was not always possible to predict how it happened, but it was clear that certain milestones were reached in each effective session. Now my challenge was to capture them in a simple and memorable format that could be used in training other coaches.

We used a variety of acronyms to capture this structure before we experienced a eureka moment and GROW was born. A simple and effective model that can be applied to all coaching interactions, it stands for Goal, Reality, Options and Wrap-up. GROW captures a key aspect of what coaching is and does: enabling people to grow, to develop their capabilities, achieve high performance and gain fulfilment.

Effective coaches have GROW or similar models internalised so that it becomes an unconscious competence. Within this framework, the coaching is fluid, natural and artistic. The coachee is not subjected to a mechanistic and linear approach. If coaching becomes too formulaic, it detracts from the human connection and interferes with the magical space of relaxed concentration where real value emerges. While our language requires us to describe the GROW model as linear, in fact most coaching sessions are cyclical in nature. A coach recaps earlier phases of the GROW model throughout a coaching interaction, helping the coachee to see clearly and move forward.

Super Model covers GROW in detail, which has now become the world's best-known coaching model, appearing in most coaching books and numerous coaching development programmes.

Diagram 13: GROW Model

TOPIC

After establishing or re-establishing rapport and connection, depending on whether it is a first session or one of a series, the coach asks his coachee what he would like to look at during the coaching session. On occasion, it may be appropriate for a coach to propose a topic, however, unless the coachee owns it, and he seriously wants to look at it, then it should be put on a backburner. A coach who prepares for a session, which is an important discipline, but then doggedly sticks to a topic he has previously identified, runs the risk of failing to connect authentically with his coachee. Another potential trap is for a coach to have a topic in his back pocket and to subtly move the session in that direction, believing that his topic is more relevant for the coachee.

For instance, a coach may think that his coachee needs to address the topic of time management because he has no white space in his schedule. However, the coachee has just had a heart-to-heart conversation with his boss about his role and responsibilities, which he wants to address. If the coach is not careful, the session could be like ships passing in the night. Although time management may be a useful topic to address at some stage, the most pressing and important one is clearly the implications of the recent conversation with his boss.

Key questions to establish the topic include:

- What topic do you want to address?

- What would be the most valuable subject to focus on?

- What would you like to discuss today?

Sometimes, a coachee may express his topic for the session in a rather general and non-specific fashion. It is often the case that a coachee is not entirely clear about what he wants to talk about, hence topics are presented vaguely, along the lines of, 'I want a better work–life balance' or 'I want more fulfilment in my work'. It's important to unravel a generalised topic and clarify what it is a coachee really wants to focus on. In some cases, gaining this insight plays a large part in resolving the topic. The following table illustrates how a nugget of gold can be sitting within a non-specific topic:

Generalised Topic	Specific Topic
Work–life balance	To say 'no' when unreasonable demands are made
Fulfilment at work	To ensure that my tasks are linked to my vision and values

It's often the case that a coachee's fuzzy thinking around a topic has immobilised him and it is only through a questioning and probing process that the real topic becomes illuminated. We will use a hypothetical coaching example to demonstrate the different stages of GROW. Firstly, establishing a topic could run along the following lines:

Coach: What topic would you like to address today?

Coachee: I've been wondering about stress, because I'm feeling pretty tense.

Coach: What specifically would you like to focus on about stress?

Coachee: I'm not sure. Probably just the fact that I'm getting irritable at work.

Coach: I've heard you say that you'd like to address the topic of stress and that you've been feeling pretty tense and getting irritable at work. What feels most pressing out of those areas?

Coachee: I don't know. They all seem quite inter-linked.

Coach: Would you be prepared to consider that stress is a non-specific topic?

Coachee: Yes.

Coach: In which case, what aspect of it would be most helpful for you to look at?

Coachee: Not getting so irritable at work.

Coach: Are you sure?

Coachee: I think so.

Coach: Think for a moment, what would make the biggest difference for you, being able to resolve your tension, or not getting irritable at work?

Coachee: Well, if I wasn't so tense, I probably wouldn't get so irritable?

Coach: Are you sure about that?

Coachee: Yes, because I know that when I've been more open and relaxed in the past irritability has not been an issue.

Coach: Okay, shall we focus on the topic of tension for today?

Coachee: Yes.

Coach: On a scale of 1–10, 10 representing maximum value, how useful would it be for you to gain new insight into the topic of tension?

Coachee: Nine.

Coach: What would you need in order to make it ten?

Coachee: To understand that by resolving tension I will be able to manage stress more effectively.

Coach: With that awareness in the background, are you prepared to agree to explore tension?

Coachee: Yes.

Although this may appear a laborious task, it is only through taking a rigorous approach to establishing the topic that a coach can ensure he is addressing what is most valuable for a coachee.

GOAL

'A goal properly set is halfway reached.'

Abraham Lincoln

'As you suggested, I made a list of my professional goals:
1) Make Ed stop blowing his nose when I'm on the phone.
2) Convince Cheryl and Sandra to wear less perfume.
3) Get to the break room faster when I smell popcorn....'

Perhaps one of the most significant steps in our own coaching work was the recognition of the critical need to differentiate between the topic of a coaching session and a specific outcome. Unless the agreed topic can be distilled into a bite-size chunk that is achievable during the agreed time frame, it can lead to a frustrating, purposeless and sometimes meandering conversation. Therefore, the intention in the goal stage of the GROW model is to set a SMART goal, so that the coachee can walk away with a result.

The way that we define the popular acronym SMART is Specific, Measurable, Achievable, Relevant and Trackable. The coach should attempt to establish a goal after agreeing the topic, but the coachee may not be able to express it clearly and specifically until he has talked it through and been able to see it with greater clarity. The use of further questioning and probing enables the coach to drill down into the topic until a realistic goal becomes clear. Then and only then should the coach proceed with the conversation.

Building on our session described above, the coaching could take the following form:

Coach: In relation to the topic of tension, if you could get anything from this coaching conversation what would it be?

Coachee: A greater understanding of why I get tense and how to stop it.

Coach: What specifically would have the greatest impact for you when you get out of your chair in the next hour?

Coachee: To stop getting tense.

Coach: How could you measure that by the end of our session?

Coachee: Well, I couldn't, because it will only be in actual situations that I can test it.

Coach: So what is achievable today?

Coachee: Getting one action point that will help me to stop tension.

Coach: What difference would that make for you?

Coachee: A big difference, because it would be the start of resolving the tension in my life.

Coach: How would you know?

Coachee: Because, upon leaving here, I would have a greater understanding about what tension is and how to deal with it.

Coach: So what I've heard you say is that when you get up out of your chair you want to walk away with one specific action that will make a measurable difference to stopping tension in your life.

Coachee: Yes.

Coach: Do you agree to focus on that goal?

Coachee: Yes.

Coach: Good.

If we were to couch this conversation in our SMART formula it would look like this:

Specific	Measurable	Achievable	Relevant	Trackable
One action to stop tension.	Yes, I would be able to feel myself relax.	Yes, we have 2 hours.	Very. It would make a tangible difference to the quality of my work and life.	On a daily basis, I would be able to see if it worked or not.

All coaching has a defined outcome and, in most cases, this takes the form of an action step or steps. On occasion, a coachee might say that he just wants to kick a topic around and see what emerges, but even that is a goal for the session.

There are a variety of questions that can ensure that the session is purposeful, focused and delivers a tangible outcome. These include:

- What would you like to take away from this session?

- What specific output would make this session worthwhile?

- What goal would you like to achieve as a result of this session?

- What would ensure that your time has been well spent?

- What would be most valuable for you as a consequence of this session?

- What outcome do you want to achieve?

- When you get out of your chair, what outcome would be most valuable for you?

While it can seem pedantic to pin down the Goal phase we encourage coaches to do just that. It is helpful for a coachee to clarify what he really wants and what it would look, feel and sound like, thus building clarity, insight and ownership. Proceeding too far into a coaching session without the necessary clarity about where it's heading and what it will look like at the end poses a risk. While the coach may have an interesting conversation with his coachee, and the latter might feel some therapeutic benefit from talking and being listened to, the session will not have the 'hard edge' of performance that differentiates coaching from other conversations that take place at work. These tend to lack value as a result of insufficient agreement about the purpose and outcome of the conversation, and serve more as a meandering 'natter' or negative 'dump'. Coaching has a defined point to it and it is the coach's responsibility to ensure that the outcome is made crystal clear for his coachee.

REALITY

The temptation for a coach, once he has a confirmed goal, is to hurry straight into action and tell his coachee what he should do to solve his dilemma. Session done! Although this might provide instant gratification and appear to save precious time, it defeats the objective of coaching and prevents the coachee from deriving long-lasting benefit as a result of the intervention.

In our experience, the bulk of time in coaching is spent at the reality phase. By presenting a rare opportunity to explore issues in a non-judgmental environment, a coachee is allowed to face his reality, often for the first time, in the cold light of day. An alchemical reaction appears to take place when honesty and non-judgement are brought together for the purpose of understanding a situation. This is the time when a coach can help shine the light of awareness onto the reality of a coachee. As it is brought into sharp focus, he may gain new insights, raise his awareness and see an issue or need with more clarity, and then he will inexorably move towards an internal confrontation about whether he is committed to moving forward or not.

The tool that enables reality to be understood is the use of open-ended questions and probing statements. These help a coachee describe his situation in rich detail and enable him to see things in a fresh light. There is no ultimate list of 'killer' questions and statements, but some of the more constructive ones include:

- Tell me about your situation.

- Describe your current reality as you see it.

- What is your current understanding of your situation?

- How do you see things at the moment?

- What's going on?

- Describe in detail your experience of reality.

- How do you feel about your reality?

- What control do you have?

- What have you already done?

- What has stopped you from doing anything more?

- What impact does the situation have?

- Who is involved?

- What resources do you already have? Support, time, money, knowledge, skill, etc.?

- What other resources will you need?

- What do you want to happen in this situation?

- What are the obstacles that you are encountering?

- In what ways would it benefit you to maintain the status quo?

- What are the consequences of staying with your current reality?

Our coachees frequently report how valuable it is to be brought up against questions that they haven't asked themselves, that they may be avoiding or that they never make time to reflect upon. In particular, senior executives and managers say how helpful it is to be challenged on their perception of reality since it doesn't often happen in their normal day-to-day interactions.

The key to the Reality phase is to create clarity and new ways of seeing things so that, when the session moves into the Option phase, the coachee has tested his reality sufficiently to have as clear a picture as possible.

In the majority of cases, the options for finding a solution become clearer as a direct consequence of having invested in the Reality phase. The intention is to help a coachee probe into things, peel away the layers of the onion, see things specifically, clarify meaning, strip away assumptions and judgements, use precise language and provide real world examples of assertions.

Our experience is that the questioning and exploration often start out on a broad base until the specific issue becomes clearer. Once this happens, the focus narrows as we help our coachees drill down into a new take on their reality. The risk of becoming too narrow too soon is that we may get involved in an issue that is not the most important or fundamental to them. By emphasising that we are going from broad to narrow, we seek to help our coachees address the cause of their issue rather than staying at a symptom level. A good indicator as to whether we have really reached the root cause of a situation is whether any fundamental change takes place following the session. If not, it will probably mean that the reality has not been reached and that the coaching has been caught up with effects rather than a cause.

The dynamic of a coachee coming with an initial issue is known as the presenting issue. However, the presenting issue is often not the core issue. For instance, if a coach was dealing with the topic of time management, a presenting issue might be working long hours. Dealing with it at a symptom level might mean that a coachee will make some marginal changes in how he uses his time. However, unless the coach has helped him locate the real issue, such as having a mind-set that dictates he has to work 12-hour days, or feeling guilty about leaving work on time, then nothing will change at a fundamental level and he is likely to default to his original pattern.

A further purpose of the Reality phase is to support a coachee in seeing the truth behind his excuses or reasons for his picture of reality. 'I can't tell my boss because he won't understand.' 'The culture forces me to work long hours.' 'My emails waste so much time.' A coach can then challenge a coachee about whether he would rather have what he wants in life or the reasons why he doesn't. It enables him to separate the fear from the fact, thus increasing his resolve and helping him to grasp nettles that he has previously avoided.

Putting the Reality phase into action by continuing our previous coaching dialogue may work out as follows:

Coach: Tell me about your current experience of tension.

Coachee: I wake up in the morning and feel a sense of dread about the day. When I consider all the things I have to do it appears overwhelming.

Coach: Tell me more.

Coachee: I get up quickly, hoping the feeling will pass, hit the shower, grab breakfast and get on with the day.

Coach: What else?

Coachee: I've never really thought about it. Let me think. Well, I suppose that there is always a background noise in my head. It's like a voice telling me that I should do this and I should do that. It tells me that I'm never doing enough and that whatever I do isn't good enough. Come to think about it, I feel tense just talking about it.

Coach: Keep describing your experience of this voice.

Coachee: It never stops. It is always present, criticising me and affecting the way I feel. When my boss requests a meeting I feel dread. The voice then gets really loud and starts predicting the worst. 'You're going to get found out now.' 'This is it. You might as well pack your bags.'

Coach: What happens?

Coachee: Nothing. My boss just wants to discuss the project we're working on and we have a useful conversation.

Coach: What is your current understanding of the cause of this voice?

Coachee: I've been criticised for as long as I can remember. I grew up in an environment where there were great expectations. My father worked hard to send me to a good school and he reminded me of it on many occasions. When I woke up in the morning, he would tell me that I would have to work hard that day or else I'd get into trouble. I realise now that I've lived with that dread all my life. In fact, I can see that I've probably set my boss up as my father, because I expect to get into trouble with him.

Coach: What does this show you about your reality?

Coachee: I'm living in the past. I'm still behaving like a child! I've never seen it like that before. It's funny, because all the things I thought would help me relax haven't. Getting promotion, earning more money, moving up the property ladder, getting engaged – in fact, the more responsibility I seem to take on, the more tension I experience.

Coach: What does this tell you?

Coachee: I need to resolve this fear, which goes back to my upbringing. Unless I stop that voice, I'll continue to be in the same situation, regardless of what happens in my life. In fact, the more I achieve the worse it gets.

Coach: What is your evidence for this statement?

Coachee: By discussing my experience of tension, without trying to fix it or get rid of it, I am able to see that it is not based on an actual situation in my life. There is nothing in my current reality to indicate that I should be waking up feeling dread or carrying it through my day.

Coach: Is there anything else?

Coachee: Well, my partner will be relieved, because whenever she tries to comfort me and tell me everything is okay I get mad. I tell her that she doesn't understand and it causes unnecessary conflict. I can now see that, because of my own lack of understanding, I thought that she was just trying to brush it off. I can now see that this is not the case.

Coach: So if you were to describe your reality now, what would you say?

Coachee: I'm living in the past. I am still being run by an old voice in my head influenced by my father. If I can get rid of that voice, I will be able to experience things as they are, not as how I think they are.

During this conversation, the coachee has moved from a position of assumption to a clearer picture of the cause of his situation and therefore his actual reality. This in and of itself has opened a door to resolving things and giving him a clear platform to look at possible options for a solution. In the process of exploring reality, it is useful to consider the following distinctions:

Perception or reality?	According to whom?	What evidence do you have to substantiate a theory?	How would you know what is true?
Fear or fact?	Based on what?	What are the concrete facts?	What are your feelings?
Excuse or reason?	What is the evidence to back up your statement?	Who have you checked this out with?	If there were no blockers in the situation what would happen?
Symptom or cause?	What is the real reason?	How do you know?	If you removed the symptom, what are you left with?

A simple model that a coach can use to further investigate reality is the 4 Fs. They stand for:

Facts
Feelings
Findings
Future

A coach can use this model to establish the hard facts in a situation. Often, a coachee will discuss Feelings as if they were Facts, for example:

- 'I can't tell my boss, because he won't understand.' Is this a fact or a feeling? What happened the last time you spoke with your boss?

- 'The culture forces me to work long hours.' Who is the culture? How does it force you to work long hours?

- 'My emails waste so much time.' Who is in charge of your emails? What have you already done to resolve the issue?

Once a coachee has distinguished the Facts from the Feelings, he can look at what it tells him. The Findings stage involves understanding the data:

- What does it tell you about yourself that you feel you can't speak with your boss? What does it tell you about your boss that you feel you can't speak with him? What do you think your boss would say if he knew that you feel you can't talk with him?

- What does it tell you about the culture? What does it show you about yourself that you feel it forces you to work long hours?

- What can you learn about yourself in relation to how you deal with your emails?

The Future stage enables the coachee to focus on his desired future state:

- What is your ideal relationship with your boss? How do you want to communicate? How do you want to feel?

- How many hours do you want to work? How do you want to perceive the culture in which you operate?

- What does your ideal email policy look like? What system do you want?

It is essential that a coach does not skimp on the Reality phase. Effective coaching dwells on current reality as a key enabler for moving forward.

OPTIONS

'Be a Columbus to whole new continents and worlds within you, opening new channels, not of trade, but of thought.'

Henry David Thoreau

Once the coachee has described his reality in rich detail and the goal for the session has been revisited to assess whether it is still relevant or in need of modification, the coach's role is to help the coachee generate some options to explore how to move forward.

In the vast majority of our sessions, we have been astonished at the inherent capability of our coachees to see their way through issues, problems and development needs. In most cases, it is not necessary for us to intrude into this natural process of self-discovery. However, asking creative questions to encourage them to think 'outside the box', put themselves in other peoples' shoes or overcome any barriers can be extremely useful. If a coachee starts looking to his coach for input and advice, it is important to revisit the initial contract and agreed expectations. If a coachee is clear about the nature of his coach's support being predominantly non-directive when the coaching engagement starts, it is less likely that he will lean on him for answers.

In the Option phase, it appears that the most effective strategy is to start by asking open-ended questions such as:

- What could you do?

- What options do you have?

- What possible solutions are available?

- What are the different ways that you could resolve this issue?

- What ideas have you had in the past?

- What have you tried before?

Using simple questions can elicit surprisingly valuable options from the coachee. Coaching sessions don't always have to draw out new or particularly novel ideas. Often, they bring previous thoughts into sharper focus and confront the coachee with whether certain choices are desirable.

After these base-line questions, a coach can become more creative with his questioning style. Useful probing questions include:

- What have you seen others do?

- If you were an expert in this area what would you do?

- If you had all the time/resource/money in the world what would you do?

At this stage, it's important for the coach to explain that he is not asking the coachee to commit to any particular actions. His aim is flush out a variety of options to be pinned down or discarded in the Wrap-up phase. It is critical for a coach to remain non-judgmental and give no evaluation of suggestions made. A coachee needs to feel free to say anything without the coach disclosing any overt or covert point of view. The coachee will evaluate his options at the next stage and test their practicality, possible implications and the level of his motivation to take action.

The coach can now step up the level of creative questioning to enable the coachee to gain further ideas. Helpful questions are:

- If you could do anything, what would you do?

- If this was the most important thing in the world to fix in the next 24 hours, what would you do?

- If you had no fear, what would you do?

- What would you do if you could have a new beginning and start again?

- What would your boss/partner/colleague tell you to do?

- What does your intuition, your inner-voice tell you to do?

The purpose of this type of questioning technique is to generate as many options (however unlikely, impractical or zany) as possible. When a coachee has exhausted the range of options he has been able to come up with, it's important to summarise what he has explored. For instance, saying, 'It seems that there are the following possibilities . . .' enables him to reflect if any stand out for future consideration or if something is missing.

At this stage, it may be that a coachee would like the coach's perspective. This can happen if he feels blocked, if the solutions he has generated are inadequate, or if he is covering old ground. This usually comes to light either in the form of a straight request from the coachee, or by the coach spotting it and asking if he would like it. As we discussed in the section on suggestions, what the coach offers is not a preferred option, nor the 'right' answer, nor is what he offers any more valuable than the coachee's ideas. Any suggestion is purely for the purpose of reflection and must only be taken on if it really fits and resonates with the coachee's position. It's also important to allow any suggestion to be dismissed (politely!) if the coachee does not feel it's relevant or would work. The more upfront the coach is about having no expectations in relation to his suggestions being used, the easier it is for the coachee to say, 'No thank you'.

At this point, the coachee has a comprehensive list of all the options available to him, which have predominantly come from his own wisdom, experience or creativity, with some possible additions from the coach. We will now look at putting the Option phase into action by building on our previous coaching conversation.

Coach: Let's check our original goal for this coaching

session and make sure that we're on track. You said that you wanted to walk away with one specific action that will make a measurable difference to ending tension in your life. In relation to the description of your current reality you said it was like, 'Being run by an old voice in your head influenced by your father'. Are you still in agreement with your stated goal?

Coachee: Yes. However, I'm not sure how I'm going to achieve it.

Coach: That is the purpose of the next stage of our conversation, where you generate a variety of options, which we can then explore as possible ideas for the way ahead. I will ask you a series of questions to reflect upon what you could do and if you want I can also offer some suggestions.

Coachee: Okay

Coach: So what could you do?

Coachee: Tough. How do I stop this voice? Well, in my experience, this voice never stops, so I don't think I could stop it, but I could change it.

Coach: How? What options do you think you have available?

Coachee: I could see that what I'm telling myself is not based in reality. I could speak with my boss to get his feedback on my performance to make sure that he is satisfied with my output. I could speak with my partner and explain the situation to her to avoid future confrontations.

Coach: What have you tried in the past?

Coachee: I have tried to talk myself out of it but to no avail. I did once check with my boss to see if I was meeting his expectations and I once attended a relaxation class at my gym, but it didn't appeal to me.

Coach: What have you seen others do?

Coachee: Well my partner doesn't suffer the same tension. She always appears pretty calm. I know that my boss gets out on the golf course when he's got a lot going on.

Coachee: Imagine that you were already an expert in this field, what would you do?

Coach: I'd just stop! If I was an expert I'd probably have some technique that could make me switch off, but I don't know what it would be.

Coach: Picture yourself in a situation with all the time, resources and money in the world, what would you do?

Coachee: I'd jump on a plane and get the hell out of here.

Coach: Really?

Coachee: I would feel like the pressure had completely come off, but it's not an option.

Coach: Let's explore some other avenues. What does your intuition tell you to do?

Coachee: Relax. It tells me there is nothing to worry about, but then the old voice kicks back in with a vengeance.

Coach: Consider that this issue was the most important thing in the world to resolve in the next 24 hours, what would you do?

Coachee: I'd speak to my father and find out what he really thought about my behaviour when I was growing up.

Coach: What advice do you think your father would give you?

Coachee: He would probably tell me to relax, that I did well at school and have exceeded his expectations in my career.

Coach: Are there any other options that you can see?

Coachee: There's got to be something in this with my father. I have never really spoken with him about it.

Coach: Don't evaluate it yet. Do you have any further ideas?

Coachee: No.

Coach: Okay. So what I've heard you say is that you could tell yourself the voice is not real, you could get feedback from your partner and your boss, you could get out on the golf course, you could just relax, jump on a plane, or speak with your father and find out what he really thought about your behaviour.

Coachee: Interesting.

The coachee is now able to move from a laundry list of ideas to a specific option that will be tested in the next stage for its potential value.

WRAP-UP

Finally, the coaching session arrives at the action phase. Given that both coaches and coachees love action, it can feel as if it has taken some time before being able to establish specific steps. However, if the coach is rigorous with the previous three stages, appropriate actions may have become obvious and he is able to pick up the pace in relation to wrapping up the session. It will be no surprise to you by now that step one is to ask more open questions to pin down the best option. Useful questions include:

- What options appeal to you?

- What options stand out for you?

- How do you feel about your options?

Having established the coachee's immediate preferences, it is important to have him describe the reasons for his choices. This tests his thinking and provides greater clarity about the level of certainty and confidence he has in taking particular options forward. The coach can ask:

- What is it about these options that appeals to you?

- What connections or links do you see in the options you have chosen?

- What potential do you perceive in the options that you've put on the table?

Before deciding on a final option, the coach makes sure that he checks out the others before discarding them. Ask:

- Do the other options have any merit?

- Could you see yourself taking them?

- If you are going to discard them what is the reason?

The coachee may still have several options on the table, therefore the crucial thing is to narrow them down. It's time to pull some closed questions out of the bag:

- Which option is the front-runner?

- Which option are you certain you should take?

- Which option would make the biggest difference?

- If you could only take the one step that you believe would add the most value, what would it be?

Through this process the coachee arrives at one final option that he is ready to break down into specific action steps. This is the moment when the coach needs him to be rigorous about evaluating the implications of the action, its practicality, any obstacles that could arise and any support he may need. The coach wants him to have the experience of success, of keeping his word and of the certainty that if an action step is identified in a session then it will be taken.

In this context, the coach shouldn't leave the coachee with any self- doubt. It is vital to address anything that could lead him to saying, 'I might', 'I think I will', 'If I get the time', 'But', 'If only', or 'When'. Otherwise, he could end up in a disempowered state where he fails to take any authentic ownership and make any real commitment. It is far better to agree to no action steps being taken than to land up with an ambiguous or wishy-washy conclusion.

To ensure that the action is thoroughly evaluated, we recommend using a variety of questions:

- What are the implications of taking this action?

- What would it mean if you did it?

- How practical is it?

- How realistic is it?

- What possible obstacles could be in the way?

- Is there anything that would stop you from doing it?

- Are there any risks or downsides?

At this point, it's important that the coach does not let up on the coachee. He needs to keep pressing him until there is clarity about the action. This is not because the coach has invested in a particular action, but to ensure that the coachee makes progress. To illustrate the Wrap-up phase, we'll continue our coaching conversation:

Coach: Let's recap the options we have on the table. You could tell yourself the voice is not real, you could get feedback from your partner and your boss, you could get out on the golf course, you could just relax, jump on a plane, or speak with your father and find out what he really thought about your behaviour. How do you feel about your options?

Coachee: Some feel more impactful than others. The option to speak with my father feels significant because I have never done it. It would probably also help to get more tangible feedback from my boss. The others don't hold a lot of interest.

Coach: What is it about these options that appeal to you?

Coachee: Hearing somebody else's perspective. Given that I get so wrapped up in my own internal voice, I believe that it would be very useful to get a reality check from people that I respect.

Coach: What potential do you see in these two options?

Coachee: A lot. If I can have this chat with my father and get honest feedback from my boss then I think it could go a long way to resolving my tension.

Coach: Before you make a final decision, is there any merit in the other options you generated?

Coachee: Not really. I've either tried them already and they haven't worked or they're just not realistic. For instance, telling myself that the voice isn't real winds me up, and jumping on a plane is a fantasy.

Coach: Which option are you certain that you should take?

Coachee: It's hard, because I feel that I should pursue both the one with my father and the one with my boss.

Coach: Which option would make the biggest difference?

Coachee: It shouldn't really matter what my father thinks today, whereas my boss has a strong influence on my future. I've got to establish a better relationship with him, so that I don't feel dutiful and dependent and can exercise more free will. This would enable me to feel more relaxed, take more risks and move forward with greater confidence.

Coach: What are the implications of taking this action?

Coachee: Well, in the worst-case scenario, my boss could either refuse to give me feedback or perceive me as weak for asking. Hopefully, he will see it as a smart move and recognise that resolving this issue will significantly improve my performance.

Coach: What would it mean if you did it?

Coachee: It would demonstrate that I'm not afraid of straight talking and it would show my commitment to overcoming the tension.

Coach: How practical is it?

Coachee: Very. I can request a meeting with my boss and let him know beforehand what I want.

Coach: Is it realistic?

Coachee: Absolutely. In fact, if I were my boss I would welcome it.

Before moving on to the final action plan, it is vital to unlock any potential interference that might prevent the coachee from committing fully to taking action. The way to do this is by exploring any blockers that he may or may not recognise. In our experience, some of the most common are:

Block	Impact
Fear	It's important to assess if the fear is fact or fiction. If a coachee is considering quitting his job and leaving himself in the lurch, the fear may be well founded. However, if it is an irrational feeling, then it will be necessary to work it through until he arrives at a satisfactory way to resolve it. Sometimes, fear is a great motivator and an inevitable part of moving forward.
Anxiety	Is anxiety a habit or a real time response to an actual situation? The trouble with anxiety is that it doesn't solve problems. It's necessary to find out what the coachee needs to do in order to turn anxiety into action.
Procrastination	Putting things off, waiting until tomorrow. Procrastination is one of the commonest ways to avoid taking action. A coach needs to make sure that a coachee is not conjuring up reasons for putting things off.

Catastrophising	Dreaming up worst-possible-case scenarios and predicting the worst. This appears like another good reason not to do anything, whereas in reality it is a false picture. It is helpful for a coach to get his coachee to express his worst-case scenario so that it doesn't lurk in the background.
Complaining	Sometimes, people would rather have their complaints than solutions. It gives them a sympathy vote and something to talk about. A coach needs to recognise when a coachee is stuck in complaining mode and challenging him in a forthright manner can help him move on.
Avoidance	A sign of cold feet is a coachee coming up with reasons to deflect the importance of the situation or going off on a tangent which seems more compelling. Avoidance is usually characterised by denying that something was a big deal in the first place once we reach the crunch point of doing something about it.
Independence	A sign of unhelpful independence is when a coachee makes out that he doesn't need any help or perceives asking for it as a weakness. In these situations, it's important to encourage him to see that it was probably his need to be overly independent that got him into a problem in the first place and therefore it certainly won't be the solution to moving forward.

Having identified any potential blockers the coach may need to spend some time helping the coachee resolve them before being able to complete the Wrap-up. Although it may appear that it's a waste of time, it is usually the blockers that have been the central reason why somebody has not taken action in the past. The coach's ability to support and challenge coachees in a non-judgmental way is the catalyst to help them overcome the interference. Continuing our session:

Coach: What obstacles could be in the way?

Coachee: None.

Coach: Are you sure?

Coachee: Well, I could get caught up in my day-to-day busyness again and therefore put it off. But I think the biggest obstacle would be my concern that my manager would see me as weak and consequently lower his opinion of me.

Coach: Imagine for a moment that you had overcome those obstacles. Is there anything that would stop you from doing it?

Coachee: Probably just finding the time. I can never get into my boss's diary, so to request something else would be hard.

Coach: What can you do about that?

Coachee: Well, he knows that I'm having coaching as part of my personal development plan. In fact, he actively encouraged it. I just need to bite the bullet, make it a priority and insist on a time to meet.

The coachee is now ready to drill down to his final action plan, including the specific action steps he will take, when he will take them, who is involved and when they will be reviewed. It's essential to write these down so that there is no room for any misunderstanding. We will now complete our coaching conversation:

Coach: What will you do?

Coachee: I can call his PA to schedule a time.

Coach: When?

Coachee: Today.

Coach: What time?

Coachee: As soon as we've finished this session. Strike while the iron is hot.

Coach: What preparation will you do for your meeting?

Coachee: I'll write down the context of the situation, explaining my tension and asking for honest feedback in order to improve my performance. I'll send it over to my boss before we meet so that he's got some time to reflect upon what he wants to say.

Coach: When will you do this prep?

Coachee: I can do it at the weekend.

Coach: How important is this to you?

Coachee: Very. Okay. I'll do it tonight and send it off in the morning.

Coach: When will you review what's happened?

Coachee: In our next session that we've got scheduled in a couple of weeks.

Coach: Is there anything else that you want to say or ask?

Coachee: No, I'm ready for this and just want to get on with it.

This is one of the key times that taking a challenging approach can be supportive. Using a variety of closed 'in the face' questions or feedback can ensure that a coachee has fully checked his position. Examples include:

- When will you do it?

- On a scale of 1–10 (in which 10 represents 100 per cent) how certain and or determined are you?

- Are you giving your word to yourself (and me) that you will do it?

Taking this approach will increase commitment and ensure that a coachee feels accountable for any output. It is the job of a coach to ensure that his coachee has made a full and complete assessment of his potential action steps and what benefit he might derive as a result. Ultimately, a coach is not responsible for what his coachee does and doesn't do. It would be extremely detrimental if a coach started to take on his actions in any shape or form. Therefore, a coach must ensure that he doesn't project an unsolicited point of view, 'You shouldn't do x, y or z because . . .' A coach may ask to give some feedback, 'I have a concern about x, y or z that I would like to share with you to see if it has any validity for you . . .' A coach might offer resources; contacts, appropriate reading, but his role is to enable a coachee to take ownership and be accountable for his actions. It is not the coach or the coaching that makes the coachee take a step. It is as a result of personal choice and heightened awareness.

Thus, a coachee can finally get up from his coaching session with one or more tangible steps that he has contracted to take and that will be reviewed in the next meeting.

SUPER MODEL SUMMARY

- GROW is not a linear model. A coach will recap the different stages to test clarity and understanding.

- GROW can be applied from short, pacey conversations to full coaching sessions.

- GROW starts with a broad topic that a coachee perceives as valuable.

- The Goal establishes an outcome for the session.

- Reality helps a coachee see his current position clearly and free of assumptions, generalisations and judgments.

- The purpose of the Option stage is to generate as many ideas as possible.

- Wrap-up ensures that options are evaluated, obstacles are removed and actions established which are specific, measurable and time-bound, with supporters identified and a review scheduled.

SuperCoaching
Exercise 7 – Developing Structure

People often describe one of the benefits of coaching as being able to have time to think. This is a precious commodity in a time-poor society, but what's needed is a framework that supports our thinking. As Thomas A. Edison said, 'To have a great idea, have a lot of them.' The GROW model provides the context in which to go beyond what you thought was possible. When you first use it, do you make sure that you inform others of your intent? Are you rigorous in establishing a topic and a goal? Do you help your coachee describe his reality in rich detail? Do you allow him to generate options? Do you ensure that he commits to specific actions? Request feedback from your coachees to heighten your awareness of the value of GROW and your ability to use it well.

CHAPTER 8

Super Tools – Increasing Capability

COACHING AND EMOTIONS

'The difference between competence and high performance often lies in emotional factors. Our ability to be resilient and confident ensures that we fulfil our potential.'

Ben: In the early days of my journey in personal development, one of my primary goals was to stop feeling. I often didn't like the way I felt and thought that by ending all emotion I could function more effectively. At times, I was consumed by feelings of fear or frustration and these often prevented me from achieving high performance. I had key relationships in which I didn't express my opinions through fear of hurting the other person. I had bouts of anxiety around my work that stopped me from taking risks. I was not alone. I found that most people I worked with also had feelings that prevented them from being more effective in their work and lives. Having specialised in working with emotions for nearly 20 years, I realise that we're missing the point if our aim is to get rid of them. The key is to learn to work with our emotions in a constructive way, to see them as enablers for our own performance and to develop strategies that help us work with our feelings rather than against them.

We're up against a legacy in the corporate world, however, as feelings and work have failed to go together. Macho cultures have encouraged people to believe that admitting to particular feelings is a sign of weakness and has led to the development of destructive behaviours such as bullying, manipulation and defensiveness, all of which can cause mayhem in the workplace. Being on the receiving end of a boss who vents his own frustration can destroy the morale of a team. Working with colleagues who play political games to hide their fear creates low trust and engagement.

Thankfully, pioneering work in the field of Emotional Intelligence, popularised by Daniel Goleman, has allowed emotions to take their rightful place as a central ingredient for being successful at work. People now recognise that in order to build relationships, lead and inspire others and achieve high performance, the ability to be self-aware, manage emotions, empathise and have advanced social skills is the order of the day. This is aside from the fact that the majority of managers are faced, at some point in their careers, with having to deal with difficult emotional situations arising from breaking bad news, redundancies, failed promotions, personal problems derived from marital or relationship breakdowns, managing alcoholism or drug use, depression and even suicide.

Super Tools explores how coaching can be used to develop emotional literacy and how we can increase our effectiveness as coaches in the domain of emotions. It then offers a series of useful tools to add to your kit.

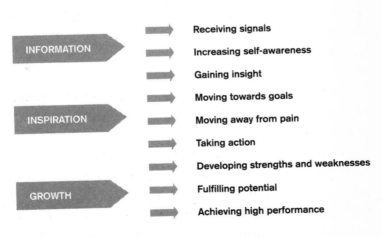

Diagram 14: Purpose of Emotions

PURPOSE OF EMOTIONS

Given the havoc that feelings can cause, it makes you wonder why we were born with them in the first place. But when we marvel at Michelangelo's David, are transported hearing Menuhin playing Elgar's violin concerto or are dazzled by Tiger Woods's swing it makes sense. Life devoid of emotion would be death. We suggest that there are three main reasons for having emotions – information, inspiration and growth.

Information Emotions are valuable information, they tell us something important. Our feelings act like the signal from a lighthouse beam, letting us know that there is imminent danger ahead, or like the beeping of a metal detector as it is about to unearth precious gold. Imagine if we had no feelings. How could we tell our desires from our suffering? How could we know about our impact on others? How could we learn about our deepest motives and desires? Although we use logic to a certain extent in making important decisions it's usually the power of emotion that is the deciding factor.

Ben: Karen wanted coaching because she felt stuck both in her work and in her life. She was separated from her husband, had a young child and a job that she no longer enjoyed. She didn't know what to do. She found herself crying a lot, which she described as 'very out of character', and had lost her motivation. I knew that if we attempted to change her external reality without facing her internal feelings we might miss a crucial piece of her jigsaw.

We agreed that for the first three coaching sessions Karen wouldn't make any life-changing decisions. Instead, I asked her to reflect upon what she thought feelings told her. Initially, she found it hard to consider the concept that feelings could be useful information, but, after some reflection, she began to see that her feelings were telling her that something was missing at the core of her life. Although she knew this on a cognitive level, she hadn't yet allowed herself to feel it. What she ultimately realised was that the 'real' Karen was absent. She had become so caught up in playing a variety of roles – as mother, wife and manager – that she had lost herself. The coaching then focused on helping Karen rediscover her passion and commitment to her own direction, which led her into making other crucial decisions.

Inspiration Emotion inspires us to move in the direction in which we want to head and away from where we don't want to be. It is energy that we can harness in either positive or destructive ways. An effective leader at times of crisis has the opportunity to tap into people's deepest emotions, which either galvanises them into taking constructive action or panics them into detrimental reactive responses. Most great accomplishments come to fruition as a result of the energy derived from being emotionally inspired.

Growth Emotions enable us to learn and develop. What makes mankind unique is our ability to combine our feelings with reason. Picture a world devoid of emotion. At the end of the film *2001: A Space Odyssey* Stanley Kubrick and Arthur C. Clarke portray the future of mankind as a space-child in a ghostly floating bubble, watching over the earth and its people. But how desirable is this? We are not free of emotion. The only way that we will fulfil our potential is through drawing upon our own emotional experience of what works and what doesn't. As parents observing our children, it is very clear that their growth comes about through their ability to harness their raw emotion and use it to their advantage. This is comparable to the workplace, where high performance is only achieved when hearts and minds are aligned.

COACHING EMOTIONS

Ben: I was running a coaching demonstration with about 20 participants. It was time for the coaching demonstration in front of the room. Alan stepped forward. When I asked him what he wanted to work on he described the topic as self-confidence. I started from a broad angle asking him what was on his mind. Alan started talking, but then became very still. I was tempted to push the session forward, because it felt uncomfortable waiting for him to respond, but my intuition forced me to keep quiet. Alan leant forward as he put his head in his hands. The emotional temperature rose. He was unable to speak. Slowly, Alan gathered his thoughts and started to explain how, two years previously, he had worked on a project that had failed within the business. It was high profile and cost the company a large sum of money. One individual had held him accountable and had made a passing remark that he had f***ed up. Alan had never allowed himself to experience the emotion around this situation. He hadn't talked it through with anyone, not even his wife, and, consequently, it had damaged his self-belief and impacted on his performance.

When we debriefed the session with the group, people commented on how uncomfortable they had felt and questioned whether I should have allowed it to continue. Checking with Alan, he said that it had been a relief to finally speak out about it and that if I had interrupted it would probably never have happened. He commented that it was having the time and space that had allowed him to feel, and the fact that I had empathised with his situation rather than tried to fix it that had made the difference.

The diagram below illustrates six key steps to work with emotions. We will now look at each one more closely.

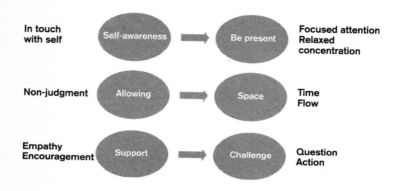

Diagram 15: Coaching Emotions

Self-awareness The ability of the coach to be in touch with himself and recognise his own responses to emotions creates a constructive environment in which his coachee can reflect. If, in the above example, Ben hadn't had sufficient self-awareness to follow his intuition he could have ruined the session. Assess your own emotional state. What are the main feelings you have and how do you work with them? Are you comfortable being in the presence of feelings or do you deflect them through humour, brush them off or indulge them? Having a high level of self-awareness means that coaches don't feel threatened when working with emotions and as a result are able to remain objective and compassionate, thereby creating a safe space for coachees.

Be present As we have already clarified, having focused attention and relaxed concentration enables coaches to stay in the moment with their coachees. The ability to be present is especially important in working with emotions because, if the coach becomes distracted when his coachee is vulnerable or distressed, it may send a potentially damaging message. The coachee could feel that he is being judged, that his coach thinks he is weak or that there are more important issues to discuss. Given that most people have not received effective support with their emotions, it's of paramount importance that the coach does not reinforce that experience. The ability to be present whilst the coachee is in an emotional state can be enough to help him turn the tide.

Allowing A coach needs to remain non-judgmental and should prevent himself from colluding with his coachee in emotional situations. We have known situations when a coachee may be crying and the coach starts crying also, or when a coachee is angry and the coach joins him in blowing off steam. This is entirely inappropriate and can result in the coachee feeling that he has to carry the coach! This is not to say that a coach is not allowed to have feelings. The coach's ability to empathise will guide him about when it's appropriate to share his own feelings and when it's crucial that he maintains a purely objective position. If a coachee has had his promotion request turned down, it may be appropriate to share his disappointment through comments such as 'I'm sorry' and 'It's bad news', but if the coach reacts too much he can hijack the session.

Space: As we saw in the example with Alan, if Ben had interrupted and tried to move on too quickly he would have lost the potency of the session. The coach's willingness to give space and be sensitive to timing is critical in working with emotions. Probably the most powerful tool available is the use of silence. When coachees experience heightened emotion, the majority would like to be allowed to feel in silence rather than have the coach to ask how they are feeling, whether they need a tissue or a cup of tea. Silence speaks louder than words. It says that the coach respects his process. He is there for his coachee. He has his time and attention. The more comfortable a coach is with silence the more effective he is.

Support It's helpful during the contracting stage to discuss feelings. The coach should always inform his coachees that he is comfortable with emotion if it does surface and that he encourages emotional honesty. He can put it in the context that if emotional issues arise which he believes require a more therapeutic approach then he will recommend counselling. However, since the obstacles to achieving high performance often have their roots in emotion it's essential that the coach can provide the right support. Explaining this provides a background to work with, so that if he feels his coachees are holding back from discussing emotions he can draw their attention to it.

Challenge A coach needs to be prepared to challenge his coachee if he believes that he is stuck in an emotion, avoiding a feeling or using an emotion as an excuse not to take action. If a coach notices his coachee returning session after session feeling pressured, insecure or anxious, it's his responsibility to help him get to the bottom of the issue so that he can resolve it. Or if the coachee keeps procrastinating about taking an important step, the coach needs to help him confront what's happening. Sometimes, it may transpire that the only way to resolve a feeling is to act. If a coachee is afraid of making a difficult communication no amount of empathy will take away the fear. Susan Jeffers book title, *Feel the Fear and Do It Anyway*, is often the solution to moving forward.

EMOTIONS AND HIGH PERFORMANCE

If we revisit the formula Performance = Potential – Interference, the interference that prevents a coachee from using more of his potential is often emotionally based. We shall now address some of the key emotions in question:

Fear: The voice of fear sounds frightening! It's no wonder that in so many situations fear impacts on confidence and prevents action. From the employee wanting to challenge up the line, to the manager wanting to address a difficult employee, to the person wanting to say 'no', fear can be the inhibitor. But is fear real? What evidence does the coachee have that causes him to doubt his capability and position? In most cases fear is False Evidence Appearing Real. As Eleanor Roosevelt put it, 'The only thing to fear is fear itself.'

The process of rationalising fear helps the coachee distinguish between whether it is an irrational fear or a genuine issue. To support this, a coach can request his coachee to provide specific evidence to back up his fear. In the case of a coachee fearing to challenge his manager on an issue, it's important to find out when he last did it and what happened. It's remarkable how often it turns out that he has never done it and his fear is based on third-hand stories or fiction. By exploring the worst-case scenario of doing it, such as losing his job, or getting a reputation as a troublemaker, the coachee is able to weigh up the reality of the possible consequences. Taking this step usually galvanises the coachee into action, and he begins to work on a strategy that enables him to move forward.

The fear of failure is also a common block to high performance. This is particularly true in the sporting world when an individual or team suffers a crisis in confidence due to a run of poor results. When Sven-Goran Eriksson took over as the manager of England the first thing he did was to address the culture of failure that had arisen around the team. He works with a Norwegian psychologist, Professor Willi Railo, whose mantra is, 'Dare to lose to win'. Together they ensured that the English players could take risks to reinstil a winning belief. Although it hasn't yet fully paid off for the England team there is a lot to be gained from this approach.

In the business world, where performance is often rated on the last project, people are terrified of failing. Ironically, one of the best ways to guarantee success is for employees to have the courage to request feedback from colleagues so that any dissatisfaction can be rectified immediately. It's often the fear of hearing negative feedback that prevents him from asking, and thereby missing out on crucial learning. Some mavericks talk about celebrating failure because they recognise that each one brings them closer to a success. Our view is that perceiving failure as part of our development is constructive, as long as we learn the lesson and don't do it again. The definition of a wise person is someone who goes on making different mistakes, whereas a stupid person is someone who goes on making the same!

Self-doubt is another manifestation of fear that can play havoc with confidence. If a coachee has a knock it's amazing how easy it is for all his other achievements to go out of the window. It's also curious how self-doubt shows up just when we need our confidence the most. Going for an interview, giving a presentation or having an appraisal with our boss are some of the occasions when the voice of self-doubt overrides logic. Coaching helps a coachee to identify, accept and ultimately control the self-doubt so that it doesn't sabotage his performance.

Anxiety An underlying belief in business today is that being responsible means having to worry. Our culture has been referred to as 'the age of anxiety'. We worry, we worry if we're not worrying and then we worry about how to stop worrying. This type of anxiety becomes a habit and usually results in people becoming hyperactive in an attempt to squash it. Unfortunately, hyperactivity is comparable to putting a sticking plaster over the anxiety – it continues to fester until it's truly resolved.

Anxiety is also the result of heightened levels of adrenalin and is caused by the hyper-stress experienced by most people in business. Hyper-stress occurs when there is an imbalance between the amount of pressure we're under and our perceived ability to cope. Short deadlines, overflowing inboxes, back-to-back meetings, constant travel, broken sleep, poor digestion and permanent exhaustion contribute to this condition.

A coach needs to offer his coachee direct feedback if he sees him in this state. When a coachee has been feeling anxious over long periods of time it becomes his norm and it's difficult for him to conceive of any other reality. A coach needs to help him think through the long-term implications of feeling anxious. He may be able to get away with it in short-term bursts, but it's not possible to sustain high performance based on adrenalin. This is where business differs from the sporting world. In sports, people are trained to deliver high performance over a short period of time, running the 100-metre race, playing a 90-minute football match. Attempting to do this day in and day out is not sustainable.

Guilt Guilt is the 'mafia of the mind'. It's an insurance policy that we sell ourselves, based on the erroneous belief that, 'As long as we feel guilty nobody else can make us feel bad because we already feel so terrible'. Unfortunately, it doesn't work. The person who struggles with work–life balance, but doesn't leave work on time because he feels guilty in relation to his boss and colleagues, is his own worst enemy. The individual who can't say 'no' out of a sense of guilt sacrifices his own life.

Like fear, guilt needs to be rationalised in order to regain perspective. The coachee struggling with work–life balance needs to discuss his hours with his boss and colleagues to find a solution. Often the act of talking about it dispels the myths of getting fired for leaving on time or letting everyone down. A coachee unable to say 'no' needs to get support from his boss to mutually decide his priorities and this will enable him to push back on other demands. Seeing guilt for what it is – a feeling that inhibits performance rather than a moral position or a solution for feeling bad – can resolve it.

It's useful for a coach to have a range of options in his tool kit to help shine the light of awareness on issues. We have derived successful results by using the following tools over the years.

CLARIFYING VISION, PURPOSE AND VALUES

'Our old mission statement was more eloquent, and dignified, but not nearly as effective.'

Graham: I was invited to coach the 34-year-old CEO of an entrepreneurial business which he had started and which had evolved very rapidly into a publicly quoted company. He was a young man of huge drive, entrepreneurial flair, presence and charisma.

As I often do at a first meeting, I asked him to describe what had driven him to achieve such success so young. He described seeing his father go broke and the hardships that had ensued for his family. He had been determined not to fall into the same traps as his father, but to achieve significant wealth for himself and for his parents, so that he could make the latter years of their lives materially secure. This quest for success and financial freedom had been his primary driver.

The business ethos and culture reflected this. The senior executives were paid significant amounts of money in return for a huge commitment of energy and hours, and the organisation was peopled throughout by self-motivated individuals who earned above the market rate. However, within the recently acquired public status (this was now a FTSE 200 company) this mission was no longer fully appropriate and anyway the business was reinventing itself into a service business as well as a manufacturing business.

My CEO had five homes, a stable full of exotic cars, a plane and boat. The question I posed was what now for his personal vision and that of the company? We worked together to plan chapter two of his career. I helped him to get in touch with what was important to him in his current reality. As well as continuing to earn well, what was going to continue to drive his success and inspire his people?

I asked him to reflect on times when he had been particularly satisfied, other than the accumulation of wealth. I encouraged him to focus on periods of his life, or indeed projects and, in some cases, single days, that had been particularly rewarding. He came up with a number of examples and we looked into these to see what were the common themes, principles and characteristics. A pattern began to emerge, which led towards the articulation of a purpose statement: 'Affecting positively the lives of people.'

I was at pains to check whether this was a 'motherhood' statement or whether it was real for him. The more he talked about it, the clearer it became that it was indeed true and was supported by the fact that, in addition to having made a great deal of money, he had enjoyed knowing that he was providing something of value for others. He decided to develop this personal mission statement with his top 40 colleagues into a purpose statement for the company that would inspire and create followership. This eventually became, 'Creating a home from home for employees', which provided the direction for the continued success of the business.

Vision	A picture of the future
Mission	A sense of purpose
Corporate Brand/ Strap Line	A marketing expression of advantage
Values	The beliefs/behaviours – a shorthand for the culture
Strategy	The plan to deliver the vision
Goals	The measurable milestones to deliver the strategy

Diagram 16: Definitions

At best, the strongest organisations have compelling visions that infect, excite and motivate their employees, and which is aligned with the CEO's personal mission and values in life. As we addressed in Chapter 1, helping people clarify their vision, mission and values is at the centre of coaching. An effective and potent mission statement captures a coachee's unique and enduring reason for being. It is the guiding light that tells him what he will achieve. It is the compass that steers him in the direction he wants to go. Typically, we start by asking a coachee the purpose of his work and life. Given that many coachees have a variety of options of what they could be doing, its essential to discover their deepest drives and aspirations. Key questions include:

- What is your vision?

- What is your sense of purpose?

- What is success for you?

- What matters most?

- What is most important?

- What do you stand for?

- What do you believe in?

- What inspires you?

It is then useful to capture this purpose in a short phrase that resonates with the coachee. We often see a visceral reaction when this is done, which is an indication of the degree of his interest. Some people are very clear about their purpose and it runs off their tongue. Others are less clear or have never consciously asked themselves the question. In the latter case, the coach should ask his coachee to look back through his work and life and identify those times when he was particularly satisfied and experienced a high degree of fulfilment. These can be either isolated incidents or more sustained periods of time, such as working on a particular project, being part of a team or doing certain activities with his family.

Having recognised a number of times or situations that meet the criteria of satisfaction and enjoyment, the coach can proceed to the next stage, which involves asking the coachee to describe the specific qualities that made those situations stand out. Common themes begin to emerge, such as the importance of making a worthwhile contribution, helping others and being innovative. These enable the coachee to reflect upon what is closest to his purpose. The final step is to encourage him to capture these themes in a purpose statement that has real meaning. For instance: to increase performance and well-being in organisations, teams and individuals through enabling insights, commitment and action.

It is important to understand that we are not talking about an aspiration that the coachee wants to bring into existence, but about an awareness that already exists within him and which the coach is helping him to articulate and bring into clearer focus. The proposition here is that we all have these driving forces within us and that, when our work and life are aligned with our true purpose, more of our potential is able to emerge, resulting in higher performance and fulfilment. Conversely, when we are off purpose, our work and life become a struggle, unsatisfying and lacking in joy.

Once a coach has helped a coachee express his purpose, he is in a position to coach him to discover how much more aligned he can become in his current situation, or, in some cases, to help him reflect on whether he needs to change his work or life circumstances. By the same token, helping a coachee clarify his mission can also put his current situation in context. It enables him to evaluate whether he is on track to achieve it or not. Useful questions are:

- What is your sense of mission?

- What does your mission look, sound and feel like?

- How would you know if you were living your mission?

Once he has created a clear picture of his mission through coaching, the coachee can compare and contrast it with current reality, identify any gaps and set about establishing specific action steps to get back on track or to accelerate his journey.

Another area to support a coachee is in clarifying his values. Research by Dr Chris Mruk at BGSU Firelands Psychological Services found that those people who were most comfortable and content with their lives were the people who set goals based around their values. Values to consider are:

- Respect

- Recognition

- Fulfilment

- Family

- Love

- Well-being

- Intellect

Helping a coachee uncover his inherent values enables him to look into his current situation and see where he is aligned with them and where he is 'selling out'. A coachee can also assess whether the environment within which he operates matches his values, in which case it will be satisfying. If it doesn't, it will be a struggle and, at worst, an alienating experience.

We would like to emphasise that if a coachee does not have the topics of vision, purpose and values as part of his original agenda, it is important to cover this ground, unless, of course, he specifically doesn't want to. Reflecting upon these topics says volumes about his aspirations, motivation, satisfaction and underlying emotional state.

RESULTS AND WELL-BEING PROCESS

SuperCoaching enables progress to take place on two fronts simultaneously – achieving results and at the same time increasing well-being. This is rare, since achieving results often comes at a cost to well-being. The following process can be used to help a coachee increase his awareness in both areas, which can either create positive change at an unconscious level or help him take conscious steps forward.

The coach creates a graph focusing on the results a coachee would like to achieve, and an aspect of well-being that he would like to improve. A coachee may want to increase his visibility with staff. At the same time, he might want to improve his satisfaction levels. The resulting graph would look like this:

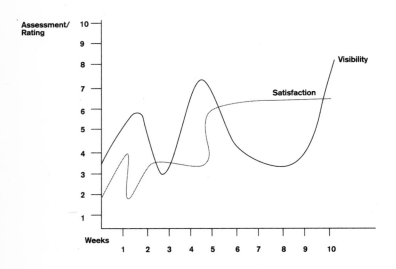

Diagram 17: Results and Well-being

In the graph, the Y-axis represents a scale of 1–10, where 0 stands for zero achievement and 10 represents high achievement; the X-axis represents dates. Over a one-month period, the coachee tracks his achievement at the end of each day on the graph. The act of bringing aspiration and performance into clearer focus enables him to move towards his goals. The Results/Wellbeing Process is deceptively simple, but graphically illustrates the value of increasing attention and raising awareness.

THE PRECISION MODEL

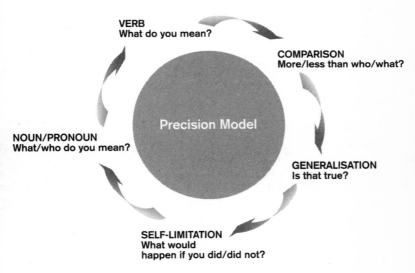

Diagram 18: Precision Model

The Precision Model is a useful tool that has its roots in the theory of language. It enables the coach to become highly attentive when helping his coachee decode what he is saying. We have found that, as coachees often use imprecise and generalised language, it is important not to make assumptions based on our own frame of reference. The Precision Model helps to clarify the meaning of nouns and pronouns, verbs, comparisons, generalisations and self-imposed limitations.

If a coachee uses a noun such as 'the team', the coach can help him clarify who and what he means. By asking, 'Who specifically do you mean?', 'Is that all the team or some of the team?' or 'What do you mean by the team?' a coach ensures that the coachee sees clearly what lies behind the statement.

When a coachee uses a verb such as 'to communicate', asking him what he means forces him to give detailed thought to what is a broad statement. For example, he may respond by saying he means 'be briefer and clearer in what I say', 'to build understanding' or 'to say what I think'.

If a coachee uses terms such as 'more than', 'better than', or 'less than', the coach can clarify what he means by asking, 'more than who?', 'more than what?', 'less than who?', 'better than what?'. Coachees often state that they want 'more money', 'more time', 'less stress', 'more success', 'more recognition', 'less hassle' or 'better lifestyle', all of which lack meaning unless compared to a previous state.

When a coachee generalises saying, 'I never have enough time', 'Nobody ever listens to me', or 'Everybody thinks the CEO is too remote,' the Precision Model challenges him to think specifically what he means. 'Do you really mean that you never have time?' 'Do you really mean nobody ever listens to you?' 'Do you really mean everybody thinks the CEO is too remote?' Putting it on the table in this manner helps him to re-evaluate the reality of his statements.

In the area of self-limiting statements, it can be revealing to challenge the coachee. If he makes comments such as, 'I must finish this report by 6 o'clock', 'I should have one-to-one's with my direct reports every week' or 'I have to be present at every meeting I'm asked to attend', asking, 'According to whom?', 'How do you know this?', 'What measure are you using?', 'What would happen if you didn't?' encourages him to test the constraint.

In summary, the Precision Model enables a coachee to move from making general statements to articulating the exact meaning of what he says. This can help him to re-evaluate his thinking, shed new light on an issue and ensure that before taking any action he has rigorously tested his hypothesis, saving both time and effort.

THE STRUCTURE OF A PROBLEM

A problem is a state in which a coachee is 'stuck' in a situation and unclear about how to proceed. Usually, it involves a topic that plays on his mind, causing distraction and internal conflict. Using the Structure of a

Problem addresses the coachee's mindset and enables him to move from a 'problem state of mind' to a 'project state of mind'. The goal is not necessarily to generate a complete solution, but to tap into his internal motivation and help him feel empowered, become unstuck and see a way forward.

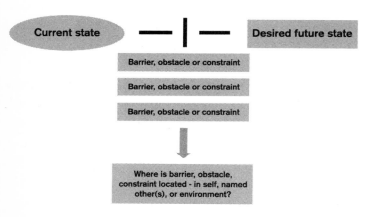

Diagam 19: Structure of a Problem

The process involves using hi-tech(!) index cards to jot down various aspects, giving the coachee a visual illustration of his situation. First, the coach gets the coachee to identify his topic. The coach captures the essence of the problem in a word, short phrase or image on a card. Next, he asks the coachee to describe his current reality and summarise it in a word. It's useful to put pace into this exercise, so that the coachee doesn't get bogged down with too much detail. Then the coach moves on to the coachee's desired future state and asks him to describe it using sensory-based language (what he wants to see, feel and hear). Again, he captures it on a card. The coach now has a clear picture of the problem and the coachee's aspirations.

Next, the coach asks the coachee to identify any barriers, obstacles or constraints he perceives exist between his current state and his desired future state and jots them down one per card. The coach needs to be patient during this stage, because there are likely to be several, and it is essential to allow enough time for the coachee to get them on the table. Simple questions such as, 'What barriers exist between where you are now and where you want to be?', 'What obstacles do you face?' and 'What constraints do you experience?' flush out the main interferences.

Having identified the obstacles, the coach asks where, in one of three places, the coachee locates them: in himself, in another named person or persons, or in his environment. This is where the power of this tool resides. It enables the coachee to see clearly where barriers exist, and thus helps him to take action where he can, and also to recognise whether there are other possible barriers outside his sphere of influence. Generally speaking, the coachee finds that the majority of the barriers exist within himself, and so he is able to act. Once he has clarified which of the obstacles to tackle, it is possible to generate options and wrap up as per a normal GROW model coaching session. Whilst using this tool may not solve the problem entirely or ensure that a coachee reaches his desired future state, it does enable him to see his situation in a fresh light and to move forward in a positive direction. He has moved from stuck to unstuck.

ISSUE RESOLUTION

Diagram 20: Issue Resolution

Index cards can also be used to clarify large or complex coaching topics such as organisational structural issues, managing teams, evaluating job options or multiple relationship issues. Helping a coachee disaggregate the different facets of a topic onto a set of cards enables him to see the various aspects of the issue in new ways. He may be able to discover a way of grouping and prioritising the different elements to shed fresh light on the situation.

It appears to be helpful to proceed through the index card notation very swiftly. The coach should encourage his coachee to jot down in shorthand the varying aspects of the issue or problem. The key is to get his inner world onto cards and laid out in front of him as quickly as possible. This act taps into the power of insight and new possibilities come into play once the coachee gains a fresh perspective.

AREAS OF LIFE CARDS

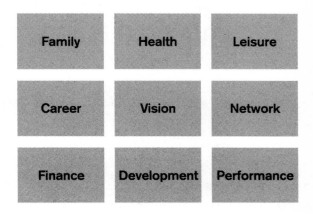

Family	Health	Leisure
Career	Vision	Network
Finance	Development	Performance

Diagram 21: Areas of Life

A further use of cards is to create a pack at the outset of a coaching programme to help formulate a coaching agenda based on each aspect of the coachee's work and life. This presents an opportunity to externalise his internal reality and begin to prioritise what's most important.

The Area of Life tool can then be used for the coachee to describe his current reality and aspirations. It also acts as a diagnostic aid to evaluate issues such as work–life balance, time management and personal fulfilment, providing information to assess where the most valuable focus can be applied. Over time, a coachee may want to add to or refine the way he has compartmentalised the different areas of his work and life.

LIFE PICTURES

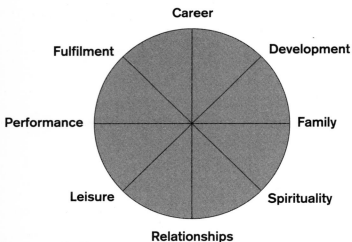

Diagram 22: Life Pictures

Life Pictures can be used if a coachee processes information visually, or to ensure that he reflects upon right-brain and emotional information. On a pie chart, a coachee draws the segments of his past. It could be based on themes from various phases of his life, for example infancy, early education, teenage years, university, career, family, friends, health and spirituality, or it could be based on his accomplishments, for example education, career, family and activities.

Having reflected upon his history, the coachee now projects onto the pie chart his future aspirations. He may want to aspire to a senior management role, wish to have a greater balance between work and family, to learn a musical instrument or to improve his golf handicap. By mapping it out into the chart, he is able to see clearly the gap between his current reality and desired future state, and establish the action steps to close it.

PERCEPTUAL POSITIONS

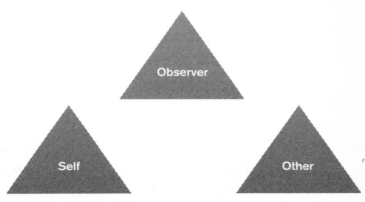

Diagram 23: Perceptual Positions

Many coaching issues have their roots in a relationship dilemma. Perceptual Positions illustrates three standpoints in a relationship: 1st position – self (how you see, feel and hear the world); 2nd position – other (his perspective); 3rd position – observer (a neutral, objective viewpoint). By taking the position of other and observer, a coachee is able to heighten his awareness of a situation and bring valuable insight back into his own reality, which may alter his perception and behaviour.

A coach uses this tool by asking the coachee to take three different physical positions, either by mapping them out on the floor, using three chairs or picturing them in his mind. The following example, involving Peter, the coachee, working on a relationship issue with his manager, Charles, illustrates how to proceed:

Coach: Step into your first position and describe how you see the situation.

Coachee: Charles is controlling and lacks understanding. He tells me what to do without consultation and gives me unrealistic deadlines.

Coach: Step into the second position and imagine Charles's reality. What does he see, think and feel?

Coachee: Charles is pressured. He has his boss breathing down his neck and although he wants to have a more collaborative style he never has the time.

Coach: Okay, now step into the third position and picture yourself as a neutral observer looking into this situation, what do you see, feel and hear?

Coachee: I see two people on different sides of a fence. It's a barbed wire fence, which means that they can see through it but had better not come too close. There has been a lack of communication, which caused a breakdown in understanding.

Coach: What advice would you give Peter?

Coachee: I would tell him that he needs to initiate a conversation with Charles, seek to understand his view and then talk to him about what he wants.

Coach: Come back and stand in the first position again. Now what do you see?

Coachee: I feel clearer. It's an approach I haven't tried. I have waited for Charles to sort it out. My going to him will represent my desire to have a more collaborative way of working.

A coach can keep moving the coachee around the three positions until he has clarity about what the real issue is and what might constitute a way forward. In the third position it can also be helpful for the coachee to imagine a mentor, boss, respected colleague or partner giving advice to add another dimension to the reflective process.

OFF THE WALL

Graham: I was invited to coach a female executive of a large retailer, with the background data that she was having trouble 'fitting in' and seemed quite stressed. At our first meeting, it was fascinating to learn that, several years previously, Emily had identified this job as her dream. It was now turning into a nightmare. Despite working round the clock she never felt on top of the job, which consequently impacted on her performance. What compounded the situation was the fact that the business was in trouble and her role, which was to communicate both internally to staff and externally to the City, was proving a daunting task.

We started our work by disaggregating her role into its component parts and estimating approximately how much time each part should take. This activity enabled Emily to see that she was attempting to achieve more work than she had hours in the week. It gave her a graphic picture of what she already knew, that she was attempting to climb an impossible mountain. Armed with this clarity, I suggested that we look at her tasks from three perspectives: stop, delegate or do them more economically. The goal was to help Emily return to her absolute 'must do's'. Although this helped, it soon became apparent that her role was too big, thus we used a series of 'out of the box' questions to explore the issue including, 'If you could do anything what would you do?', 'If you had an unlimited budget what would you do?', 'What would others do in this situation?' and 'If you were braver what would you do?'

The two front-runners emerged as to work four days

a week at the office and the fifth from home, allowing her to have essential think time, and to recruit an effective number two. The trouble was she felt they were both impossible. There had been head count freeze and she had not yet established sufficient credibility in the eyes of the CEO to ask to work from home. Since, as a coach, I operate on the premise that there's almost always a solution, I suggested that her assignment should be to make a business case for recruiting a number two. We decided that she would hold off on working from home until she was on top of the job, but that she would flag it up with the CEO as an option for the future.

I'm happy to report that Emily did get approval for her extra support, which set her on the path to getting on top of her job. She also defined a motto for herself, to keep her on track, which stated, 'Play my role as if my life depends on it, always remembering it doesn't'. This proved to be a potent set of words, as it enabled her to adopt a more flexible attitude to her workload and to recognise that her best was enough to satisfy herself, the CEO and to make a difference in the business.

On occasion, it's appropriate for coachees to consider radical concepts that challenge their habitual frame of reference. This does not mean that they suddenly quit their jobs or go bungee jumping, but it forces them to look at unusual or creative steps. The most strategic time to employ this tool is during the option stage of GROW. Key questions that draw out 'off-the-wall' responses include:

- If you could do anything without any constraints, what would you do?

- If you had no fear, what would you do?

- If you had all the time in the world, what would you do?

- If taking this step had no implications, what would you do?

- If you were a free agent, what would you do?

- If you were an expert at this, what would you do?

- If you didn't tackle this issue, so what?

- I know that you don't know the answer, but imagine if you did, what would you do?

These questions open up new possibilities and encourage coachees to consider different options.

DO IT NOW

The Do It Now tool is useful both when a coachee procrastinates and when necessary action steps get delayed. The length of time available in a coaching session may mean that a coachee can take specific action steps there and then. This is particularly helpful when the step is either quite small, for example making a phone call, scheduling a meeting or throwing out superfluous paper on a desk. If a coachee feels uncomfortable about taking an action step and continues to procrastinate, even after a coaching session, then the added leverage of having a coach present ensures that he follows through, for example discussing a difficult issue with his PA or deleting umpteen backlogged emails.

Taking this approach is an example of how it is sometimes necessary for a coach to be uninhibited and strong enough to break with predetermined ways of working. Provoking a coachee into taking immediate action and tackling something that had previously been avoided can produce tremendous relief.

SHADOW COACHING

An unusual characteristic of most business coaching is that it takes place away from the day-to-day activities of the coachee, as a result a coach has to work with a coachee's memories and perceptions rather than having the opportunity to witness his direct experience. This contrasts with most sports coaching, where the coach is present as the coachee performs, whether he is Sven Goran Eriksson watching England from the touchline or Brad Gilbert sitting in the stands observing his tennis protégé Andy Roddick.

Shadow coaching enables the coach to observe his coachee in action, which allows him to arrive at a much more realistic picture of how he operates. When a coachee permits, a coach can shadow him for a period of time in his work and life. It's important that he sets up clear expectations, boundaries and confidentiality agreements with whomever the coachee is meeting and working. Once these have been established the coach can either observe his coachee for one or more days, and then give general feedback at a subsequent session, or agree to watch for specific things, such as how well he communicates, how effective his meetings are or how well he manages his time, and report back on the day.

SUPER TOOLS SUMMARY

- The purposes of emotions are information, inspiration and growth.

- Coaching emotions takes self-awareness, being present, non-judgment, giving space, support and challenge.

- The key emotions that inhibit high performance are fear, anxiety and guilt.

- The key emotions that enable high performance are confidence, happiness and calm.

- It's useful for a coach to have a range of options in his tool kit to help shine the light of awareness on issues in different ways.

SuperCoaching
Exercise 8: Developing Coaching Tools

A world-class coach has a large collection of tools in his bag. Out of the selection explained in this chapter, identify three that you want to incorporate into your work. Ensure that you test them yourself in a self-coaching or co-coaching context, for example set aside some time to clarify your Mission, Purpose and Values, use the Results and Well-being Process for the next 30 days, or apply Structure of a Problem to a specific issue. Once you are comfortable with the tools, commit to using them at the first available opportunity in your coaching sessions.

CHAPTER 9

Super Effectiveness – Ensuring Best Practice

Graham: It was a sunny morning and I was awaiting the arrival of my coachee. I was still quite new to coaching and wondered what we would cover in the session. Paul came in, sat down and, just as I was about to embark on my normal pleasantries about the weather or football, he said, 'Graham, I'm thinking of killing myself'.

The earth stood still. I felt my heart begin to pump violently, beads of sweat built up on my forehead. Little did I know at the time, but this was my first acid test of putting into practice what I've now come to view as pure coaching. Would I stay non-judgmental? Could I help him look at his current reality and see the possible implications of his actions? Could I enable him to see another way forward? Or, would I become judgmental and manipulative and attempt to steer him towards my agenda – making sure he stayed alive?

Largely because I wasn't sure of the best way to proceed, and feeling that I couldn't just recommend that he talk with somebody else, I applied the basic coaching principles and was able to have a powerful conversation exploring his reality and options. What transpired was that he moved away from the idea of killing himself (I was never sure whether it was a real threat or a cry for help), started to dig himself out of a dark hole, and the last I heard he was leading a happy and fulfilled existence.

In those early days of coaching, we felt that developing coaching skills was the most important element in ensuring best practice. In fact, when we were first asked to help build coaching capability in managers and HR professionals it was the primary area that we focused upon. As our experience grew, we came to recognise that the 'relationship' and 'being' domains were more important than techniques. The experience with Paul showed that if a coach gets the relationship right and achieves a state of being conducive to increasing awareness, insight and learning, then even those starting out as a coach can make a significant difference to the lives of others.

Super Effectiveness explores how a coach monitors himself, his coachees and his coaching sessions to ensure that his coaching is on track and delivers best value.

SELF-MONITORING

When a coach comes face-to-face with his coachee, there is no doubt that the coachee has high expectations of what he wants to achieve and is relying on the coach to help. It is in moments like these that a coach needs to know what to pay attention to in himself, to make sure that he is in the best possible shape to deliver.

Attention A coach must be able to focus his attention on the conversation and on his coachee. It is an obvious point to make; however, it's not always straightforward to execute, because if a coach gets distracted his attention will slip away. Thus, his ability to notice where his attention is focused at any given time, and in particular when it strays from the conversation, is critical. This gives him a fighting chance of being able to refocus on his coachee.

The essence of this skill is for the coach to be able to pay attention to his coachee and to himself simultaneously. He needs to become a thought-watcher, monitoring his internal voice without letting it dominate the interaction. The most effective coaching occurs when he processes information unconsciously. In other words, coaching arises from a quiet mind. It is unnecessary, and usually a distraction, to do too much thinking about what the coachee is saying, what question to ask next and about how to proceed in the session.

If a coach becomes absorbed in his coachee without

the tyranny of trying to solve his problem, he provides the best chance for valuable coaching to take place. This does not mean that he is in a comatose state. On the contrary, like sports people who are in a state of peak performance, his actions are wholly appropriate to the situation and emerge unconsciously as a function of his attentiveness. The process of watching his thoughts enables the coach to recognise when they are contributing to or hijacking the session. It helps him to become freed up from them; in other words, thoughts can come and go, but he only pursues those that are valuable to the interaction.

Hot Buttons On a similar theme, a coach needs to notice whether any of his 'hot buttons' get pushed during a coaching conversation. If, in the normal course of life, a coach has particularly strong views on subjects such as culture, race, gender, disability, ethnicity, age, religion, sexual orientation, beliefs, education, experience, thinking style or class, he must be aware if and when what his coachee discusses activates these. If he is unable to spot these 'knee-jerk' reactions, he may adopt a position that is unhelpful to his coachee and, in the worst-case scenario, become judgmental and adversarial. If the coach is able to pay attention to his 'hot buttons', he can ensure that he doesn't succumb to them when they are in danger of being activated.

Energy A coach needs to be able to monitor his own energy levels. Coaching is an intense activity. We often receive feedback from managers attending our training programmes that they found the experience exhausting, as a result of the level of concentration demanded. Coaching requires a coach to be totally absorbed in the interaction and fully committed to his coachee walking away with something profoundly useful. This requires a significant amount of energy, so a coach needs to be able to recognise when it slips, and have strategies for maintaining it. When he does begin to feel tired, and loses concentration, he must have the confidence to address the situation. He could use humour, take a stretch-break, drink a glass of water or have a healthy snack.

Body Language Another element to self-monitor is body language. Research from the psychologist Albert Mehrabian shows that approximately 55 per cent of communication is through body language, so it is important for a coach to be alert to the signals he gives off. He needs to pay attention to his posture, facial expression, eye contact and physical gestures. Although we don't necessarily subscribe to the NLP approach of mirroring and matching (using body language as a mechanistic technique can detract from its power), we feel that it's essential to notice if body language interferes with the coachee's experience. If a coach breaks eye contact, crosses his legs or scratches his neck when his coachee is in deep thought, the coachee could perceive that he is not interested. Heightened awareness about the impact of body language ensures that if a coach does something that causes interference he can address it immediately and alleviate any concern.

Ambiguity A final part of self-monitoring is for the coach to observe his ability to operate for significant periods of time in a state of ambiguity. As we have previously stated, it is critical to have a clearly defined outcome for a session alongside the capacity to allow it to be achieved rather than forcing or pushing. Highly effective coaches notice when they have begun to push a coachee in a particular direction, or have become uncomfortable and are subtly pushing towards a certain end point in the conversation. If a coach notices himself doing this, he needs to ease off and trust the process.

MONITORING THE COACHEE

The next stage in ensuring best practice is for a coach to assess whether a coachee is absorbed in the coaching process and finding it useful, or if there is any lack of congruence in his responses. The ability of the coach to monitor the coachee effectively ensures that the latter gets the most out of the process in an effortless way.

Ben: Simon admitted that he was wary of coaching because it was the antithesis of his normal operating style as a manager. He'd said that his key criterion for selecting me as his coach was because I was so different to him. In our first session, I kept a watchful eye on his energy level and interest to ensure that he was ready and willing. Consequently, we spent a considerably longer time than usual bulding the relationship and establishing a contract. After over an hour of background conversation, the coaching got underway and we addressed critical leadership issues that Simon had with his team. Here was an example of needing to really put myself in my coachee's shoes in order to make sure that he got the most from the process and was in the right state of mind for coaching. I am convinced that unless I had paid sufficient initial attention to his needs we would not have achieved a successful outcome. The following are the essential aspects to observe in a coachee:

Awareness The starting point is for the coach to put himself in the shoes of his coachee before he walks into the room, in order to gain a sense of his possible state. The coach can ask himself:

- What is my coachee thinking?

- What is he feeling?

- What does he want?

It's important that the coach recognises his coachee is in the middle of the journey of his life, in other words he will have many things going on in his current situation, as well as a wealth of experience from his past and aspirations for his future. Adopting this approach ensures that the coach does not make any assumptions about his coachee and raises his awareness about him.

Attention As important as monitoring his own attention, a coach needs to assess the attention of the coachee. It should be obvious whether he is completely engaged in the conversation. It can be equated with those moments in life where we lose ourselves within an activity, for example hitting a golf ball, preparing a presentation, watching a movie or playing with our children. Nothing disturbs. Nothing distracts. If the coach observes this level of attention on the part of the coachee, the likelihood is that he is absorbed in the interaction. But if his attention appears to wander and his concentration is shallow, it is a signal that he is not fully engaged. This awareness provides an opportunity to challenge him about his level of engagement and either renegotiate the topic being discussed or explore the interference.

Focus Where is the coachee focusing his attention? Is he going more deeply into a specific aspect of a topic or is his focus shifting around? In the early stages of a coaching session, it may be entirely appropriate for his focus to move. While the coachee is scoping out an issue, or exploring a set of related issues, a broad focus may be required. However, once he has homed in on what is most useful to discuss, his focus needs to become like a laser beam. If the coach witnesses it continuing to shift through a session, it may mean that the goal was not clear enough or that other things are diverting him. It may prove more valuable to discuss these than to continue with the original agenda.

Energy Level A coachee will usually display a high level of energy, due to the relevance and significance of the conversation. If his energy level begins to drop, it could either mean that his attention is moving elsewhere, and that the coach needs to redirect the conversation, or that he needs a break. Although coaching is often invigorating (as it unleashes motivation), it can also be draining. It requires an extremely high level of attention and focus on the part of a coachee. Asking him to examine his thoughts and emotions can be an intense experience, far removed from how he spends the rest of his life. Agreeing to have restorative breaks from time to time can be of assistance.

Another way to monitor the energy level of a coachee is to compare it during various aspects of the session, or in relation to specific topics within the conversation. This can be very revealing, and may warrant the coach pointing it out and questioning what it might mean. If the coach sees a coachee getting particularly energised when talking about his boss, it could mean that there is an unresolved issue he feels strongly about, whereas if it drops when he is discussing a certain project, it may imply less interest.

If a coach encounters low energy levels over a period of time, it can be useful to challenge the coachee. It may be that he is so exhausted or distracted by other things in his life that he is unable to fully engage with coaching. In this case, it may be useful to reschedule the sessions at a time when he can give 100 per cent. It might provide him with an opportunity to reflect upon his lifestyle and work on how he could achieve greater balance to regain his vigour, or it could simply mean that the topic does not hold enough value for him, in which case the coach needs to establish one that does.

Hot Buttons A coach will obtain a great deal of information by monitoring his coachee's reactions. How does he respond to potentially contentious subjects? Does he have any particular hobbyhorses to which he keeps returning? It is the responsibility of the coach to bring to his coachee's attention any area that could possibly have a detrimental affect on his behaviour and reputation, and to provide a constructive environment in which they can be addressed.

Body Language It's important to reflect upon the coachee's body language. Does he sit back when discussing certain things? Does his face look enthused, angry, aggravated or sad during certain aspects of the conversation? Does he lean forward and exhibit significant hand movement as he describes something? Although the coach doesn't need to comment on most responses, it can be useful to make occasional comments such as, 'I notice that each time you talk about managing upwards you frown and cross your arms', or 'When you mention spending more time with your family you visibly relax and sit back in your chair'. These types of interventions can enable a coachee to raise his awareness about a topic and allow more significant aspects of an issue to be uncovered. A coach does not have to be an expert in the field of body language. Even if he is unsure about what the body language of his coachee specifically means, he can ask his opinion. If it proves to have no particular importance, he can simply return to the point before the interjection and continue the coaching process.

Avoidances There may be occasions when a coachee avoids an issue. The coach might ask a question and find that the coachee responds to a different train of thought, or, while reflecting upon a range of options, he avoids talking about one of them. The coach might notice something in the coachee's work or life that appears significant and yet he doesn't talk about it. It is useful for the coach to test the understanding of these possible avoidances by pointing out what he has noticed, in order to establish the best way of moving forward. However, in the final analysis, he must respect his coachee's wishes if he doesn't want to address them.

Having said that, there are times when the coach should at least challenge the coachee's position if he appears to be avoiding an area that has significant implications. If a coachee has received 360-degree feedback, with a consistent theme in it about a negative behaviour, and he brushes it off, it may have serious consequences for his career. Our view is that the coach owes it to him to point out the possible implications, so that, if he chooses to avoid it, then at least he is making a potentially damaging decision consciously rather than burying his head in the sand.

Interest Although great value is derived from following the interest of a coachee during sessions, there can also come a time when it is the responsibility of the coach to bring to his attention important areas to discuss, such as vision, purpose, strategy and relationships. The coachee may not mean to avoid them, but is so swamped by urgent tasks that he finds it difficult to keep his head above water. It may be that the coachee has a great interest in exploring people's potential, but has had to put it on the back burner as he gets on with his day job. Ironically, raising his awareness about a topic can trigger his interest and commence a valuable conversation.

At the end of the day, where the source of a coaching

topic derives from is not as important as reaching a point where the coachee is genuinely interested in discussing it. As we have already shown, it's not possible to coach people who do not want to be coached, and it's not possible to address issues that do not hold a coachee's attention.

Language The language a coachee uses tends to say a lot about his state of mind, feelings and reference points. It is extremely helpful, therefore, for a coach to monitor the language of a coachee, in order to check that it is aligned with what he wants in his work and life. On his original coaching agenda, a coachee might state that he wants a promotion, but then use derogatory language about himself, saying, 'I'm just not up to this job' or 'What's wrong with me that I can't fix this problem?' Sometimes, he might use arrogant language, such as, 'I don't know why the company doesn't just give me the job, because I could do it better than the person in charge.' He may also use judgmental language about others, such as, 'My boss is useless. He never gives clear instructions and expects me to pick up the pieces behind him.' Questioning his language can bring to his attention the possible implications, both positive and negative, of using it, and begin a process of changing it if he chooses to do so.

The coachee might also have small habits that he is unaware of, such as a tendency to give long-winded or scrambled responses, or saying, 'Okay', 'Um' and 'You know'. These can detract from the way he is perceived, so it is the responsibility of the coach to point them out so that he can decide whether to change them. At other times, a coachee will use language in an imprecise way. Using the Precision Model illustrated in Chapter 8 can help him to become clearer in his use of language. If he says, 'My boss always works long hours, forcing me to stay late', the coach can ask, 'What do you mean by always?', 'How does your boss force you?' and 'How late is late?'. Sometimes, a coachee uses language in a way that cuts down his options. This is particularly true of statements that include phrases such as, 'I should', or 'I must', which are words of obligation. Helping a coachee become more precise clarifies thinking, encourages him to see things differently and ensures that he derives more benefit from the discussion.

Environment Another valuable way to monitor a coachee is to meet in his working or home environment. Is his working environment warm, relaxed and welcoming, or stark, austere and threatening? Is his desk organised and clear or clogged with seemingly chaotic paper? Does he appear at ease in his environment or out of place? Making these types of observations can provide fresh insight for him, as he may not have previously received direct feedback about his environment.

The coach needs to be wary of making assumptions about what a coachee's environment reveals about him.

While he may be able to make a generalised observation, such as, 'A cluttered office indicates a cluttered life', this is not necessarily true. There is more to be gained from helping a coachee explain what his environment says about him than from making judgments.

Appearance What does the physical appearance of a coachee reveal? Does his appearance represent him well or does it appear out of context? If he is at a senior level, does he look comfortable in his attire or strained? Is he well groomed or somewhat dishevelled? As physical appearance is a vital component in how we are viewed, it is an important issue for a coachee to reflect upon when hoping to achieve his aspirations. The point about appearance is that it's less about the stereotype of a particular style and more about whether the way a coachee presents himself works for or against him. If a coachee doesn't bring up the subject, it's the responsibility of a coach to offer useful feedback and challenge him on his current approach if it appears incongruent.

Emotional Temperature It's important to be skilled at monitoring the emotional temperature of a coachee. Often, a coachee will arrive in a harassed state, revealed in his appearance, energy level or initial exchange. If he does appear stressed, a coach should give him a few minutes to unwind, so that he can bring his focus to the coaching. There are a variety of ways to help aid his mood, including offering a cup of tea, discussing the previous night's football results, using humour to describe his terrible journey getting to work or talking about his children. Although a coach should make maximum use of the allocated time, it is pointless to rush into a serious conversation until a coachee is ready and in the right emotional state.

Once under way, the coach's ability to keep an eye on how the coachee is feeling will have a big impact on the effectiveness of the session. He can observe different emotional states through indicators such as breathing patterns, body language, vocal quality and phrases. Indicators of stress could be increased breathing rate, the wringing of hands, sitting on the edge of the chair, eyes widening, a higher pitched voice and speaking quickly. Indicators of concern might be a slower breathing rate, hands covering face, slouching in the chair, eyes looking away, a lower pitched and quieter voice and speaking more slowly.

It can be most helpful to check the emotional temperature when there is incongruence between what a coachee is saying and the signals he gives off. He may, for instance, talk about a project deadline using positive language and yet his body language and breathing pattern display an air of concern. Drawing the coachee's attention to the discrepancy may provide an opportunity for him to talk about how he really feels.

MONITORING THE INTERACTION

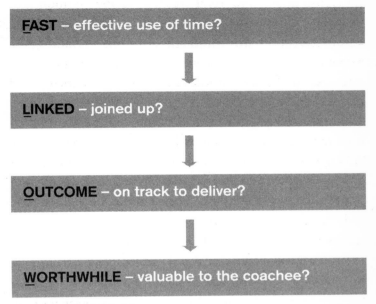

Diagram 24: FLOW Model

Once the coach has monitored himself and his coachee, the third element to assess is the quality of the interaction. With this in mind, we developed the FLOW model. This plays on the idea of 'being in flow' within a conversation, but, as an acronym, it stands for 'Fast, Linked, Outcome and Worthwhile'. We suggest that a coach initially uses it as a checklist with his coachee, enabling him to know when he is hitting the mark. Over time, it can be internalised and used implicitly to monitor interactions as they unfold.

FAST

Ben: I worked in one particular organisation when it was suggested that a manager come and see me for a trial session. As soon as he entered the room, it was obvious that he was reluctant to be there and that time was a big issue. His first comment was that he had only 20 minutes and that there were several pressing issues that required his presence back at his office. My opening line was that I recognised the importance of his time and that I guaranteed he would leave the room in 20 minutes with a clearer idea of whether coaching had any value for him. I then found myself making a reference to how much time we had left about every 2–3 minutes. In any other context, this would have sounded insane. However, in this case, it seemed to do the trick, because he read it as an indication of my valuing his time, which (surprise surprise) turned out to be his biggest issue. I also kept up a furious pace during the interaction, which held his attention and gave the impression that we had no time to waste.

A coach needs to check if a coaching session moves too fast or too slowly, if it is on track to complete in the given time and if the time allocated is appropriate to the needs of the coachee. There is no one answer to the correct use of pace. Some coachees, particularly highly-driven ones, want to proceed quickly in order to achieve an outcome. Others find it helpful to proceed more slowly, providing the opportunity to talk broadly around issues and move less hastily towards a conclusion. It's important that a coach understands his coachees' preferences in order to meet their needs.

There are several elements that can interfere with the effective use of time. Sometimes, a coachee may feel he needs to provide large amounts of detail and background history, so that a coach can understand his situation. We usually find that this is not necessary and therefore it is the coach's responsibility to tactfully point this out and ensure that the coachee 'cuts to the chase'.

Another potential interference occurs when a coach fails to set a realistic or clear outcome for a session, such as when someone is working on the future of his career and states that he wants to achieve complete clarity about where he is heading as a result of one session. A topic of this importance requires considerable reflection following a session, as well as the consideration of a range of other possible interventions. It is the responsibility of the coach to manage expectations and ensure that any goal can be achieved in the available time.

It is also possible for a coach to feel that he wants to give so much value that he lets a session run on, thinking that it will offer more. Or if he has a strong, 'be perfect' driver, he could keep going in an attempt to make the session as good as possible. This is where the coach's own level of self-awareness will determine the effectiveness of his timekeeping. It's important that he doesn't become a clock-watcher, as this would send out a negative message, but if he is unsure about the pace then a coach should check with his coachee. If the relationship is strong and open, the coachee will give an honest answer about what works for him.

Linked The next aspect of the interaction to monitor is whether the conversation appears to be joined up or not. Does it flow? Is it connected? Does it unfold naturally? Or is it jagged, disconnected and too random? While coaching conversations are by their very nature unpredictable, they should not be disjointed and lacking coherence.

There are several ways to ensure that the content under discussion stays linked and relevant. It is the coach's responsibility to point out to a coachee if his train of thought jumps about in a manner that detracts from the potency of the session. If the topic under discussion is about managing a difficult employee, but the conversation keeps going off at a tangent about other people or various work issues, then it is up to the coach to challenge the coachee about his level of focus. Very often, when someone is talking about a subject that is uncomfortable for them, they become distracted to avoid facing the reality of it. It may also transpire that letting a conversation jump around is a habit for a coachee and not unique to the coaching interaction. Bringing this to his attention can provide him with a valuable opportunity to become more effective in the way that he communicates generally.

Another option is for the coach to suggest 'parking' any additional issues that emerge in a conversation. The coachee may be discussing how to influence his team to become more cross-functional when other issues surface, such as team briefings, delegation and working hours. Agreeing to have a 'parking' lot provides a framework in which the coach can capture these items and then, if they are still relevant, revisit them at a later date, or, if that is no longer the case, remove them from the agenda. It also reassures the coachee that he can continue with his train of thought, knowing that he won't lose anything of value.

At times, the coach may need to agree with his coachee that he take some time to 'brain dump' before he is able to sustain a flow. He might have just come out of a stressful meeting or have a difficult situation to address later in the day, which keeps playing on his mind. In these cases, it can be helpful to allow him to move around until his mind settles. Ironically, being non-judgmental will enable him to focus more quickly than trying to dictate a joined-up conversation.

Coaching conversations should be fresh and unpredictable without a linear, mechanical or rehearsed quality. In order to achieve this 'flow', a coach needs to follow his coachees' interests, whilst remaining alert to whether he is avoiding an issue, adopting a habit of distraction or genuinely moving into new territory that will provide greater insight and awareness.

Outcome As we have previously highlighted, one of the key differences between coaching and other inter-personal interactions is the significance coaching places on delivering measurable output. One of the main challenges for a coach in meeting this criterion is to ensure, while in the midst of an absorbing conversation, that he is on track to deliver an agreed outcome. Despite any complimentary noises that a coachee may make along the way, a coach won't know that he has assisted him in reaching his desired outcome until he has final verbal and non-verbal confirmation. This requires him to be vigilant to the emergent and unpredictable nature of the coaching process, which often causes the outcome to be shrouded in mist until the final moment.

While in many sessions it will be apparent to the coach that he is on course to deliver, at other times he will be uncertain and, indeed, may fear that he is off track. When this happens, he needs to be prepared to 'stop the action' and ask his coachee how he feels about the value of the dis-cussion and, more importantly, whether he believes that it's moving him in the direction he wants. This requires the coach to hold his nerve, because he may receive negative feedback. If he does, it's essential to find out from his coachee what he needs, to ensure that the interaction gets back on course. A coach's willingness to put himself on the line is a sign of strength. The act of asking for an honest opinion is a trait of someone with a high level of self-awareness, who has the courage to face, rather than shirk, reality.

A closing thought to be aware of is that what a coach pays attention to increases its probability of being achieved. Therefore, it is the coach's responsibility to be accountable, to keep an eye on progress and to stay focused on achieving the desired outcome.

Worthwhile The final aspect of the interaction to monitor is the necessity that a session is worthwhile for a coachee, whether it's producing greater insight, raising awareness, generating motivation, providing inspiration or resolving issues. Ideally, sessions have clearly identified outcomes, which the coach monitors to ensure that the coachee achieves them. It may be that he does not have a specific outcome. Often, the further up an organisation a coachee is, the less opportunity there is to discuss situations in a non-judgmental environment, so a coachee's requirement may be simply to have an open dialogue without needing to pin anything down. The session will be less likely to have a tangible output, so a coach must make sure that the conversation provides value as it proceeds. Although evidence can be gained from reading a coachee's level of absorption in the conversation – via his body language, energy levels, emotional temperature and language used – it's also useful for the coach to be able to draw upon his intuition. Listening to and then following his gut instinct is an important method of checking if an interaction is worthwhile.

A coach can gain greater kinaesthetic clarity from his intuition by asking himself the following questions:

- Do I sense the interaction is worthwhile?

- Do I feel that the coaching is adding value?

- Do I experience the conversation as beneficial?

If a coach has a more visual sense, he could use the following questions:

- Do I see the interaction as worthwhile?

- Do I view the coaching as a worthwhile exercise?

- Do I picture the conversation as adding value?

On the other hand, if a coach's dominant preference is auditory, he could ask:

- Does it sound like a worthwhile conversation?

- Do I hear benefit coming out of the interaction?

However, nothing can replace asking a coachee whether he feels the interaction is valuable. Only direct feedback will enable a coach to ensure that the coaching is worthwhile.

Having identified the internal mechanisms for ensuring best practice, we will look now at other possible interventions that enable coaches to hone their skills or indeed benefit from coaching in their own lives.

CO-COACHING

A Super Coach should also be a Super Coachee, continuing to receive coaching himself. This has two primary benefits, firstly, he enhances his own personal effectiveness by constantly raising the bar on his performance as a coach, and, secondly, he keeps in touch with the reality of his coachees. It would be hypocritical of a coach to support other people to take action in their lives and not to use the same support himself.

A co-coaching relationship is a mutual exchange of coaching sessions set up with a colleague. When we run SuperCoaching programmes within organisations we stipulate that participants must follow-up with co-coaching relationships. We recommend people contract together either in alternate sessions, in which they reverse roles as coach and coachee, or in a single session, where they elect to give a proportion of time to being in each role.

If a coach wants to use co-coaching to increase his effectiveness as a coach, he can assess himself and request feedback from his co-coach using the following questions:

- What was the topic of coaching? Make sure that you both have shared clarity about the topic being addressed.

- What was the goal? Check that you were both agreed on the outcome for the session.

- What was the process used? Ensure that you can clearly explain your methodology and that your coachee can recognise the framework.

- What were the outcome and benefit delivered? Be specific about the value added and check that no assumptions were made.

- What worked? Find out what specifically went well, such as types of questions asked, use of silence, pace of the session, suggestions offered.

- What didn't work? Be rigorous about any mistakes made, such as interrupting, steering the agenda or a woolly goal.

- Any new or reaffirmed learning? Focus on any learning that came out of the sessions in order to use and apply it.

We encourage both individuals to note their answers quickly and to share them with each other. This allows the coach to generate a set of learnings or action steps for future coaching. As the relationship builds, the coach can contract with his co-coach to monitor particular aspects of his development needs. If a coach tends to operate in a push or tell mode he could use the co-coaching relationship and future sessions to develop himself in this area.

There is no doubt that being on the receiving end of

skilled coaching is a challenging process and helps a coach keep in touch with the reality of his coachees. It's easy to underestimate what it feels like for a coachee to have to confront issues and to be prepared to do something about them. The willingness of a coach to be coached himself ensures that he has greater empathy and prevents him from thinking in abstract terms. Managers may acknowledge that they should invest in one-to-one time with their people, but it can be quite another matter when they have gruelling deadlines to meet. It is only when a coach demonstrates best practice in his own life, or is honest about his own shortcomings, that he can support his coachees with integrity.

EXTERNAL COACHING

Graham: I was once invited to become one of the external coaches available for senior managers in a high street retail chain. I was unsure about whether I wanted to be on their list, not because it wasn't a large and prestigious business, but because I was unsure that being part of a stable of coaches was going to deliver them the value they wanted.

On speaking with the HR director, it emerged that, out of the numerous external coaches they were working with, were trying to reach a definitive list and find out what difference was being made. I believed that here was an opportunity to help, over and above just being on a list, and therefore suggested that I conduct a coaching audit to show what was occurring with their use of external coaches.

Through a series of interviews, and by reviewing current documentation, I compiled a report that painted a clear picture of who was being coached by whom, the agendas that were being worked on, the results that were being achieved and the costs that were being incurred. I also made some general observations about the quality of the coaching, which included highlighting the fact that there was an insufficient link to the business agenda (this was exemplified by the majority of the coaches not having seen the company's current strategy and values documents). There was no consistent coaching methodology being used, it lacked a robust definition and failed to ensure the necessary success measures and review procedures that effective coaching requires. The audit matched the company's fears of what was taking place. Consequently, they asked me to suggest a way of pulling the external coaching together, by agreeing best practice which ensured that they gained a higher return on their investment.

An article by Steven Berglas in the June 2002 edition of the *Harvard Business Review* suggested that there were at least 10,000 professional coaches working for businesses in the US, and this figure was expected to exceed 50,000 by 2007. A recent survey by The Hay Group, International showed that between 25–40 percent of *Fortune 500* companies use executive coaches. Within this exponential growth of external coaching, one of the dilemmas faced is that, whilst it can bring enormous value to the business and individuals concerned, it can also become a high-ticket item that delivers value to the coachees involved but not to the business in general. To counteract this possible scenario, it is essential to link any external coaching directly to the business strategy and operational objectives, and to the line management and HR processes. This ensures that it will meet the needs of the business, and allow for an individual agenda to emerge that has agreement with all parties. This agenda must include measurable outcomes, with a specific review process to ensure that the coaching is on track to deliver expectations, and a final review to sign off with the coachee and business stakeholders, to make sure that they got what they paid for.

External coaching can fall down when people receiving it fail to make an authentic choice to be coached. As we have already emphasised, coaching cannot be an imposed solution, and thus people considering whether to work with external coaches must be willing, at least, to participate in an exploratory, no obligation meeting. A reluctant person submitting himself merely at the behest of his manager or HR will get little or no value, and risks eroding the credibility both of the coaching process and of the external coach.

External coaches should be more accomplished and

experienced as coaches than anyone within an organisation. It is rare to find full-time internal coaches within companies and when they do exist there are often issues around perceived credibility and confidentiality. External coaches should have no axe to grind other than the need to support the individual and the organisation. The complication of line management or HR coaching, where there is a possible conflict within the coachee as to whether he should be fully open and honest, is removed. Understandably, coachees often fear that real honesty may cost them in their jobs, which is a different situation to working with an external coach with established protocols of confidentiality.

From a commercial standpoint, contracting with external coaches puts the onus on the coach to deliver. As with any service provider, he won't last long unless the organisation perceives value in what he brings. From an organisation's perspective, the most efficient way is to contract with an external coaching provider that has a number of coaches who share a similar methodology. Larger organisations today are certainly looking to work with one provider, so that there is a consistency of approach. It is easier to manage and enables the coaches to build up a picture of the organisation, helping them to form a consistent approach. Having a pool of external coaches to draw upon means that it is more likely that employees will find the right fit and allows for different levels within an organisation to be coached. We recommend introducing different coaches at different levels, to rule out any concern that what is said in coaching sessions travels up or down the hierarchy. Although coaches aim to operate with absolute integrity, often coachees don't believe this to be possible.

The following diagram illustrates our suggested approach for delivering external coaching:

RESEARCH COMPANY	COACH
COACHING CONTEXT AND NEED DESCRIBED	COACH CLIENT REPRESENTATIVE
NO OBLIGATION EXPLORATORY MEETING	COACH COACHEE
BACKGROUND DOCUMENT REVIEW	COACH
PROPOSAL WRITTEN AND SIGNED OFF	COACH COACHEE STAKEHOLDERS
SESSION 1 DRAFT SUCCESS MEASURES AND AGENDA INPUTS AGREED	COACH COACHEE
AGENDA AND SUCCESS MEASURES FINALISED VIA 360, PROFILING, 3-WAY MEETINGS, SELF-ASSESSMENT	COACH COACHEE STAKEHOLDERS
SESSIONS 2-5	COACH COACHEE
MID-POINT REVIEW	COACH COACHEE STAKEHOLDERS
SESSIONS 6-10	COACH COACHEE
FINAL REVIEW	COACH COACHEE STAKEHOLDERS

Diagram 25: External Coaching

SUPER EFFECTIVENESS SUMMARY

- The extent that a coach works towards ensuring best practice is the extent of his commitment to coaching.

- Monitoring his own effectiveness through paying attention to himself, his coachee and the interaction provides the best chance of adding value in every coaching session.

- The FLOW model helps make sure coaching interactions use time effectively, unfold through a linked conversation, stay on track for delivering specified outcomes and are worthwhile throughout.

- Forming co-coaching relationships continues to develop skills and capabilities, as well as helping coaches receive the benefits of being coached.

- Organisations benefit from external coaches if they establish coaching contracts with highly professional and credible external providers whose processes are clearly defined and whose measurable outcomes are identified and delivered in line with business objectives.

SuperCoaching
Exercise 9 – Using the FLOW Model

Put FLOW into practice. Agree with a coachee to use it as a checklist in a session to ensure that you are delivering value. During the session, ask your coachee if he thinks the pace is appropriate. Be prepared to accelerate or slow down, depending on his feedback. Check to see how cohesive the conversation is. Ask your coachee if he feels that there is a natural sequence to it, or if it is too broken up and disjointed. Make sure that you are on course to deliver the agreed outcomes by checking progress. Most importantly, request feedback on the value that your coachee received from working with you. Was it worth his precious time? Did you exceed his expectations? Which aspects of FLOW will you improve during your next coaching sessions? Be prepared to put your coaching on the line to become even more accomplished.

CHAPTER 10

Super Value – Receiving the Benefits

'I never cease to be amazed at the power of the coaching process to draw out the skills or talent that was previously hidden within an individual, and which invariably finds a way to solve a problem previously thought unsolvable.'

John Russell, MD, Harley-Davidson,
Europe Ltd

Graham: 'Graham, you ought to be charging us at least five times what you are doing'. I did a double take and checked how much wine my dinner guest had drunk. Sitting opposite me was the HR director of a leading retail chain. I had invited him out to thank him for the work he had put my way and to get to the bottom of why he perceived that my colleagues and I had brought so much value to his business.

'Did I hear what I think I heard, Steve?' I exclaimed.

'Yes, I'm serious,' Steve continued. 'We pay vast amounts of money to strategic consultants and trainers, but it is often very difficult to measure the value of what they produce. Some assignments cost hundreds of thousands or millions of pounds, whereas the recent job that you did with the top team cost a fraction of that amount. They walked away with a genuine commitment to the strategy going forward, a plan to address a number of the key operational issues and enhanced working relationships. I would say that you were cheap, and that if we were paying you on a value basis, we would have paid significantly more than you charged us.'

'Thank you for saying so, and my supplementary invoice is on the way,' I responded jokingly. 'I have felt for a long time that many of our projects do provide similar value to more expensive interventions. My challenge has been to help clients understand this, but nowadays I am much better at translating what we're offering into measurable terms, and relating it to the bottom line.'

I continued, 'Let me reciprocate by thanking you, not just for the money that we've earned, but for the quality of the relationship we have with you, which I truly believe is an effective partnership. We have gained intense satisfaction from working with your senior colleagues, watching them open up and become more genuine with each other. We've also had the satisfaction of knowing that we've played a part in helping the business take its next step forward, which should have a positive impact on the lives of tens of thousands of your employees. We feel blessed by what we do – to be doing something we love, to be constantly learning about it and to have a positive effect on both individual lives and business success. On this basis, I ought to return what you've paid me, and pay you for the privilege and joy of doing what we do.'

Although coaching can, and does, help individuals and organisations achieve high performance, thereby boosting the bottom line, its real value goes far beyond keeping shareholders satisfied. The implications of integrating a coaching philosophy and approach to work, life and relationships allow for new levels of success and fulfilment. Super Value explores how we can maximise the potential of coaching as individuals, within teams and organisations, and, ultimately, within our families and communities, thus improving our quality of life.

AS A COACH

Our wish is for everyone to have coaching as a core skill. Not only would it make communication, and hence business, easier, but there are immense rewards to be gained from doing something of intrinsic value and receiving direct proof of its usefulness. There is an added benefit that through coaching others a coach will often gain insights himself. Coaching someone on a particular topic such as work–life balance enables a coach to identify new strategies to achieve greater balance himself. Indeed, he may go away and take immediate action after a coaching session as a direct result of what has emerged with his coachee.

Ben: I was recently working with a coachee on her career development. She wanted to further it, which necessitated stopping certain activities that no longer supported her. As we explored her various options, I realised that there was one particular activity that I myself needed to stop. At the time, I wrote a column for a national magazine which had passed its shelf life. I recognised that I was holding on to it because it had been an earlier aspiration and used to work for me. Later that day, I pulled out my contract and handed in my notice.

Depending on the nature of the relationship between coach and coachee, the coach may also get direct or indirect benefit from his coachees' outcomes. If a line manager coaches one of his direct reports, the more the coachee increases his personal effectiveness and raises his performance, the more the manager benefits. We have often seen the profile of managers raised as a result of improved output by their team. As external coaches we, too, benefit from the success of our coachees as our reputations are enhanced.

A further benefit a coach can receive is the satisfaction of continuous learning and of enhancing his capability as a coach. Coaching is an art form and, as for any artist, there is always room for development. Every coaching conversation provides an opportunity to hone skills, explore new options and attempt new ways of helping others achieve outcomes in a more effective way.

Ben: I used to marvel at Lord Menuhin's life-long commitment to perfecting the art of the violin. Right up until his unexpected death, he played with a passion and inquisitiveness which defied his years and expertise. He would often display more curiosity and eagerness to learn than the class he was teaching! It was a humbling experience and left me with the awareness that at the heart of a world-class performance is someone who has a beginner's mindset, who is always keen to learn more. When a coach commits to lifelong learning, he will discover endless fascination and room for improvement as each day offers numerous opportunities to grow and develop. Another benefit of being an external coach is that it can also provide a good living!

SELF-COACHING

One of the great assets to be gained from coaching is the ability to coach ourselves. In our speeded-up world, a single thought or action can make the difference between success and failure. Carving precious time out of our busy lives to reflect upon particular topics and to become more strategic in our thinking and behaviour is often the best investment we can make.

Developing the ability to self-coach is a discipline and we recommend using the GROW framework to channel our focus and thoughts effectively, rather than just turning something over in our minds. We often receive feedback that, although people may have thought about issues for quite some time, it isn't until they apply structured thinking that they are able to push forward to some form of resolution or action.

The potential downside of self-coaching is that, if we're blocked on an issue, we may not be able to break out of our imprisoned thinking. But there is great satisfaction to be gained if we are able to coach ourselves through a block and come out the other side. Not only does it give us an immediate solution, it also builds our confidence in the long-term, allowing us to raise our game.

CO-COACHING

In the previous chapter, we explored how to set up co-coaching relationships to ensure best practice. The offshoot of this activity is that a coach gains tremendous value from being coached himself, learning from observing others in action and receiving feedback about his own coaching expertise. Since a coach mostly works on his own, it is rare to get direct feedback from other experts who are able to assess his capability from an objective standpoint. Although receiving feedback from coachees is helpful, it's unrealistic to expect enough constructive comments to enable a coach to make significant advances. With this in mind, it's useful to contract with a variety of co-coaches, so that we are able to witness different styles and get feedback from different viewpoints. One of the great values of the Alexander team of Super Coaches is that it encompasses a broad spectrum of styles, enabling us to draw upon each other as a learning resource.

Most people love to talk about themselves, so having the opportunity to indulge this preference by reflecting upon our own life is a gift. Co-coaching means that we are constantly able to move our lives forward and achieve our goals. Indeed, our collaboration in writing this book came about as a result of a suggestion from our colleague, Dr Robert Holden. Robert was coaching Ben about where to channel his energies after completing his last book and this coincided with Graham's desire to publish his vast experience of coaching. The result lies in your hands!

EXTERNAL COACHING

Ben: Clare is a director within a financial department. One of her goals was to become more efficient in the way she worked, especially with regard to her time management. We kicked off by looking at the topic of time. It was very revealing when she began to describe her current reality because, as we pinned it down, she realised that she lost up to an hour a day through IT difficulties, up to 30 minutes as a result of personal requirements and another half an hour from interruptions caused by people wanting social chit-chat. Clare was staggered when she quickly multiplied this over the course of a year to 440 hours. Before she even started work she had lost 52.5 working days per year.

The benefits of external coaching can range from helping someone to save an extra precious hour per day to transforming lives and the performance within organisations. Research that has investigated the views of coachees generally gives very positive findings. The *Ivy Business Journal* reported that, 'Executives and HR managers know coaching is the most potent tool for inducing lasting personal change' and CNN said, 'Once used to bolster troubled staffers, coaching now is part of the standard leadership development training for elite executives and talented up-and-comers at IBM, Motorola, J.P. Morgan, Chase and Hewlett Packard. These companies are discreetly giving their best prospects what star athletes have long had: a trusted adviser to help reach their goals.' A recent study by the International Coach Federation found a wide range of benefits reported by individuals who took part in coaching. These included:

Increased self-awareness	68%	Improved quality of life	43%
Better goal-setting	62%	Enhanced communication skills	40%
More balanced life	61%	Increased project completion	36%
Lower stress levels	57%	Improved health or fitness level	34%
Enhanced self-discovery	53%	Better relationship with co-workers	33%
Increased confidence	52%	Better family relationship	33%

As we discussed in the previous chapter, the key to the success of external coaching lies in ensuring that a rigorous methodology is used, which is consistent throughout an organisation.

RELATIONSHIP COACHING

Graham: I had been called into the Italian office of an international management consultancy because the two senior partners were finding it difficult to work together. There was a lot of bad feeling between them, which was having a knock-on effect throughout the business. There were various factions and siloed teams, and the consequent drop in morale was affecting performance.

My first step was to meet with each of the partners individually, to ensure that they were committed to enhancing their working relationship and to being coached together. I helped them to see that the cost of the current situation was high in relation to personal anguish, staff morale and business performance. Having agreed that there was a need to change and that they were willing to be coached, I asked them to prepare for a three-way meeting by answering the following questions:

- What's working and not working in the relationship?

- What do you attribute the difficulties to?

- How do you see yourself in the relationship?

- How do you see the other partner in the relationship?

- How do you think the other partner sees you in the relationship?

- How do you think the other partner thinks you see them in the relationship?

- How would you like the relationship to be?

When we came together, my job was to create an environment where they could share their perceptions and hear each other's points of view. They agreed to be open and honest and to work through potentially difficult conversations. We also established a contract for authentic commitment, meaning that any action steps had to be genuinely intended or else they would be struck off the agenda.

With the scene set, I orchestrated a discussion that started with them sharing their different perceptions of the various questions that I had posed. As they listened closely, it became very apparent that they had made one or two faulty and costly assumptions about each other. One assumption had been that a partner's frequent trips to Sweden had implied a lack of commitment. What transpired was that his attempts to resolve a difficult marriage were interfering with his ability to perform. Another key misperception had been that the other partner had interpreted the style of his colleague as highly 'command-and-control' and uncaring of his subordinates. In fact, when he shared various reports from team members of how they had experienced his leadership of various projects, the comments were very positive such as, 'This partner sets high standards and drives us hard, but it's highly stimulating, we learn a lot and deliver high value to our clients'.

As we flushed out these different perceptions and faulty assumptions, they grew more aware of their current reality. They began to see that they both wanted the same thing and were on the same side. One of the outcomes that emerged was the establishment of a weekly lunch together to ensure that communication was maintained and there was no scope for further false assumptions. As their relationship improved, and they found more effective ways of working together, the morale and business results improved across the entire office.

Coaching is a valuable asset in a variety of one-to-one relationship contexts, such as a chairman and chief executive, or a sales and marketing director needing to perform well together. A coach can work to establish greater understanding and alignment, to build trust, to resolve outstanding issues and to gain consensus. It is also possible for a coach to work with individual departments within an organisation to support and challenge operational procedures. For example, to ensure that buying and operations work well together within a retail organisation, research and development in an engineering company, or IT and anyone in any company (apologies to IT staff). Given that people operating within these environments tend to have higher levels of technical competence than people skills, a coach can play an extremely useful role in the areas of communication and co-operation.

Another potential use of relationship coaching is between a client and supplier or customer. We sometimes get asked to work with this type of relationship following the breakdown of an agreement or when trust is low. The aim is to help re-focus the original intent of working together, and match expectations against the actual experience of working together, so that their behaviours and processes can realign.

TEAM COACHING

'At lunch I devised this brilliant team organization chart on a napkin. Unfortunately, you're not on the team anymore because I had to wipe some gravy off my mouth.'

Graham: Following the merger of two UK high street banks, I was asked to help the top team integrate as quickly as possible. The CEO felt that with my help he could significantly reduce the inevitable period of forming, norming, storming and performing that occurs within teams.

At the first off-site workshop, the purpose of which was to establish a shared vision, mission and strategy, I became aware that one of the team members before, during and after dinner drank excessive amounts of alcohol. My concerns were compounded when he did not appear the following morning. I am always inclined to start meetings on time, but checked with the chief executive how he wanted to play it. He brushed off the 'no-show' as if expected and informed me that the team member would join us when he was ready. I found this an odd response given the critical importance of our time together and the need for the team to reach consensus.

The team member finally appeared during the coffee break, looking somewhat worse for wear. He mumbled an apology and proceeded to contribute very little for the rest of the morning. He perked up during the afternoon, only to repeat the drinking that evening. Fearing that we might have a repeat performance the next day and being concerned about his drink problem, I decided to tackle the chief executive over breakfast. He initially dismissed my concerns saying, 'Oh, he likes a drink, but it's not a problem.' I was in a dilemma, but felt that I had to pursue it and challenged him to take a strong look at the impact of the behaviour on the team. Coming at it from this angle, the chief executive saw that it was having a detrimental effect on all concerned. Reluctantly, he decided that it was best not to do anything during the workshop, but that he would tackle it back at the office. It transpired that the team member did in fact have a severe drink problem, which was known in his part of the business, but had been kept under wraps during the acquisition. Eventually, the individual received professional help and left the business. This situation was an example of when a coach could support and challenge a team to confront the consequences of certain behaviours which were damaging performance.

When we are asked to help build coaching capability within organisations, one of the most hotly demanded subjects is team coaching. Once individuals begin to see the potential of coaching, they want to apply it to their teams. A similar approach to one-to-one coaching can be brought to bear on all sorts of team issues, except that a coach will also need to apply facilitation and team dynamic skills to make it effective.

Before commencing any team-building coaching, a coach should challenge the request for it. He needs to question the group about what they mean by 'team' and why they need to operate as one. Is there a compelling business reason why a group of people needs to work closely together? Can they proceed effectively as independent units? Not all business groupings necessitate close team working. The acid test is to determine the added value to the business of a group working together as a team.

Assuming that there is a compelling business case for a team, the first step is to agree a contract about how they are going to approach team coaching. This can run along similar lines to a one-to-one contract, but what usually stands out are the needs to be open and honest, respectful and to have a good sense of humour. The coach will then work with the following six dimensions:

Diagram 26: The Six Dimensions of Team Coaching

Although there is a logical sequence to the way we have laid out the six dimensions, a coach should not deal with them strictly in order. He will often move forward on a number of fronts and if, for instance, he has helped a team on the first five dimensions the level of motivation and fulfilment will have increased by default. We will now look at each area in more detail:

Vision and Direction A team coach, irrespective of what he has been asked to do, should always start by checking the team's level of alignment in relation to its vision and direction. If these are lacking, he can guarantee that any team coaching will have much less value and, indeed, may actually work against the team, as there is no context within which to place it. The starting point, then, is to work with the team to define its vision and direction. This requires deep thought about why it exists, where it is heading and what is its purpose. When there is a need to formulate vision and direction, it can help to economise time and speed up the task to ask individual members to prepare their thoughts in advance of the team coaching session.

Vision and direction statements are most useful, and have the greatest potency, when they are an expression of a deep-seated passion within the team which is linked to a commercially sound intention. They need to be authentic, brief and powerful, in order to inspire, inform and steer everything that takes place within the team.

Goals and Strategy A team coach can be used to ensure that there are measurable, individual and collective goals spelt out within a manageable time frame. The individual goals should add up to the collective ones in order to maximise the resource. The value of having a coach facilitate this process is that it can help a team become clear about what needs to be delivered over what period, without the manager driving the agenda. If the process is solely in his hands, there may be conflict within the team, because they feel uncomfortable about challenging him in a group context. As a consequence, thoughts remain unexpressed and niggles build up. On countless occasions, we have been brought in to work with teams where damage has been done as a result of lack of communication. In most cases, this has not been the wilful intention of the manager, but simply has arisen through his inability to create a level of honesty and openness that allows for sufficient challenge. The coach can ensure that all team members are clear about expectations and can test levels of motivation and commitment to achieve the goals.

Having established these goals and action plans, the coach can then help the team to agree a review process and any problem-solving or support mechanisms required. It can be useful if teams operate on a win/win understanding, recognising that if one person wins, everybody wins. This approach encourages individual and collective commitment to achieving the goals and to creating a supportive and challenging environment along the way.

Roles and Accountabilities The next step is for individuals to agree and understand their roles and responsibilities. It can cause numerous problems when there is a lack of clarity in these areas. The challenge is that, in these complex times, no one individual or team can achieve their goals in isolation. People are dependent on colleagues and on other teams, departments and divisions, and it's often the clarity and commitment demonstrated at these interfaces that makes the difference. The coach can make sure that the team thinks carefully about who they need to work with and how they're going to work together in order to reach their goals.

Process Another role for a coach is to enable the development of effective working processes, such as communication protocols, meetings and performance reviews. Teams often recognise the importance of having clear structures, but get taken over by tasks, which prevent these from becoming established. The coach can ensure that sufficient time and attention are given to defining the mechanics of working together and can then build in regular reviews to check that progress is being made. A lot has been written over the years about the value of learning organisations and yet they are still rather thin on the ground. A coach can ensure that the team has regular reviews of different aspects of their work. This provides good opportunities to highlight the areas that are working well and those which need improvement. The review sessions also enable teams to assess themselves against a range of criteria, from hard and objective measures such as business results, to the quality of relationships, level of openness, honesty, trust and confidence. Reviews provide a useful entry point for important conversations to take place and for feedback to be given.

Interpersonal Relationships A team's overall direction and defined goals are only as useful as the effectiveness of its working relationships. Since we all have different working styles, communication preferences, strengths and weaknesses, relationships within a team can easily fall apart. A coach is able to help develop these relationships so that they support the team. This does not necessarily mean that the team has to spend large amounts of time together, or that people have to become the best of friends, but it is a requirement that the relationships need to enhance performance and not inhibit it.

The value of a coach is that in being outside the group he can help teams have the conversations amongst themselves, or within subgroups, that they would ordinarily find difficult or impossible to conduct. It is all too easy for people to adopt dysfunctional behaviour, such as being defensive or closed when the pressure is on. If the coach is able to support an environment of openness and honesty in relation to vital team conversations concerning roles, expectations, interpersonal feedback, successes and disappointments, then trust and respect will build. This will ensure that the team becomes aligned and reduces the likelihood of misunderstandings and resentments occurring. It is all too easy for team members to have blind spots about how they are perceived by each other and the impact of their working style. Giving feedback can be especially difficult if it involves either pointing out an area where a team member is creating difficulty for others, or if it's about his part of the business. It requires great skill to be able to give constructive comments, so the value of the coach is his ability to help the team develop this capability. He can also ensure that positive reinforcement is given, helping them to celebrate their achievements as well as focusing on their development needs.

Motivation and Fulfilment A key component of team success is to understand members' core drivers. However, coupled with fulfilment, these are probably the two most overlooked topics on any team agenda. While a team might achieve short-term results driven by fear or anxiety and accompanied by low levels of fulfilment, they are not sustainable in the long-term.

High performance comes about from a state of relaxed concentration, focused attention and absorption, satisfaction and enjoyment, not from the relentless stress and fire-fighting activity so prevalent in teams today.

The benefit of having a team coach is that he can ensure motivation and fulfilment are priorities. He can facilitate team conversations about how motivating and enjoyable their work is and how committed they are to working together. When motivation wanes, he can make sure that the reasons are addressed, implications identified for performance, and agreements made about the way forward.

Thus, if a coach does an outstanding job in addressing the six dimensions of team coaching, he will add enormous value to the teams he works with and, hence, the businesses in which they operate.

COACHING CULTURE

In recent years, many organisations have striven to develop coaching cultures. We have yet to come across one, however, where a coaching culture predominates, although it exists within a growing number of departments and teams. One of the primary starting points to develop a coaching culture is to help managers become more effective coaches. As stated in the *Harvard Business Review*, 'The goal of coaching is the goal of good management: to make the most of an organisation's valuable resources.' If a manager who is responsible for up to thousands of people is brilliant at bringing the best out of others, he is obviously more likely to achieve high performance and retain and develop people for the long-term benefit of the business.

Despite the potential value to a business, we often find that the development of a coaching culture is attempted in an ineffectual way. Taking a 'sheep dip' approach of trying to train managers in a two-day training programme will produce few results. Coaching is a complex activity which impacts deeply on attitudes and states of being, as well as on skills and behaviour. These elements cannot be addressed in a superficial way or they will have little value and may indeed be counter-productive.

As well as having sufficient learning opportunities managers need to be able to operate in an environment conducive to coaching, which is hard to achieve in our task-focused economy. It requires understanding from the leaders of the business to promote the development of people as part of the vision and values of the company, and to demonstrate it themselves. It creates confusion and cynicism if managers are encouraged to attend a coaching programme yet feel forced to revert to being dictatorial bosses back in the business.

A further challenge for organisations is to establish how coaching fits within the issues of hierarchy, performance management, reward and hiring and firing. It requires very advanced behaviour on the part of an internal coach and coachee to have sufficient openness and honesty within a hierarchical relationship when, in other contexts, the coach would be sitting in judgment on the coachee.

Although this obstacle can be overcome, it can help accelerate the development of a coaching culture to populate an organisation with internal Super Coaches who make coaching a significant part of what they do, and who are not sitting in judgment over their colleagues. Another option is to use external coaches working in partnership with HR departments. As with any culture change programme, it is imperative for coaching to be aligned to other management and HR processes. It needs to relate directly to performance management, annual appraisal and career data. It also requires clarity in relation to any other developmental programmes, such as mentoring, that an organisation may have introduced.

If successful, a coaching culture can lead to a dynamic environment where people value each other in tangible ways, play to their strengths, exchange feedback, have clear expectations, roles and responsibilities, continue to learn, enjoy their work and relationships, achieve high performance and outstanding results. Our recommended approach for the development of a coaching culture is illustrated in the following diagram:

Vision High performance/people development as competitive advantage **Strategy** Behaviours linked to execution of strategy **Leadership Style/Support** • Role modeling • Communication • Participation **Linked to Performance Management** • Objectives • Appraisal • Reward	**Attitudes/Skills** • Development programmes • Colleague feedback • Personal development plans • Workshops • Implementation plans • Management follow-up • On-going support • Review and reinforcement **Super Coaches** • Specialist internal coaches • Culture development • One-to-one coaching practice **Continuous Improvement** • Measurement • Best practice • Communiction • Success stories • Refinement

Diagram 27: Coaching Culture Development

FAMILY COACHING

Ben: George was a director within a macho engineering environment that did not lend itself to discussions of a personal nature, with whom I was working in regard to achieving his annual targets. One day he arrived looking exhausted, but when I asked him how he was feeling I got the standard 'fine' in response. I probed further until he finally exclaimed that he felt exasperated by his wife and daughter.

Given that this was not the type of topic we usually addressed, I checked with him to see whether it was affecting his work performance and if he was okay to discuss it. George acknowledged that it was off our main agenda, but agreed that it was preventing him from focusing on his objectives, so I invited him explain his situation. He went on to say that, as soon as he walked in the door at the end of a day, he had his wife and daughter both moaning to him about each other. When I asked him about the cause of the problem, he said that his daughter was difficult, moody, spoilt, selfish, needy and whiny, whereas he had a son who was good as gold and could do no wrong. It turned out that his daughter was six years old, so I challenged him on who was the adult in the relationship. He admitted that they had never established a happy pattern with her. When his son, who was two years younger, came along, he was so easy in comparison that all the attention went to him. I asked him to consider what it would be like to be labelled difficult, moody, spoilt, selfish, needy and whiny in the workplace or, even worse, at home, in the environment where you're supposed to be loved. He recognised that it would be tough and would probably lead to disruptive behaviour.

I asked George to consider a new way of regarding his daughter, in terms of his ideal future state. He admitted that his greatest wish would be to see her as easy, fun, happy, co-operative and loving. He felt completely helpless about how to make that happen, so I coached him on his first step, which turned out to be to speak with his wife and establish a mutual understanding of the situation and then to explore options of how they could work together to influence their daughter's behaviour.

I offered some suggestions about how they could

reinforce her positive behaviour, such as by keeping a success diary and entering her achievements each day. They could also hold family meetings, where each would be allowed airtime to voice their opinions and draw up agreements about contentious issues such as bedtime, going to school and sharing toys. They discovered that the way to get something done was to turn it into a game. Gradually, the daughter's behaviour changed, but only as a result of George and his wife adopting a different tone.

It would be crazy to limit coaching to our working lives and thus prevent the most important and precious relationships, namely our family, from benefiting. Although we have advised against coaching friends and family, there is tremendous value to be gained from having family on a coaching agenda, as well as adopting a coaching style for handling certain family conversations and parenting issues.

While family is not typically on the explicit agenda of those in the business world, there is no doubt that the quality of our family relationships impacts on performance. If a coachee is struggling in a marriage or with his children, he can behave in detrimental ways, becoming short-tempered and aggressive, moody and irritable or closed and defensive. Even if he tries to hide it, people will pick up on the signals, leading to potentially damaging outcomes. While we're not suggesting that a coach takes on the role of family therapist, as with other coaching topics, new insights can be realised, motivation generated and specific actions identified through open and honest dialogue.

Within the family context, a coaching style, as distinct from formal coaching sessions, can be extremely useful when dealing with certain issues and conversations. Naturally, emotions run high, so it can be difficult to retain an objective viewpoint. Keeping a coaching hat on can save the day when our children are home late yet again, fail to tidy their room, refuse to do their homework or sit all day in front of the XBOX. It may also help when dealing with difficult conversations about emotive issues such as sex, drugs and rock 'n' roll. Using the basic skills of listening, asking questions and summarising to test understanding can prevent us from jumping in with a reactive response and alienating our children.

At less emotive moments, we can also use the GROW model to help our children resolve issues. If one of them is having a hard time in a particular relationship at school, getting him to identify his goal in the relationship, explore his current reality, generate options and agree to a next step may give him a greater sense of empowerment and boost his confidence.

We can also use our understanding of coaching within our marriages and partnerships. The stereotyped images of men and women exemplified by John Gray's *Men Are From Mars, Women Are From Venus* suggests that there is a great need for better understanding between the sexes! Given that coaching is a communication tool, it would make sense to apply the skills liberally to give our primary relationship the best chance of succeeding. Following our coaching events, we hear amusing remarks of male managers exclaiming that their wives no longer recognise them now that they have started to listen! We recommend letting your partner know what you're up to. Suddenly using coaching techniques could leave him or her rather confused.

EDUCATION

We have a vision where all teachers add coaching to their portfolio of skills. Having classroom environments in which children are encouraged to tap into their own wisdom, and where their own ideas are drawn out of them, is an advanced concept in some parts of the educational world. Moving away from the traditional talk/chalk style to a more individual approach that places a greater emphasis on self-reflection and personal discovery could make learning more attractive.

Being confined to a National Curriculum that prioritises school grades above the learning process is a challenge. A coaching approach might make learning take longer, but in the long run we would probably see higher levels of motivation, interest and, maybe, even more academic success.

Coaching could be a considerable help in building

relationships between staff and pupils. Imagine if people applied the principles of respect, non-judgment, acceptance and encouragement, and used the skills of listening, questions, summarising, feedback and suggestions. These are essential social skills, which allow for better understanding and co-operation.

Probably the greatest benefit would be increased enjoyment. We've talked about how fulfilment is one of the most under-utilised elements for achieving high performance. It's quite rare to find children, particularly older ones, leaping out of the bed in the morning looking forward to another enjoyable day at school. However, when learning is fun it's remembered and applied.

COMMUNITY

Many people go through life with a nagging sense of guilt that they ought to be doing more for the community in which they live – yet don't do anything about it. Coaching can help either to turn this subliminal angst into a commitment to act, put it on the back burner for a later period in life or create a resolution about the current level of contribution. Often, the view that we ought to be doing more has been conditioned into us in earlier years and therefore it is important to examine our own values and beliefs so that whatever we decide to do is an authentic and personal choice.

We salute the many organisations that pay great attention to the community through their social and environmental acts. Coaching can support people who want to take a more proactive role in thinking it through and making a realistic commitment to contributing in a significant way.

QUALITY OF LIFE

Probably the greatest benefit coaching can offer is its ability to satisfy the desire to have a better quality of life, whilst at the same time ensuring that we adhere to a deeply-felt purpose. When we ask people to rate the quality of their life, most admit to feeling dissatisfied. Sometimes, this is down to suffering from the 'grass is greener' syndrome, but often it is the result of an imbalance or loss of focus on what is really meaningful in life. It is so easy to get caught up in the rat race that we forget what matters most. As the saying goes, 'Even if you win the rat race you still end up a rat.'

Coaching serves coachees in a profound way when it enables them to raise the quality of their life. This has a positive impact on their families, friends, communities and organisations. The way people express this will differ from person to person, and a coach must not force his own values and views onto them. For some, an improved quality of life could be learning to live in the present, or simply appreciating what they already have. For others, it could be a radical life change in terms of occupation, location or lifestyle.

There are many ways to play life. It is a highly individual journey. But it's a rare person who doesn't want to experience a high quality of life. Since we have but one shot at it, let's use the gifts that coaching offers to ensure that we use every opportunity to make the most of life.

SUPER VALUE SUMMARY

- A career as a coach means doing something with intrinsic value and yielding a financial gain.

- Self-coaching is an effective way to create solutions.

- Co-coaching provides support and challenge to improve performance.

- External coaching helps businesses to be competitive, as well as employees to attain their potential.

- Relationship coaching enables difficult conversations to occur.

- Coaching teams assists with the development of vision and direction, goals and strategy, roles and accountabilities, process, interpersonal relationships, motivation and fulfilment.

- A coaching culture develops if managers are excellent coaches.

- Coaching can assist families in dealing with difficult issues and providing a healthy framework for communication.

- Coaching in education could unlock a passion for learning.

- Coaching helps people clarify how they want to support the community.

- Ultimately, coaching helps improve the quality of life.

SuperCoaching
Exercise 10 – Gaining Value

As you can see, there is enormous potential for deriving a wide range of benefits from coaching. Check to see that you're providing and receiving the most value from it by asking yourself, What is your promise to yourself as a coach? What do you commit to taking forward as a coach? What value will you bring to organisations and people's lives through coaching? In one sentence, write a purpose statement outlining your intention for coaching and use it to measure the value that you give and receive.

CONCLUSION

It is only since the early 1980s that coaching has become a recognised activity in the business world. Now, the idea of it not being on the agenda of leading organisations, as a key component for achieving high performance, developing people and gaining fulfilment, is inconceivable. In the hurly-burly of our modern working life, where the pace of change has become bewildering and we seem to be working harder than ever without necessarily making progress, there is a critical need for this new approach, to help us steer the most effective path through the undergrowth, to raise our eyes to the skies and to release more of our potential to succeed.

In new times we need to change. Most of our parental and educational conditioning was to prepare us for a world that no longer exists. Learning how to manage the increased pace and demands of our work–life, the tyranny and freedom that personal choice brings, the changing values in society and the expectations of our partners and children can be overwhelming. Coaching can be the catalyst that enables us to change and adapt to these new circumstances.

What makes coaching such a unique solution is its highly personalised approach, coupled with the immediate return on investment over a short period of time. Since most people succumb to the collective mentality, whether climbing the corporate ladder or shopping at the supermarket, coaching stands out as an intense and focused activity tailored to meet the needs of an individual or team. Given the irony that the more we do and have, the less successful and fulfilled we can feel, coaching enables us to punctuate our permanent busyness and review our progress. It helps us to recognise which areas of our work and life we are enjoying, where we are performing well, what we need to develop and what we have achieved. This gives us a true sense of our own success, which will rub off on those around us. It is rare to be able to explore one's own agenda without interference. Since we usually have the solutions to our dilemmas within us, coaching provides a precious opportunity to gain insight, clarity and motivation, leading to personal and professional fulfilment, and to close the gap between our potential and performance.

SUPERCOACHING CORE COMPETENCIES

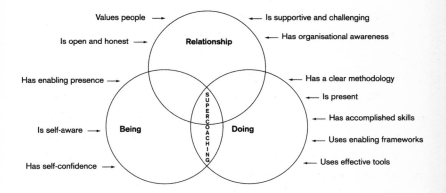

Diagram 28: SuperCoaching Competencies

We developed the 12 Core Competencies to provide a framework for measuring effective coaching. They are grouped into the three critical domains of 'Being', 'Doing' and 'Relationship', however, there is no level of priority in these. They are all essential for any Super Coach to demonstrate.

BEING DOMAIN

1. Has Enabling Presence

- Is authentic, genuine and able to be himself.

- Believes in the inherent ability of others.

- Is able to transcend personal beliefs, prejudices and biases.

- Sets a positive intention to see the best in the coachee, whilst remaining aware of any resistance or difficulties that arise.

- Demonstrates acceptance of coachee.

- Trusts the coaching process and is able to live with uncertainty and ambiguity long enough to allow something unique and valuable to occur.

2. Is Self-aware

- Is aware of own internal state, including emotions and intuitions.

- Is able to prevent own ego interfering with the coachee's agenda.

- Is able to be an observer of self, the coachee and the coaching process.

- Ensures that his inner dialogue is constructive and enabling.

3. Has Self-confidence

- Has a high level of self-worth.

- Has inherent belief in the process of coaching.

- Is able to self-regulate in order to be in a resourceful state.

- Is non-defensive by having nothing to prove and no hidden agenda.

- Is comfortable with ambiguity.

- Is secure with insecurity.

- Has certainty with uncertainty.

- Is open to not knowing and taking risks.

RELATIONSHIP DOMAIN

4. Values People

- Demonstrates respect for the coachee's personality, perceptions and preferences.

- Recognises the coachee as an expert in his work and life.

- Believes that the coachee has the inherent potential to generate his own solutions.

- Is committed to 'win/win' relationships.

- Is non-judgmental of coachee.

- Seeks to understand the coachee through empathy.

- Shows genuine concern for the coachee's well-being.

5. Is Open and Honest

- Accurately describes his level of coaching expertise, experience and qualifications.

- Ensures that the coachee has clear expectations about coaching.

- Recognises the compatibility between himself and the coachee and will make referrals when appropriate.

- Establishes and sustains clear confidentiality protocols.

- Discusses any potential conflict of interests between himself and a coachee.

- Is aware when a coachee is no longer benefiting from coaching and makes appropriate recommendation for either continuing coaching elsewhere or stopping.

- Obtains agreement with a coachee before using his name as a client or reference.

6. Is Supportive and Challenging

- Is willing and able to both support and challenge the

coachee's perceptions and behaviours.

- Is able to stretch the coachee to raise the bar.

- Is committed to the coachee extending his options and/or making real advances that matter to him.

7. Has Organisational Awareness

- Is aware of the vision, mission and values of the organisation in which the coachee works.

- Understands how the coaching assignment fits into the business context and performance management of the organisation.

- Is aware of, and understands, the culture dynamics of the organisation and, therefore, the expectations, pressures and constraints in which the coachee operates.

- Has done background work on the key stakeholders in the business.

DOING DOMAIN

8. Has a Clear Methodology

- Demonstrates a non-directive coaching approach.

- Uses a pull style to encourage self-discovery in the coachee.

- Ensures that the coachee takes responsibility for his commitment to the coaching process.

- Establishes a clear contract, which includes a well-defined agenda and measurable outcomes.

- Effectively prepares and documents coaching sessions to summarise main topics and agreed next steps.

- Builds in review to assess progress made.

9. Is Present

- Is able to have one-pointed concentration.

- Demonstrates a clear mind that is free from distractions.

- Has 100 per cent absorption in the coaching conversation.

- Demonstrates an effortless approach, allowing coaching to flow.

10. Uses Enabling Frameworks

- Uses *The Inner Game* model (Performance=Potential-Interference) to establish high performance.

- Uses the GROW model to achieve results.

- Uses the Feedback model to raise self-awareness.

- Uses the FLOW model to monitor the interaction.

- Uses other models for problem-solving, generating solutions and decision-making.

11. Has Accomplished Skills

- Listens with the intention to understand the meaning behind what the coachee says.

- Asks insightful questions to enable change and/or transformation.

- Is able to summarise clearly and effectively.

- Provides relevant, timely suggestions in a direct way.

12. Uses Effective Tools

- Uses self-assessment processes (e.g. self-assessment, 360-degree feedback, psychological profiling, performance and development data, PDPs).

- Performs 'shadow coaching' if applicable.

- Provides relevant reading material if required.

SUPERCOACHING SELF-ASSESSMENT

Whether you are a leader, manager or coach, the following self-assessment encourages you to explore your own understanding of coaching, to identify your success stories, to learn from your challenges and to focus on your development areas in order to enhance your capability.

- What does coaching mean to you?

- What have been your successes as a coach?

- What have been your difficulties and disappointments as a coach?

- What are your development needs as a coach?

- What are your principal strengths as a coach?

- What are your aspirations as a coach?

- What contribution would you like to make to the coaching profession?

SUPERCOACHING SELF-ASSESSMENT FORM

This questionnaire can be used before commencing a one-to-one coaching programme to enable the coachee to reflect upon and gain insight about his current situation and his measurable success criteria for coaching.

Date _____

Name _____

Company _____

Position _____

Work telephone _____

Email address _____

Secretary's name _____

Home address _____

_____

_____

Home telephone _____

Preferred mailing address ☐ Home ☐ Business (tick one)

Date of birth _____

Please fill in this questionnaire completely prior to your meeting with . . . Our recommendation is that you set aside at least one hour to work quietly on your own to complete this form. Please return by email to: . . . or send it to: . . . so that he/she has a chance to see it before your next session.

WHERE AM I NOW?

As you fill in this questionnaire, begin to use the SuperCoaching programme to get an 'aerial' view of your own life. It is rare that you get the opportunity to put distance between yourself and your everyday concerns to make an honest and objective assessment of the current status of your life. This form is confidential; it will only be seen by your coach.

Using a scale of 1–10 (with 10 being the highest), how would you rate yourself against each of the following?

- ☐ being a leader
- ☐ sense of achievement
- ☐ career development
- ☐ physical fitness
- ☐ personal direction
- ☐ inner peace
- ☐ job security
- ☐ challenge
- ☐ personal effectiveness
- ☐ relationship with boss
- ☐ relationship with subordinates
- ☐ keeping my word
- ☐ inspiration
- ☐ confidence
- ☐ use of time and talent
- ☐ freedom
- ☐ ability to produce results
- ☐ succeeding
- ☐ balanced lifestyle
- ☐ stress (high score = low stress)
- ☐ planning
- ☐ relationship with peers
- ☐ developing others
- ☐ commitment

What do you consider to be your five major achievements of the past 12 months?

1. _____
2. _____
3. _____
4. _____
5. _____

What have been the major disappointments over the same period?

1. _____
2. _____
3. _____
4. _____
5. _____

Consider each of the major areas of your life. Briefly describe the current status of each:

Career_____
Family/intimate relationships _____
Friends/leisure _____
Health_____
Finances _____

What concerns and/or problems have taken most of your attention over the past year?

List the topics, issues, areas where you would like particular attention paid in this coaching programme.

What are your particular skills, strengths and abilities?

What are your areas for development?

What specific objectives would you like to achieve as a result of your participation in coaching?

What success criteria will you use to measure the value of your coaching programme?

SUPERCOACHING DOCUMENTATION

We recommend using the following format to document sessions. The key is to ensure that a coachee derives value from the reports, so you may need to adapt them to meet his requirements.

Session 1

Coach:

Coachee:

Date:

Draft Agenda

Draft Coaching Success Measures / Outcomes

In the eyes of the coach:

In the eyes of the coachee:

In the eyes of the business:

Agenda Data Inputs

- Self-assessment
- Profiling
- 360-degree feedback

Finalised Agenda and Success Measures

Coach:

Coachee:

Stakeholder:

Date:

Finalised Agenda

Finalised Coaching Success Measures / Outcomes

In the eyes of the coach:

In the eyes of the coachee:

In the eyes of the business:

Finalised Agenda Data Inputs
- Self-assessment
- Profiling
- 360-degree feedback

Finalised Coaching Process, Schedule and Sessions Numbers Agreed

<u>**Sessions 2–5**</u>

Coach:

Coachee:

Date:

Review of Action Steps

Review of Agenda

Coaching Topic 1

Coaching Topic 2

Coaching Topic 3

Next Steps

<u>Coaching Progress Review – use half way through the programme</u>

Coach:

Coachee:

Stakeholder:

Date:

Review of Agenda

Review of Coaching Success Measures / Outcomes

In the eyes of the coach:

In the eyes of the coachee:

In the eyes of the business:

Review of Process

Review of Schedule

Review of Coaching Relationship

Review of Results Achieved

Next Steps

<u>Sessions 6–10</u>

Coach:

Coachee:

Date:

Review of Action Steps

Review of Agenda

Coaching Topic 1

Coaching Topic 2

Coaching Topic 3

Next Steps

<u>Final Review</u>

Coach:

Coachee:

Stakeholder:

Date:

Coaching Agenda and How It Developed

Coaching Success Measures / Outcomes Agreed

Coaching Process

Results Achieved

Sign-off Process

SUGGESTED READING

Lucy West and Mike Milan, *Reflecting Glass: Professional coaching for leadership development*, Palgrave Macmillan, 2001 ISBN: 0333945298 Includes chapter by Graham Alexander.

Ben Renshaw, *Successful But Something Missing: Daring to enjoy life to the full*, Random House, 2000 ISBN 071267053X

Ben Renshaw, *Together But Something Missing: How to create and sustain successful relationships*, Random House, 2001 ISBN 0091855934

Ben Renshaw, *The Secrets: 100 ways to have a great relationship*, Random House, 2002 ISBN 0712629483

Ben Renshaw, *The Secrets of Happiness: 100 ways to true fulfilment*, Random House, 2003 ISBN 0091887542

Robert Holden & Ben Renshaw, *Balancing Work & Life: Essential Managers Series*, Dorling Kindersley, 2002 ISBN 0751333654

Robert Holden, *Success Intelligence: Timeless wisdom for a manic society*, Hodder Modius, 2005 ISBN 0340830174

Robert Holden, *Shift Happens; Powerful ways to transform your life*, Hodder Modius, 2000 ISBN 0340716886

Robert Holden, *Happiness Now: Timeless wisdom for feeling good fast*, Hodder Modius, 1998 ISBN 0340713089

Susan Lucia Annunzio, *Contagious Success: Spreading high performance throughout your organization*, Portfolio, 2004 ISBN 1591840600

Susan Lucia Annunzio, *eLeadership: Proven techniques for creating an environment of speed and flexibility in the digital economy*, Simon & Schuster, 2001 ISBN 0743204387

Timothy Gallwey, *The Inner Game of Work: Overcoming mental obstacles for maximum performance*, Texere, 2000 ISBN 1587990474

Timothy Gallwey, *The Inner Game of Tennis*, Random House, 1975 ISBN 0679778314

Deborah Tom, *Find The Balance: Essential steps to fulfilment in your work and life*, BBC, 2004 ISBN 0563521384

ABOUT SUPERCOACHING

SuperCoaching is a service offering from Alexander, a leading provider of one-to-one executive coaching, leadership, team and culture development. Founded by Graham Alexander in 1986, Alexander has worked with many of the FTSE 100 and Fortune 500 companies. Extensive client relationships include: Cadbury Schweppes, Kingfisher Group, PriceWaterhouse Coopers, LloydsTSB and BAE Systems.

Mission statement

We maximise performance, development and fulfilment in people and organisations everywhere.

Our vision

To ensure the achievement of measurable results in alignment with explicit business needs beyond what people thought was possible. Thus we have a life enhancing impact in the world of work.

Our Core Beliefs

- People have far more potential than they exhibit

- People have an innate ability to discover their own solutions

- Openness and honesty are key enablers for high performance

- Most organisations spend a disproportionate amount of time focusing on under-peformers rather than high-performers

- Most organisations are only paying lip service to their claims that they value their people and believe in work–life balance

- Most organisations fail to recognise and celebrate their successes

Our services

- Executive Coaching

- First 100 Days Coaching

- Master Classes

- Keynote Speeches

- Coaching Training

- Coaching Audits

- Leadership Development

- Culture Development

- Team Coaching, Development and Facilitation

To learn more about Alexander and SuperCoaching, please call +44 (0) 207 435 7194 or visit www.supercoaching.net

Alexander
200a West End Lane
London
NW6 1SG